JOHANNESBURG

ONE CITY

COLLIDING WORLDS

publishers pty ltd

First published in 2004 by STE Publishers
4th Floor Sunnyside Ridge
Sunnyside Office Park
32 Princess of Wales Terrace
Parktown 2143
Johannesburg, South Africa

ISBN 1-919855-28-9

Printed by Colors Print

For Nina and Joshua

Kilometres

Freeways
Main roads
Mines & quarries
Built-up land
Administrative regions

REGION 1

COUNTRY VIEW
BLUE HILLS
NOORDWYK

REGION 2

Boulders Shopping Centre

Grand Central Airport

KYALAMI ESTATES

EBONY PARK

IVORY PARK

VORNA VALLEY

Gallagher Estates

TEMBISA

Leeukop Golf Club

RABIE RIDGE

Fourways Gardens

FOURWAYS

Montecasino

SUNNINGHILL

N1

REGION 3

M1

REGION 7

HONEYDEW

RANDPARK RIDGE

RANDBURG

SANDTON
Nedcor HQ

ALEXANDRA

N3

REGION 5

WELTEVREDEN PARK

MELROSE ARCH

ROODEPOORT

ROSEBANK

ZOO LAKE

REGION 4

KILLARNEY

MELVILLE
AUCKLAND PARK

Bruma Lake

YEOVILLE

See Insert

Ellis Park

BRAM FISCHERVILLE

REGION 8

M2

REGION 6

ORLANDO WEST

DOBSONVILLE
ZONDI

Hector Peterson Museum

ORLANDO EAST

GOLD REEF CITY
Apartheid Museum

ZOLA JABULANI

DUBE

DIEPKLOOF

NALEDI EXT. 1

THOKOZA PARK

MAPETLA
PROTEA NORTH

Chris Hani Settlement

PROTEA CHIAWELO

REGION 10

REGION 9

LENASIA

REGION 11

Insert: Johannesburg CBD

M1

YEOVILLE

Civic Theatre

Metropolitan Centre

Ellis Park

Carr Gardens

Market Theatre

Fashion District

Oriental Plaza
Mary Fitzgerald Square

Newtown

Absa Bank

Gandhi Square

M2

CONTENTS

CONTENU

INHALT

MESSAGE

AngloGold Ashanti is very pleased to be associated with this collection of essays. They define some rich perspectives of the city which is our home and the commercial capital of our country, even our continent. They offer a contemporary picture of a city which has had a turbulent history in its rise from mining camp to city of global significance.

The perspective and picture is drawn in bold strokes and decisive shades. Lindsay Bremner's voice is an emphatic one. Her judgments are strong: some might even say strident. This seems entirely appropriate for the subject of these essays. Johannesburg is no place for sissies. It is a city for the tough, the quick, the resilient. Indeed, there is no one Johannesburg. Rather it is the coincidence in time of space of many societies: suburban matrons and township tsotsis; mining magnates and street vendors; ethnic enclaves (drawn from all continents, including especially our own) and office parks which could belong in Perth or Denver. Joburg is a stage on which many different plays are running contemporaneously. You need a loud voice and a pithy speech to be heard.

Hopefully many will find Lindsay's questions important ones in considering the future of our city. Many

MESSAGE

AngloGold Ashanti est très heureux d'être associé à cette collection d'essais. Ils définissent quelques riches perspectives de cette ville que nous considérons comme notre foyer, et qui également est la capitale commerciale de notre pays, et même de notre continent. Ils offrent une image contemporaine de la ville qui a connu une histoire tumultueuse dans son accession de statut de campement minier à celui de ville de renommée mondiale.

Des coups de peinture audacieux et des ombres décisives sont utilisés pour rendre la perspective. La voix de Lindsay Bremner est très énergique. Ses jugements sont puissants: véhéments, diraient même certains. Cela semble entièrement approprié pour le sujet de ces essais. Johannesburg n'est pas un lieu pour les femmelettes. C'est la ville de l 'endurci, de celui qui réagit rapidement et qui est flexible. En fait, Johannesburg n'est pas constituée que d'une seule catégorie sociale. Elle est plutôt une rencontre dans le temps et l'espace de plusieurs sociétés: ces dames des riches banlieux et les pickpockets des townships; les magnats de l'industrie minière et les vendeurs ambulants; les enclaves ethniques (en provenance de tous les continents le nôtre y compris) et les bureaux qui n'auraient rien à envier à Perth ou à Denver. Jo'burg est une

NACHRICHT

AngloGold Ashanti ist es eine große Freude, mit dieser Sammlung von Essays in Verbindung gebracht zu werden. Die Texte erlauben wertvolle Einblicke in diese Stadt, die unser Zuhause und die wirtschaftliche Metropole unseres Landes, ja sogar des ganzen Kontinents ist. Sie zeichnen das moderne Bild einer Stadt, die es im Laufe ihrer turbulenten Geschichte vom Minencamp zu einer Stadt von globaler Bedeutung gebracht hat.

Die Perspektiven und Bilder sind mit kräftigem Federstrich und feiner Nuancierung gezeichnet. Lindsay Bremner ist eine emphatische Stimme, ihre Urteile sind streng. Einige mögen sogar sagen: provokant. Dies scheint bei der Thematik dieser Essays durchaus angemessen. Johannesburg ist kein Platz für den, der schwache Nerven hat. Es ist eine Stadt für die Zähen und Schnellen, für die, die hart im Nehmen sind. Und es gibt nicht nur ein Johannesburg - es treffen in dieser Stadt viele Gesellschaftsgruppen aufeinander: Hausfrauen aus den 'suburbs' und Gangstertypen aus den Townships, Minenbosse und Straßenhändler, ethnische Enklaven, deren Bewohner aus allen Kontinenten stammen, nicht zuletzt aus unserem eigenen, und Büroparks, die in Perth oder Denver stehen könnten. Johannesburg ist eine Bühne, auf der viele Stücke

will disagree with her answers. That is fine. Controversy is part of Johannesburg's heritage and character.

AngloGold Ashanti will be fighting its corner, promoting its vision and working hard to make its contribution to ensuring that the Johannesburg of the future will be one of Africa's most dynamic and successful cities.

Bobby Godsell
CEO
AngloGold Ashanti

scène sur laquelle plusieurs pièce-se jouent à la même époque. Votre voix, pour être entendue, doit être forte et vigoureuse.

Nous espérons que beaucoup trouveront pertinentes les questions soulevées par Lindsay au regard du futur de notre ville. Plusieurs personnes seront en désaccord avec ses réponses. Tant pis. La controverse fait partie du caractère et de l'héritage de Johannesburg.

AngloGold Ashanti se battra pour ses opinions tout en assurant la promotion de sa vision et en travaillant dur pour contribuer à faire de la Johannesburg du futur une des villes les plus dynamiques et let plus susceptibles de réussir.

Bobby Godsell
DG
AngloGold Ashanti

gleichzeitig spielen. Es braucht eine laute Stimme, eine kraftvolle Sprache, um gehört zu werden.

Viele werden hoffentlich, wenn sie an die Zukunft unserer Stadt denken, Lindsays Fragen für wichtig halten. Viele werden mit ihren Antworten nicht übereinstimmen. Das ist gut so. Auseinandersetzung ist Teil von Johannesburgs Vermächtnis und Charakter.

AngloGold Ashanti wird sich dafür einsetzen und mit ganzer Kraft, zielbewusst und beharrlich dazu beitragen, dass das Johannesburg der Zukunft eine der dynamischsten und erfolgreichsten Städte Afrikas wird.

Bobby Godsell
Generaldirektor
AngloGold Ashanti

AngloGold Ashanti

PREFACE

The influence of a city does not depend only on how powerful its industries are, how strong its army is, how extended its infrastructures are, how big its finances are or how audacious its traders are. It also and mainly proceeds from how ready it is to transform its material power into a cultural and symbolic capital.

Three things are included in the notion of cultural and symbolic capital. Firstly, a series of formal institutions such as monuments, museums, libraries, opera houses, theatres. Secondly, a set of public life infrastructures like parks, gardens, boulevards, cafés and restaurants, clubs — without which urban social life is hardly possible. Lastly, a series of cultural practices and the place given to debate, which offers a self representation of the city, the idea of the city in itself, and thus builds its own identity while exposing itself to the world.

This explains why old countries give such an importance to arts and architecture, to music and written work, generally speaking. In brief, the importance that is given to the work of the mind.

Modern metropolises are born from this combination between material power and cultural creativity. By definition, a modern metropolis is a

PRÉFACE

Le rayonnement d'une ville ne se mesure pas seulement à la puissance de ses industries, la force de ses armées, l'étendue de ses infrastructures, le poids de ses finances ou l'intrépidité de ses commerçants. Il découle aussi, et surtout, de son aptitude à convertir sa puissance matérielle en capital culturel et symbolique.

Par capital culturel et symbolique, il faut entendre trois choses. Et d'abord une série d'institutions formelles telles que les monuments, les musées, les bibliothèques, les opéras, les théâtres. Ensuite un ensemble d'infrastructures de la vie publique telles que les parcs, les jardins, les grands boulevards, les cafés et restaurants, les clubs — infrastructures sans lesquelles il n'y a guère d'urbanité. Enfin, un ensemble de pratiques culturelles et une culture du débat, à travers lesquelles la ville se représente elle-même; se donne une idée d'elle-même et, ce faisant, construit son identité propre tout en se projetant dans le monde.

D'où l'importance accordée, dans les vieux pays, aux arts et à l'architecture, à la musique et à l'écriture en général — en un mot le soin que l'on accorde aux œuvres de l'esprit.

C'est de cette combinaison entre la puissance matérielle et la créativité culturelle que naissent les métropoles modernes. La métropole moderne est,

VORWORT

Der Glanz einer Stadt wird nicht allein an der Leistungsfähigkeit ihrer Industrie, an der Stärke ihrer Ordnungskräfte, am Ausmaß ihrer Infrastruktur, an ihrer Finanzmacht oder an der Entschlossenheit ihrer Geschäftsleute gemessen. Er entwickelt sich auch und vor allem aus ihrer Fähigkeit, dieses materielle Potential in kulturelles und symbolisches Kapital zu verwandeln.

Unter kulturellem und symbolischem Kapital sind drei Dinge zu verstehen. Zum einen Bauwerke wie Denkmäler, Museen, Bibliotheken, Opernhäuser, die Theater. Dann die Infrastruktur des öffentlichen Lebens wie Parkanlagen, Gärten, große Boulevards, Cafés, Restaurants und Clubs, ohne die Urbanität kaum möglich ist. Und schließlich die Gesamtheit kultureller Aktivitäten und eine Gesprächskultur, in der die Stadt sich darstellt und vermittelt. So findet sie zu ihrer eigenen Identität und strahlt zugleich nach außen.

Von daher auch die Bedeutung, die die alten Länder den Künsten und der Architektur, der Musik und der Literatur beimessen, mit einem Wort: der Pflege, die sie dem Geistesleben zuteil werden lassen.

Aus diesem Zusammenspiel von materiellem Potential und kultureller Kreativität entstehen moderne Metropolen. Die moderne Metropole ist per definitionem ein kosmopolitischer

cosmopolitan entity. It mainly characterises by its hospitality towards foreigners and its opening to the world in general. It is the place where all differences mix together, whether ethnic, racial or religious.

With this book, Lindsay Bremner leads us implicitly to realise how far Johannesburg still is from the status of a modern and cosmopolitan metropolis. And she does so in a subtle way: she takes her readers by the hand and shows them around either building sites or derelict buildings, reporting the speech of politicians, architects or urban planning authorities and the words of ordinary people, users or citizens concerned by the becoming of their city and by what its unity is made of.

These different sites, voices and itineraries show a city which is at the same time rich and poor, fragmented, polycentered, bearing the aftermath of a racist past and inequalties coming down from an extremely brutal period — a city that develops, following several simultaneous directions.

Lindsay Bremner insists heavily on these transformations, wonders what their nature is, analyses their limits and possibilities, sometimes from an aesthetic and architectural point of view, and sometimes from a socio-political point of view. Her approach is clever and courageous as she mixes open criticism, subtle analysis and a

par définition, un espace cosmopolitain. L'éthos de l'hospitalité envers l'étranger et de l'ouverture au monde en général fait partie de ses caractéristiques essentielles. Elle est le lieu de brassage des différences, qu'elles soient d'ordre ethnique, racial ou religieux.

A travers ce livre, Lindsay Bremner nous invite implicitement à mesurer le chemin qui sépare encore Johannesburg du statut d'une métropole moderne et cosmopolite. Elle le fait sans en avoir l'air: en prenant son lecteur par la main; en lui faisant visiter tantôt des sites en construction et tantôt des sites en déréliction; en lui faisant écouter tantôt les voix des autorités politiques, des architectes ou des fonctionnaires du plan, et tantôt celles de simples gens, usagers ou citoyens préoccupés par ce que devient leur ville et par ce qui fait son unité.

De ces multiples sites, voix et itinéraires émerge une ville à la fois riche et pauvre, fragmentée, polycentrée, marquée par un passé raciste et par des inégalités héritées d'une période de brutalités sans nom — une ville qui avance vers plusieurs directions simultanément.

Lindsay Bremner s'appesantit sur ces transformations, en interroge la nature et en analyse les limites et les possibilités, tantôt à partir d'une perspective esthétique et architecturale, et tantôt à partir d'une perspective socio-politique. Elle le fait de manière

Raum. Zu ihren wesentlichen Eigenschaften gehören das Ethos der Gastfreundschaft gegenüber Fremden und allgemein die Öffnung zur Welt. Sie ist der Ort, wo sich Unterschiede, mögen sie ethnischer, rassischer oder religiöser Art sein, vermischen.

Lindsay Bremner fordert uns mit diesem Buch auf, selbst zu beurteilen, wie weit Johannesburg noch vom Status einer modernen und kosmopolitischen Weltstadt entfernt ist. Sie macht es unmerklich: Indem sie die Leserinnen und Leser bei der Hand nimmt und ihnen die Orte zeigt, die im Begriff sind zu entstehen, und die Plätze, die vom Zerfall gezeichnet sind. Indem sie sie die Stimmen der Politiker, Architekten und Planer hören lässt, aber auch die der einfachen Leute, der Verbraucher und Bürger, die sich Gedanken darüber machen, was aus ihrer Stadt wird und was ihre Einheitlichkeit ausmacht.

All diese mannigfaltigen Orte, Stimmen und Wege lassen eine Stadt zum Vorschein kommen, die gleichzeitig reich und arm ist, zersplittert, mit vielen Zentren. Eine Stadt, die geprägt ist von ihrer rassistischen Vergangenheit und der aus einer Zeit beispielloser Brutalität stammenden Ungleichheit — eine Stadt, die sich nach vielen Richtungen gleichzeitig bewegt und deren jüngste Veränderungen doch von einer erstaunlichen Dynamik zeugen.

Lindsay Bremner befasst sich mit diesen Veränderungen, hinterfragt ihre

lot of fondness for this place which she evidently likes very much.

The author's ability to reproduce a kaleidoscopic city is one of the strengths of this book. Bremner achieves the amazing feat of depicting a city, avoiding the numerous clichés given to Johannesburg by many a commentator. This is done in a simple language that succeeds nevertheless in restoring Johannesburg's complexity.

Achille Mbembe
Research professor in history and politics
University of the Witwatersrand

habile et courageuse, mêlant chaque fois la critique franche, la subtilité dans l'analyse et beaucoup d'affection pour ce lieu pour lequel elle a manifestement beaucoup de sympathie.

L'une des forces de ce livre réside dans la capacité de l'auteur à restituer une ville kaléidoscopique. Bremner réussit le tour de force de peindre une ville qui échappe largement aux nombreux clichés dont maints commentateurs affublent Johannesburg. Elle le fait dans une langue simple, mais qui parvient à restituer la complexité de Johannesburg.

Natur, analysiert deren Grenzen und Möglichkeiten, sowohl aus ästhetischer und architektonischer Sicht als auch unter sozio-politischen Gesichtspunkten. Sie macht dies in einer klugen und mutigen Weise, verbindet offene Kritik mit scharfsinniger Analyse und viel Zuneigung für diesen Ort, für den sie ganz offensichtlich eine große Sympathie empfindet.

Eine der Stärken dieses Buches liegt in der Fähigkeit der Autorin, den vielfältigen Bilderreigen einer Stadt ausdrucksvoll wiederzugeben. Lindsay Bremner gelingt es, ein Johannesburg zu zeichnen, das sich weitgehend den unzähligen Klischees entzieht, die manche Kommentatoren der Stadt anhängen. Lindsay Bremners Sprache ist einfach, aber es gelingt ihr damit, die komplexe Beschaffenheit Johannesburgs darzustellen.

INTRODUCTION
INTRODUCTION
EINFÜHRUNG

these five essays on the city of Johannesburg were first published in the *Sunday Times* newspaper in February and March 2002, as the first Bessie Head Fellowship articles. A year previously, in February 2001, Mike Robertson, then Editor of the *Sunday Times*, had announced his newspaper's sponsorship of a new literary award — the Bessie Head Non-fiction Fellowship Award, aimed at promoting the development of narrative non-fiction writing in South Africa. Writers were invited to submit proposals for a series of 5 or 6 newspaper articles fitting this genre, and, on the basis of which, an award of R100 000 would be made, allowing the author to research and write the articles for the newspaper over a period of six months.

I submitted a proposal entitled 'Contemporary Johannesburg: cultures, spaces, identities', in which I proposed to research and record the new geographies, new practices and new citizens shaping the transforming landscape of the city of Johannesburg.

For Johannesburg was re-inventing itself. Like most cities in the country, but more intensely, it had undergone major changes over the previous 10 years. The end of apartheid, the beginnings of democracy, entry into the global economy and burgeoning neo-liberalism had, in many ways, created a new city. Its streets and

Ces cinq essais sur la ville de Johannesburg furent publiés pour la première fois dans le quotidien *Sunday Times* en février et en mars 2002, et constituent les premiers articles de la "Confrérie Bessie Head". Un an plus tôt, Mike Robertson, alors Editeur du *Sunday Times*, annonça son sponsor au quotidien pour un nouveau prix littéraire — le Prix de la Confrérie Bessie Head pour les œuvres non-romanesques, qui visait à développer les récits narratifs non-romanesques en Afrique du Sud. Les écrivains étaient invités à soumettre leur proposition pour une série de 5 à 6 articles de journaux correspondant à ce genre, sur la base desquels un prix d'un montant de 100 000,00 Rands serait décerné, permettant à l'auteur de faire ses recherches et d'écrire les articles pour le quotidien en six mois.

J'ai soumis une proposition intitulée "Le Johannesburg contemporain: cultures, espaces, identités", où je proposais de faire des recherches sur les nouvelles géographies, les nouvelles pratiques et les nouveaux citoyens qui donnaient forme au paysage en transformation de la ville de Johannesburg, et de répertorier ces nouveautés.

Car Johannesburg était en train de se réinventer. Comme beaucoup d'autres villes du pays, mais avec une plus forte intensité, elle avait entrepris des changements majeurs au cours des

diese sechs Essays über Johannesburg wurden zum ersten Mal im Februar und März 2002 in der südafrikanischen Wochenzeitung *Sunday Times* veröffentlicht. Sie waren die ersten Artikel, die durch das "Bessie Head Stipendium" gefördert wurden. Ein Jahr zuvor, im Februar 2001, gab der damalige Herausgeber der *Sunday Times*, Mike Robertson, die Ausschreibung eines neuen Literaturpreises bekannt, der der 1986 verstorbenen südafrikanischen Schriftstellerin Bessie Head gewidmet war. Mit der Vergabe des "Bessie Head Non-fiction Fellowship Award" wollte die Sunday Times einen Beitrag zur Förderung des narrativen, nicht-fiktionalen Schreibens in Südafrika leisten. Autoren waren aufgerufen, Vorschläge für eine fünf- bis sechsteilige Artikelserie dieses Genres einzureichen; das Preisgeld von 100.000 Rand sollte es der Stipendiatin oder dem Stipendiaten erlauben, innerhalb von sechs Monaten das eingereichte Thema für die Zeitung zu recherchieren und zu schreiben.

Ich legte einen Vorschlag mit dem Titel "Das moderne Johannesburg: Kulturen, Räume, Identitäten" vor; es ging mir darum, die neuen Orte und Räumlichkeiten, die neuen Lebensgewohnheiten und die neuen Bewohner der Stadt zu erkunden; denn sie sind es, die Johannesburgs wandelnde Landschaft prägen.

Johannesburg war im Begriff, sich nach innen und außen neu zu definieren.

office spaces, suburbs and parks, once manicured and controlled, had taken on the character of most cities in the developing world. They were crammed with unregulated informal economic activity — survivalist street trade, small-scale manufacturing, cross border trade. Ethnic enclaves had found their place in the shadows of corporate headquarters. Middle-class residents had secured themselves behind electric fences, guardhouses and patrols. Townships had virtually disappeared from view. The casino economy had taken hold. The city had become more fragmented, more polarized and more diverse than ever before. On the other had, it had become a city for the first time. Its leaders struggled to find out what this meant. Through telling the stories of some of Johannesburg's peoples, institutions and practices, I hoped to frame a view of the rapidly transforming city and to explore the new identities, bonds and intimacies forming in the midst of or in between the new rigidities and spatial enclosures of the emerging Johannesburg. Somehow this captured the imagination of the Bessie Head selection panel, and I was honoured by being made the first recipient of the award. Six months later, in February and March 2002, these essays were published, contributing, in a small way, to the growing literature, fictional and

10 années précédentes. La fin de l'apartheid, les débuts de la démocratie, l'entrée dans l'économie internationale, le bourgeonnement du néo-libéralisme avaient, de bien des manières, créé une nouvelle ville. Ses rues et ses espaces de bureaux, ses banlieues et ses parcs, à une époque parfaitement manucurés et contrôlés, avaient pris l'apparence de la plupart des villes du monde en développement. Une activité informelle non-réglementée les saturaient — commerce de rue de survie, production à petite échelle, commerce inter-frontalier. Les enclaves ethniques avaient trouvé leur place à l'ombre des sièges sociaux d'entreprises. Les résidents des classes moyennes se protégeaient au moyen de clôtures électriques, de cabines de gardiennage et de patrouilles de sécurité. Les townships avaient virtuellement disparu du paysage. L'économie du casino était lancée. La ville devenait plus fragmentée, plus polarisée et plus diverse qu'elle ne l'avait jamais été auparavant. D'un autre côté, c'était la première fois qu'elle devenait une ville à proprement parler. Ses dirigeants luttaient pour essayer de comprendre ce que cela signifiait. En racontant les histoires de certains habitants de Johannesburg, de ses institutions et des pratiques de cette ville, j'espérais donner un aperçu de cette ville qui se transformait rapidement et explorer les nouvelles identités, les nouvelles frontières et les nouvelles

Wie die meisten Städte Südafrikas, nur noch intensiver, hatte die Stadt im vergangenen Jahrzehnt große Veränderungen erlebt. Das Ende der Apartheid, der Beginn der Demokratie, der Eintritt in die globale Wirtschaft und in den aufkeimenden Neoliberalismus schufen auf vielfältige Weise eine neue Stadt. Ihre Straßen und Büroviertel, die Parkanlagen und 'suburbs' (früher ausschließlich Weißen vorbehaltene Stadtteile), alle einst sauber gepflegt und überwacht, hatten ihr Gesicht verändert und glichen nun dem der meisten Städte in Entwicklungsländern. Überall schossen ungeregelte, informelle Wirtschaftsaktivitäten aus dem Boden: Straßenhandel um zu überleben, Kleingewerbebetriebe, Handel mit Produkten aus dem Ausland. Ethnische Enklaven entstanden im Schatten großer Firmensitze. Vertreter der Mittelschicht verschanzten sich hinter Elektrozäunen, bewacht von Sicherheitsposten und Patrouillen. Townships verschwanden buchstäblich aus dem Blickfeld. Die Kasinowirtschaft übernahm. Die Stadt war zersplitterter, polarisierter und vielschichtiger als je zuvor. Andererseits — sie wurde zum ersten Mal Stadt. Und die, die diese Stadt regierten, versuchten verzweifelt herauszufinden, was das bedeutete. Mit Geschichten über Menschen aus Johannesburg, von neuen Gewohnheiten und Einrichtungen wollte ich ein Bild von der sich schnell verändernden Stadt zeichnen. Ich wollte

non-fictional, popular and academic, on this intriguing, infuriating and excessive city.

The essays capture a particular moment in the city's history; a wild, dynamic, unsettled moment, when the city was moving in many directions all at once and when a myriad countervailing trajectories criss-crossed its terrain. My attempt to capture these took shape around a number of themes, woven into the final essays.

The first was the theme of 'home', of the changing ways in which people were making the city their home. Framed by conditions of insecurity, fear, migration and an increasing sense of "not-at-homeness", the complex problematic of dwelling in the contemporary city became apparent — the appropriation of space by the city's homeless and immigrant populations, the security enclaves, the burgeoning "Tuscan" landscape of the northern suburbs, the sprawling informal settlements wrapping its periphery. How are people living in Johannesburg, I asked myself? Where is home? What are the conceptions people have of home? How are these transforming our urban landscape? How at home/transient are Johannesburg's citizens?

The second theme was that of public space, historically something to avoid in Johannesburg. Synonymous

intimités qui se formaient au milieu de cette ville, ou entre les nouvelles rigidités et fermetures spatiales du Johannesburg émergeant. D'une manière où d'une autre, ceci captura l'imagination du jury de sélection du Bessie Head, et j'eu l'honneur d'être la première à recevoir ce prix. Six mois plus tard, en février et en mars 2002, ces essais étaient publiés, contribuant, bien modestement, à la littérature toujours grandissante, qu'elle soit romanesque ou non-romanesque, populaire ou académique, sur cette ville intrigante, horripilante et excessive.

Ces essais capturent un moment particulier de l'histoire de la ville : un moment sauvage, dynamique, instable, à un moment où la ville se dirigeait simultanément dans plusieurs directions à la fois et où elle était parcourue d'une myriade de trajectoires contradictoires. Ma tentative pour capturer ces moments prit forme autour d'un certain nombre de thèmes, tissés dans ces essais qui en sont l'aboutissement.

Le premier fut le thème de la "maison", celui des manières changeantes par lesquelles les gens faisaient de leur ville leur maison. Au centre des questions d'insécurité, de peur, de migration et du sentiment croissant de "ne pas se sentir chez soi" apparaissait la problématique complexe des habitations dans la ville d'aujourd'hui — l'appropriation de l'espace par les populations de sans-abris et d'immigrés de la ville, ses

wissen, was hat sich inmitten neu entstandener Zwänge und räumlicher Abgrenzungen an neuen Identitäten, Beziehungen und Gemeinschaften herausgebildet. Dies hat wohl das Interesse der Jury des "Bessie Head-Literaturpreises" gefunden, und mir wurde die Ehre zuteil, die erste Preisträgerin des neuen Stipendiums zu werden. Sechs Monate später, im Februar und März 2002, wurden die Essays veröffentlicht. Sie leisten einen kleinen Beitrag zu der wachsenden Zahl fiktionaler und nicht-fiktionaler, populärer und wissenschaftlicher Bücher über diese faszinierende, aufwühlende und exzessive Stadt.

Die Essays beleuchten einen bestimmten Augenblick in der Geschichte Johannesburgs — einen stürmischen, dynamischen, unruhigen Augenblick, als die Stadt sich nach allen Seiten hin bewegte, und eine Vielzahl unterschiedlicher und doch gleichwichtiger Strömungen sie erfasst hatte. In dem Versuch, diese festzuhalten, kam ich auf eine Reihe von Themen, die in diesen Essays aufgegriffen werden.

Das erste Thema ist "home", das Zuhause, die sich ändernde Art und Weise, wie Menschen sich die Stadt zu ihrem Zuhause machten. Umgeben von Unsicherheit und Angst und angesichts des Phänomens der Zu- und Abwanderungen und des wachsenden Gefühls von "Nicht-zu-Hause-sein" offenbarte sich die vielschichtige

with loitering or insurrection, it was frequently declared undesirable in the apartheid days, and erased. Since democracy, streets and parks, pavements and intersections had been overrun by practices claiming space in messy and overlapping ways. I sought to explore this new landscape by recording the ways in which people were remaking the public space of the city, and the reactions to these emerging practices.

The third theme was a particular part of the city, central Johannesburg — present and yet absent from most people's experience — present because its absence gives the city its unstable meanings. The issue for me was how to speak about the Johannesburg city centre without simply repeating what had already been said, how to approach it from new angles, give it new perspectives. I chose to do this, initially, through understanding the story of ABSA Bank's far-reaching R400 million investment into its central-city administrative head office in the late 1990s, and what that had done not only to the city, but also to conceptions of its future.

Since the late 1980s, Johannesburg has attempted to reinvent itself as a city through constructing itself as a world-class city. This theme now pervades official policies and representations and has spawned a

enclaves sécurisées, les paysages bourgeonnants de style "Toscan" des banlieues nord, les camps d'habitation informels tentaculaires enveloppant leur périphérie. Comment les gens vivent-ils à Johannesburg, me demandais-je ? A quel lieu appartiennent-ils ? Quelle conception les gens ont-ils de leur maison ? Comment tout cela transforme-t-il notre paysage urbain ? Comment se comportent les citoyens de Johannesburg à la maison / sur leur lieu de passage ?

Le deuxième thème fut celui de l'espace publique, un espace à éviter à Johannesburg d'un point de vue. Synonyme de vagabondage et d'insurrection, cet espace a souvent été déclaré indésirable et fut effacé pendant l'apartheid. Depuis la démocratie, les rues et les parcs, les trottoirs et les carrefours ont été envahis par des échoppes réclamant l'espace de manière désordonnée en se chevauchant les unes les autres. J'ai pensé à explorer ce nouveau paysage en observant la manière dont les gens reformaient l'espace publique de la ville et les réactions à ces pratiques émergeantes.

Le troisième thème fut celui d'un quartier particulier de la ville, le centre de Johannesburg — présent, et pourtant absent de l'expérience de la plupart des gens — présent parce que son absence donne à la ville ses significations instables. La question pour moi était de

Problematik von Wohnen in der modernen Stadt: Die Besetzung von Raum durch Obdachlose und Zuwanderer; die abgeschotteten Enklaven mit ihren Sicherheitssystemen; die blühende "toskanische" Landschaft der nördlichen 'suburbs'; die wuchernden, illegalen Siedlungen, sie sich um die Peripherie legen. Wie leben die Menschen in Johannesburg, habe ich mich gefragt. Wo ist ihr Zuhause? Welche Vorstellungen haben die Menschen von ihrem Zuhause? Und wie wirken sich diese Vorstellungen auf die urbane Landschaft aus? Wie zuhause fühlen sich Johannesburgs Bewohner — oder auch nicht?

Im zweiten Thema geht es um den öffentlichen Raum, etwas, das in der Vergangenheit in Johannesburg gemieden wurde. Synonym für Herumlungern oder Aufstände, erklärte man ihn zu Apartheidzeiten regelmäßig für unerwünscht und beseitigte ihn. Doch mit der Demokratie nahmen neue Lebensformen Raum für sich in Anspruch und eroberten in ausschweifendem Durcheinander die Straßen und Parks, Gehwege und Kreuzungen der Stadt. Ich wollte diese neue Landschaft erkunden, wollte festhalten, auf welche Weise Menschen den öffentlichen Raum in der Stadt neu gestalten, und ich wollte die Reaktionen auf diese neue Lebensart kennen lernen.

Das dritte Thema beschäftigt sich mit einem bestimmten Stadtteil, mit der Innenstadt von Johannesburg. Sie ist

useless terms "urban + rural".

→ lived space complexities.

View across the roofs of Charter Square informal settlement, Kliptown

Vue du camp de peuplement informel du Charter Square

Blick über die Dächer von Charter Square, Kliptown

new language, new imagery, a new politics and, inevitably, new disparities. Adopted, seemingly unquestioningly by the city's new leaders, I sought to interrogate the idea and raise questions about its consequences for the city — what kind of city is it likely to produce? Who does it incorporate and who does it exclude?

One of the themes that has recently emerged in thinking about the post-colonial city in Africa is that the traditional opposition of urban and rural is not only useless and inaccurate, but also obstructive. In Johannesburg for instance, the intricate web of the mealie trade on the streets of the city overlays its quintessentially modern urban fabric with traditionally rural patterns of food consumption; patterns of living from the rich, white northern suburbs of the city are transposed, with new cultural meanings, onto the south; in Soweto, people still cook with firewood, whereas in rural mud-plastered huts, electric stoves are used; chickens are slaughtered on the pavements of central-city suburbs, while a rural chief drives the latest BMW. There is simply no urban alternative to the rural place, but rather complex configurations of lived space, neither rural nor urban. I sought to investigate the complex interweaving of institutions, practices and value systems and how these different worlds were being mapped

parler du centre ville de Johannesburg sans me contenter de répéter ce qui avait déjà été dit, comment l'approcher sous un nouvel angle, apporter de nouvelles perspectives sur cette question. Dans un premier temps, j'ai choisi d'étudier cette question par le biais de l'histoire d'ABSA, une banque dont les investissements consacrés à l'installation de son siège administratif en centre-ville s'étaient à élevés à 400 millions à la fin des années 1990, et ce que cela avait non seulement apporté à la ville, mais également à sa propre conception du futur.

Depuis la fin des années 1980, Johannesburg a essayé de se réinventer en tant que ville, en essayant de se développer comme ville de classe mondiale. Ce thème est désormais prévalent dans les politiques officielles et dans les représentations que l'on en a et a engendré un nouveau langage, une nouvelle imagerie, une nouvelle politique et, inévitablement, de nouvelles disparités. Adoptée, apparemment sans questionnements par les nouveaux dirigeants de la ville, j'ai pensé à interroger cette idée et à soulever des questions sur ses conséquences pour la ville — quel genre de ville cela est-il susceptible de produire ? Qui est incorporé à ce phénomène et qui en est exclu ?

L'un des thèmes qui a récemment émergé de la pensée sur la ville post-colonialiste en Afrique est que

präsent und doch in der Erfahrung der meisten Menschen nicht vorhanden. Präsent, weil ihr Nicht-Vorhandensein der Stadt ihre wankende Bedeutung gibt. Die Frage für mich war, was ich zu Johannesburgs Innenstadt sagen sollte, ohne zu wiederholen, was ohnehin schon gesagt worden war. Unter welchen neuen Gesichtspunkten könnte ich mich der Stadt nähern und neue Perspektiven aufzeigen? Ich beschloss zunächst, mich mit der Geschichte der Absa Bank zu befassen, die Ende der 1990er 400 Millionen Rand in ihre City-Zentrale investiert hatte. Was bedeutet ein solch weitreichendes Vorhaben für die Stadt, aber auch für zukünftige Planungen?

Mit dem Bestreben, Johannesburg zu einer 'world class city' zu machen, versucht die Stadt seit den späten 1980ern sich ein neues Image zu geben. Dieses Thema zieht sich durch offizielle Planungsstrategien und Darstellungen und hat eine neue Sprache, neue Bilder, eine neue Politik und — unvermeidbar — neue Ungleichheiten geschaffen. Ich wollte dieser Idee, die von den neuen Stadtvätern anscheinend ohne zu hinterfragen übernommen worden war, nachgehen. Welche Konsequenzen ergeben sich daraus für die Stadt? Wie würde sie sich entwickeln? Wen schließt sie ein, und wen aus?

Ein weiteres Thema, das seit kurzem in der Diskussion über die post-koloniale Stadt in Afrika debattiert wird, ist, dass der traditionelle Gegensatz zwischen Stadt

onto one another in increasingly complex ways.

And finally, the themes that inadvertently emerge when one looks at Johannesburg today — themes of identity and universality, of enclosure and exclusion, of inside and outside, of centre and edge, of self and the other. Almost symmetrically around the axis of 1994, the city has constructed new definitions of place, replacing the old, race-based seclusions with new boundaries, identities and enclosures. I sought to interrogate how and why people were configuring the city in this way and whether any more hybrid conceptions of society and space were becoming evident.

Eighteen months after the stories were written, half-way into the city's first executive mayor's term of office, much about the Johannesburg I described has changed. Most noticeably, its fluidity has congealed into a more rigidly defined landscape. From the window of my apartment in Killarney, I have watched as the tentative, fragile practices that were supplementing the incomes of the suburb's domestic workers have been eradicated. Magnes Mabaso no longer sits on the street corner — she has been driven away by the no-tolerance policing of the metropolitan police. I have watched as children playing ball games in the park have been banned by new by-laws — the park has been

l'opposition traditionnelle entre l'urbain et le rural n'est pas seulement inutile et imprécise, mais qu'elle pose également des obstacles. A Johannesburg par exemple, la toile compliquée du commerce du maïs dans les rues de la ville recouvre le tissu urbain moderne en quintessence avec les schémas ruraux de consommation de nourriture ; les modes de vie des riches, des banlieues nord de la ville, sont transposées, avec de nouvelles significations culturelles, vers le sud; à Soweto, les gens cuisinent toujours avec du bois de chauffe, alors que dans les huttes rurales enduites de boue, on utilise des cuisinières électriques; les poulets sont tués sur les trottoirs des banlieues proches du centre-ville, alors qu'un chef rural conduit le dernier modèle de BMW. Il n'y a tout simplement pas d'alternative urbaine au milieu rural, mais plutôt des configurations complexes d'espaces vécus, ni ruraux, ni urbains. J'ai pensé à enquêter sur les interrelations complexes des institutions, des pratiques et des systèmes de valeur et comment ces différents mondes se superposaient les uns aux les autres de manière de plus en plus complexe.

Et finalement, les thèmes qui émergent par inadvertance lorsque l'on se penche sur Johannesburg aujourd'hui — les thèmes de l'identité et de l'universalité, de la fermeture et de l'exclusion, de l'intérieur et de l'extérieur, du centre et de la périphérie, de la

und Land nicht nur keinen Sinn macht, sondern auch nicht stimmt und sogar hinderlich ist. In Johannesburg zum Beispiel greifen das komplizierte Netz des Straßenhandels mit Maiskolben und damit einhergehend traditionelle, ländliche Essgewohnheiten auf die moderne Großstadtstruktur über. Lebensformen der reichen, weißen, nördlichen Stadtteile werden mit neuer kultureller Bedeutung auf die Viertel im Süden übertragen. In Soweto wird noch mit Holz gekocht, während in den Lehmhütten auf dem Land schon Elektroherde in Gebrauch sind; Hühner werden mitten in der Stadt auf der Straße geschlachtet, während ein 'chief', ein Dorfchef, den neuesten BMW fährt. Die Stadt ist nicht einfach Gegensatz zum Land, vielmehr existieren miteinander verwobene Strukturen von gelebtem Raum, der weder ländlich noch städtisch ist. Ich wollte dieses Ineinandergreifen von institutionellen Strukturen, Gewohnheiten und Wertesystemen erkunden und herausfinden, wie sich diese unterschiedlichen Welten in immer komplexerer Weise anordnen.

Und schließlich die Themen, die unweigerlich zur Sprache kommen, wenn man das Johannesburg von heute betrachtet — die Themen von Identität und Universalität, von Sich-Einschließen und Ausschluss, von drinnen und draußen, Zentrum und Rand, die Frage nach dem Selbst und den anderen. Fast zeitgleich mit den ersten freien Wahlen

returned to its former patrons — middle-aged white women walking their dogs at sunset. I have witnessed, and not impassionately, the awarding of the redesign of Freedom Square to a scheme that eradicates much of Kliptown as it now exists, in favour of a formal architectural arrangement of monumental squares and colonnades.

One cannot help but feel some sense of loss at these measures of progress and of the reassertion of authority, the sense that, for the city, something has been lost. For what has passed is that moment of spontaneity, a space that allowed people to experiment with the city and to make it work in new ways. In its place is a growing alignment of power, an eradication of mess and a singularity of vision. Fortunately for the city, this will always be contested, exceeded, transgressed, by the countless unpredictable practices of ordinary people engaged in the complex problematic of belonging to modern society and living in a modern city.

Finally, I would like to thank my two children, Nina and Joshua, without whose encouragement none of this would have happened. Thanks also to Mike Robertson, editor of the *Sunday Times* at the time, for his vision in setting up the Bessie Head Fellowship Award, Charlotte Bauer, editor of the Bessie Head stories, and the *Sunday Times* team, for having faith in my

personne et de l'autre. Quasiment symétriquement par rapport à l'axe de 1994, la ville a développé de nouvelles définitions du lieu, remplaçant les anciennes retraites basées sur la race par de nouvelles frontières, de nouvelles identités et de nouveaux moyens de fermeture. J'ai pensé à interroger comment et pourquoi les gens configuraient de la sorte la ville et si d'autres conceptions hybrides de la société et de l'espace apparaissaient de manière évidente.

Dix-huit mois après avoir rédigé ces histoires, à mi-chemin du premier mandat du maire de la ville, beaucoup de ce que j'ai décris sur Johannesburg a changé. Le plus remarquable est que sa fluidité s'est mue en un paysage défini de manière plus rigide. Depuis la fenêtre de mon appartement de Killarney, j'ai vu des tentatives de commerces fragiles qui permettaient aux employés de maison des banlieues d'augmenter un peu leurs revenus être éradiquées. Magnes Mabaso n'est plus assise au coin de la rue. Elle a été emmenée par la police métropolitaine, intolérante envers de telles pratiques. J'ai observé à mesure que les enfants qui jouaient au ballon dans le parc ont été bannis par les nouveaux règlements de la municipalité — le parc est retourné à ses précédents propriétaires — des femmes blanches d'âge moyen qui promènent leurs chiens au coucher du soleil. J'ai été le témoin, et non pas sans passions, de la

1994 hat die Stadt neue Definitionen von Raum formuliert und die alten, auf Rassentrennung basierenden Räume durch neue Grenzen, Gemeinschaften und abgesonderte Areale ersetzt. Ich wollte der Frage nachgehen, wie und warum Menschen die Stadt auf diese Weise strukturieren, und ob noch andere Mischformen in Gesellschaft und Raum sichtbar werden.

Achtzehn Monate, nachdem ich meine Geschichten geschrieben hatte, und nach der Hälfte der Amtszeit des ersten Johannesburger Regierenden Bürgermeisters hat sich vieles verändert in dieser Stadt. Was am meisten auffällt: Das, was damals im Fluss war, ist ins Stocken geraten und nun einer strenger geordneten Landschaft unterworfen. Vom Fenster meiner Wohnung in Killarney aus habe ich beobachtet, wie die zögerlichen, vorsichtigen Versuche der im Stadtteil arbeitenden Hausangestellten, ihr Einkommen aufzubessern, abgeschmettert wurden. Magnes Mabaso sitzt nicht mehr an der Straßenecke - sie wurde von einer intoleranten polizeilichen Ordnungsmacht vertrieben. Ich habe gesehen, wie Kinder, die im Park Ball spielten, aufgrund neuer Verordnungen daraus verbannt wurden, der Park fiel an seine frühere Klientel zurück — weiße Frauen mittleren Alters, die ihre Hunde bei Sonnenuntergang spazieren führen. Ich war — nicht ganz ohne persönliches Interesse — bei der Preisverleihung für die Neugestaltung des Freedom Square-

contribution, and from whom I learnt a great deal, mostly about the importance of populating a text with people; to the many people I met and interviewed in the preparation of the stories, for the generous sharing of their time and experience; to Sydney Sechebedi and Lori Waselchuk for the wonderful photographs in this book. And a great thank you to Reedwaan Vally and his staff at STE Publishers, particularly Marie Human and editor Laura Grant for their willingness and dedication to publish these stories, a reflection of their commitment to the city of Johannesburg.

Lindsay Bremner
Killarney
June 2003

condamnation du Freedom Square, qui avait été rénové en un plan éradiquant la majeure partie de Kliptown tel que le quartier existe maintenant, pour un arrangement architectural officiel de places et de colonnades monumentales.

On ne peut s'empêcher d'éprouver un certain sentiment de perte à la vue de ces mesures du progrès et de la réaffirmation de l'autorité, le sentiment que, pour la ville, quelque chose s'est perdu. Car ce qui s'est envolé est ce moment de spontanéité, un espace qui permettait aux individus d'expérimenter avec la ville et de le faire fonctionner d'une nouvelle manière. Au lieu de cela, c'est un alignement grandissant de puissance, une éradication du désordre et une singularité de la vision. Heureusement pour la ville, ceci sera toujours contesté, dépassé, transgressé par les innombrables pratiques imprévisibles des gens du commun engagés dans la problématique complexe d'appartenir à une société moderne et qu'est d'appartenir à une société moderne.

Enfin, je souhaiterais remercier mes deux enfants, Nina et Joshua, sans les encouragements desquels rien de tout cela n'aurait pu voir le jour. Merci également à Mike Robertson, alors éditeur du *Sunday Times*, pour sa vision en mettant en place le Prix de la Confrérie Bessie Head, à Charlotte Bauer, éditrice des histoires Bessie Head, et à l'équipe du *Sunday Times*,

Viertels dabei. Danach wird das alte, heute noch existierende Kliptown zu einem großen Teil durch neue formale architektonische Arrangements von monumentalen Plätzen und Kolonnaden ausgelöscht.

Man kann nicht umhin, sich irgendwie verloren zu fühlen angesichts dieser am Fortschritt orientierten Maßnahmen und des neuen Durchsetzungsvermögens der Behörden: für die Stadt ist etwas verloren gegangen. Was vorbei ist, ist dieses Moment der Spontaneität, ein Raum, der es Menschen erlaubte, mit der Stadt zu experimentieren, neue Funktionen für sie zu finden. An dessen Stelle trat eine zunehmende Orientierung an der Macht, die Beseitigung von Durcheinander und eine visionäre Einmaligkeit. Zum Glück für die Stadt wird dies immer wieder in Frage gestellt, wird immer wieder dagegen verstoßen und darüber hinweggegangen werden. Denn zu einer modernen Gesellschaft und zum Leben in einer modernen Stadt gehören ganz gewöhnliche Menschen mit ihren zahllosen, nicht vorhersehbaren Lebensformen und Gewohnheiten.

Zum Schluss möchte ich meinen beiden Kindern Nina und Joshua danken, ohne deren Unterstützung dies nicht zustande gekommen wäre. Mein Dank geht auch an Mike Robertson, dem damaligen Herausgeber der *Sunday Times*, für seinen Weitblick, den "Bessie Head Fellowship Award" ins Leben zu rufen, und an Charlotte Bauer,

pour avoir foi en ma contribution, et grâce à laquelle j'ai énormément appris, en particulier sur l'importance de peupler un texte de personnages; aux nombreuses personnes que j'ai rencontrées et que j'ai interrogées pour préparer ces histoires, pour avoir généreusement donné de leur temps et de m'avoir faire partager leurs expériences; à Sydney Sechebedi et à Laurie Waselchuk pour les superbes photographies illustrant ce livre. Et un grand merci à Reedwaan Vally et à son personnel chez STE Publishers, en particulier à Marie Human et à l'éditrice Laura Grant pour leur enthousiasme et leur dévouement pour la publication de ces histoires, un reflet de leur engagement envers la ville de Johannesburg.

Lindsay Bremner
Killarney
Juin 2003

Herausgeberin von Bessie Heads Geschichten. Dank auch für das Vertrauen, das mir die Mitarbeiter der *Sunday Times* erwiesen. Von ihnen lernte ich sehr viel, vor allem, wie wichtig es ist, Menschen zu Wort kommen zu lassen. Mein Dank gilt auch all denen, die ich im Laufe meiner Recherchen getroffen und interviewt habe, dass sie mir so bereitwillig ihre Zeit opferten und ihre Erfahrungen mit mir teilten; er gilt auch Sydney Sechebedi und Laurie Waselchuk für die wundervollen Fotografien in diesem Buch. Ein besonderer Dank geht an Reedwaan Vally und an die Mitarbeiter von STE Publishers, insbesondere an Marie Human und an die Lektorin Laura Grant für ihre Bereitschaft und ihr Bemühen, diese Geschichten zu veröffentlichen — Zeichen ihres Engagements für die Stadt Johannesburg.

Lindsay Bremner
Killarney
Juni 2003

OUTER SPACE(S), EDGE CITY ESPACES PERIPH

QUES, SUR LES MARGES DE LA VILLE *VORSTÄDTE*

in an arc stretching around the northern edge of Johannesburg lies a tiara of sparkling outer cities that stand at the new frontier of urban life. They are further out than the old suburban towns of Sandton, Randburg and Roodepoort. Spinning off the concrete highway encircling the city they include Weltevreden Park, Randpark Ridge, Honeydew, Fourways and Sunninghill, and further out Lanseria, Midrand and the Edenvale Kempton Park complex.

These emerging outer cities are connected to each other and their urban forerunners by an almost continuous swathe of development: busy local and international airports, corridors of low-rise office buildings, acres of distribution warehouses and glazed-roofed shopping malls, health and fitness clubs, rowdy Pentecostal churches, get-away conferencing facilities, casinos and golf courses. Housing includes pre-packaged bungalows for clerks and sales personnel, armed and guarded estates and electrified country mansions for executive families, and ever-sprawling informal settlements for those seeking the unskilled work that is no longer being generated fast enough.

These complexes, while still overshadowed by the metropole's most glamorous edge city, Sandton, are the laboratories, the works in progress, of contemporary capitalist

dans un arc de cercle qui s'étend autour des marges septentrionales de Johannesburg se trouve un diadème de brillantes cités périphériques qui représentent la nouvelle frontière de la vie urbaine. Elles se trouvent au-delà des anciennes villes suburbaines de Sandton, de Randburg et de Roodepoort. S'enroulant autour de l'autoroute de béton qui encercle la cité, elles incluent Weltevreden Park, Randpark Ridge, Honeydew, Fourways et Sunninghill, et plus loin encore Lanseria, Midrand et le complexe d'Evendale et de Kempton Park.

Ces cités périphériques émergeantes sont connectées entre elles et avec leurs précurseurs urbains par une rangée presque continue de développement: aéroport local et international à activité intense, corridors d'immeubles de bureaux de quelques étages, demi-hectares dédiés à la distribution. Se succèdent des entrepôts et des centres commerciaux aux toits vernis, des clubs de santé et de remise en forme, des églises pentecôtistes actives, des salles de congrès et de conférences, des casinos et des terrains de golf. Les logements sont composés de bungalows tout-équipés pour les employés et le personnel de vente, de propriétés gardées et armées et de demeures de style campagnard électrifiées pour les familles du personnel dirigeant, et enfin de camps d'habitation informels, toujours en expansion pour

am nördlichen Stadtrand von Johannesburg liegt in einem weiten Bogen ein Kranz glitzernder Vorstädte — die neue Grenzlinie urbanen Lebens. Noch hinter den alten weißen 'suburbs' Sandton, Randburg und Roodepoort gelegen, breiten sie sich jenseits des Autobahnrings aus, der sich um die Metropole zieht. Weltevreden Park, Randpark Ridge, Honeydew, Fourways and Sunninghill gehören ebenso dazu wie, noch ein Stück weiter draußen, Lanseria, Midrand und Edenvale Kempton Park.

Diese aufstrebenden Vorstädte sind untereinander und mit ihren städtischen Vorläufern durch eine fast ununterbrochene Aneinanderreihung von Wohn- und Gewerbeflächen verbunden: nationale und internationale Flugplätze mit regem Verkehrsaufkommen wechseln ab mit endlosen Reihen niedriger Bürogebäude, riesige Lagerhallen folgen Glas überdachten Einkaufszentren, Fitness- und Gesundheitsclubs glänzen neben Kirchengebäuden, in denen Gläubige enthusiastisch singen und klatschen, Konferenzzentren reihen sich an Kasinos und Golfplätze. Dazwischen Fertighäuser für Angestellte und Verkaufspersonal, gesicherte und bewachte Wohnparks, Landhäuser hinter Elektrozäunen für Familien der Oberschicht und die immer weiter wuchernden, keinen Verordnungen gehorchenden, informellen Siedlungen für ungelernte Arbeiter auf der Suche nach

urbanisation. In their expedient, badly planned, or even unplanned, developer-driven landscapes are to be found many of the clues needed to understand the implications for our post-apartheid cities of advanced industrial production and links to global flows of capital, information, commodities and people.

Midrand is the uncontested jewel in this outer-city crown. Even its nondescript name, telling us nothing more than that it is in the middle of the Rand, places it in the A-team of edge cities worldwide along with Massachusetts Turnpike and Route 128 outside Boston, North Sydney and London's M25. These names offer no biographical intrigue like "Johannesburg" or "Pretoria", conjure up no picturesque magic like "Suikerbosrand" or "Sterkspruit". Instead, highways, intersections or a vague designation in relation to something else serve to name these bland sprawls at the sharp edge of new urban development.

Just 25 years ago, Midrand was a small strip village called Halfway House, about 35 minutes' drive from Johannesburg. Lorraine King, a Midrand estate agent who sells R1-million-plus homes in high-end Midrand suburbs like Kyalami Estates, has lived in the area since she was 12 years old. "My father bought a plot here in the 1960s," she said of

les demandeurs d'emploi sans qualification en recherche de travail, travail qui ne se crée plus suffisamment rapidement.

Ces complexes, quoi qu'encore éclipsés par la plus glamour des cités périphériques de la métropole, c'est-à-dire Sandton, constituent le laboratoire, le chantier de l'urbanisation capitalistique contemporaine. Emporté par l'opportunisme, mal ou pas du tout planifiés par les développeurs immobiliers, on peut lire dans ces paysages bien des clefs qui permettent de comprendre les implications pour nos cités post-apartheid de la production industrielle avancée et des liens avec les flux globaux de capitaux, d'informations, de marchandises et de personnes.

Midrand est incontestablement le bijou de cette couronne de cités périphériques. Même son nom, qui n'est pas très descriptif car ne signifiant rien d'autre que le milieu du Rand, la situe parmi l'équipe gagnante des villes périphériques mondiales au côté de Massachussetts Turnpike et de la route 128 en dehors de Boston, du Nord de Sydney et de la M25 de Londres. Ces noms n'offrent guère d'intrigue biographique comme "Johannesburg" ou "Pretoria"; pas plus qu'ils n'évoquent une certaine magie picturale comme "Suikerbosrand" ou "Sterkspruit". Les autoroutes, les intersections, ou une vague désignation en relation avec quelque chose d'autre, servent à

Jobs, die es kaum noch in ausreichender Menge gibt.

Auch wenn all diese Gebiete noch im Schatten von Johannesburgs elegantestem Stadtteil Sandton stehen, sind sie doch die Versuchslabors, die Baustellen moderner kapitalistischer Urbanisierung. In ihrer auf Funktion ausgerichteten, oft schlecht oder überhaupt nicht geplanten und den Vorstellungen der Bauherren unterworfenen Landschaft finden sich Anhaltspunkte, die helfen, die Auswirkungen einer hoch entwickelten Industrieproduktion auf unsere Post-Apartheidstädte zu verstehen und zu begreifen, wie die globale Vernetzung von Kapital, Information, Rohstoffen und Menschen funktioniert.

Midrand ist das unangefochtene Juwel in diesem außerstädtischen Kranz. Selbst der belanglose Name, der uns nichts weiter sagt, als dass der Ort mitten in Witwatersrand liegt, stellt ihn in eine Reihe mit anderen Vorortstädten der Spitzenklasse, wie Turnpike in Massachusetts und Route 128 außerhalb Bostons, mit Nord Sydney und Londons M25. Diese Namen erinnern an keinen biographischen Lebenslauf wie "Johannesburg" und "Pretoria" und rufen auch keine liebenswürdig-pittoresken Assoziationen hervor wie "Suikerbosrand" ("Zuckerbuschhöhe") oder "Sterkspruit" ("Starker Strom"). Vielmehr sind es Nummern von Schnellstraßen, Namen von Kreuzungen oder irgendwelche vagen

Traffic congestion where the Allandale onramp meets the N1 freeway, looking south towards Johannesburg

Embouteillage sur la route, au croisement de la sortie d'Allandale et de l'autoroute N1, en direction du sud de Johannesburg

Hohes Verkehrsaufkommen bei der Autobahnauffahrt Allandale mit Blick nach Süden auf Johannesburg

Midrand's rustic past. "We used to come out to ride our horses, fish in the river or picnic on Sundays. All the village was then, was the Halfway House Hotel and Van's Café."

Today Midrand is a speeding, on-the-make city of 240 000 people, expected to grow to 380 000 by 2010. It is home to somewhere between 2 500 and 4 500 businesses — mainly in the pharmaceutical and information technology sectors — and is growing by 20 percent a year. About R500 million worth of building plans are approved annually and 65 percent of the land is under development.

Despite these impressive figures, Midrand remains geographically and economically divided, the fault line being the concrete wall of the N1 freeway and the exhibitionist, state-of-the-art corporate head offices — Siemens, BMW, Vodacom, Midrand Virgin Active — which front it.

To the west of these lie ever-expanding suburbs of mostly new affluence, where seven percent of the population lives on large plots, in walled estates or in cluster or townhouse developments. Vorna Valley, the first of Midrand's suburbs laid out in the 1970s, is now smug and settled, home to the city's established lower-middle-class office workers, tradespeople and artisans. To its north lie Noordwyk (uniformly face-bricked) and Country View (stylish townhouses

nommer ces fades banlieues tentaculaires qui sont à la pointe du nouveau développement urbain.

Il y a tout juste 25 ans, Midrand était juste un tout petit village s'étirant en longueur appelé "la Maison du Milieu", à environ 35 minutes de voiture de Johannesburg. Lorraine King, un agent immobilier de Midrand qui a vendu pour plus d'un million de Rands de maisons au fin fond de la banlieue de Midrand, comme pour l'ensemble immobilier de Kyalami, y a vécu depuis qu'elle a douze ans. "Mon père a acheté un terrain ici dans les années 1960" dit-elle en parlant du passé rustique et campagnard de Midrand. "Nous avions l'habitude de venir monter à cheval ici, de pêcher dans la rivière ou d'y pique-niquer le dimanche. Au village, il avait alors seulement l'Hôtel de la Maison du Milieu et le Café Van's".

Aujourd'hui, Midrand est une cité de 240 000 personnes en construction perpétuelle, qui vit à toute vitesse et dont la croissance atteindra les 380 000 personnes d'ici 2010. C'est le siège d'environ 2500 à 4500 sociétés — principalement dans les secteurs pharmaceutiques et des technologies de l'information — et ce chiffre augmente d'environ 20 % par an. Environ 500 millions de Rands de projets de construction sont approuvés chaque année et 65% des terrains sont promis au développement urbain.

En dépit de ces chiffres

Kennzeichnungen, die diesen langweiligen Gebäudeansammlungen in den äußersten Randgebieten neuer urbaner Entwicklung ihren Namen geben.

Vor nur 25 Jahren war Midrand ein kleines Straßendorf. Damals hieß es noch Halfway House, und von Johannesburg fuhr man 35 Minuten. Lorraine King, Immobilienmaklerin in Midrand, die in Toplagen von Midrands Außenbezirken wie Kyalami Estates Häuser für 1 Million Rand (100 ZAR = ca. 13 EUR) und teurer verkauft, lebt seit ihrem zwölften Lebensjahr hier draußen. "Mein Vater kaufte hier in den 1960ern ein Grundstück", und dann erzählt sie von Midrands ländlicher Vergangenheit. "Wir kamen zum Reiten hierher, wir fischten im Fluss oder picknickten sonntags. Das ganze Dorf bestand damals aus dem Halfway House Hotel und dem Van's Café."

Heute hat Midrand 240.000 Einwohner, die Stadt wächst rasch, und bis 2010 rechnet man mit schätzungsweise 380.000 Bewohnern. 2.500 bis 4.500 Unternehmen — hauptsächlich der Pharmabranche und des IT-Sektors — haben sich hier angesiedelt, und jedes Jahr steigt ihre Zahl um 20 Prozent. Jährlich werden Baupläne im Wert von 500 Millionen Rand genehmigt, 65 Prozent des Gebiets ist ausgewiesenes Bauland. Trotz dieser eindrucksvollen Zahlen ist Midrand in geographischer und wirtschaftlicher Hinsicht eine in zwei Teile gespaltene Stadt; Schuld daran ist die Betontrasse

with names like La Hacienda), two of South Africa's earliest racially mixed suburbs, now middle-class new-arrivals halls.

To their south-west is the prestigious Kyalami Estates, where everyone earning enough (and many who aren't) to afford a starting price of R1,5 million for a 400-square-metre house whose plaster is barely dry, is clamouring to get in. In between, the horsey types are threatened but holding their own in the agricultural holdings of Kyalami and Blue Hills.

Mid-level Country View was one of South Africa's first "grey" areas, declared a township in 1990. Susie Naidoo, along with a handful of families from the Indian township of Laudium, and the black townships of Tembisa and Soweto, was one of its first residents. This was, then, the brave new world. "We came here," she said, "because we did not want to live in racial ghettos." Though strangers to one another, they fast became a close-knit community and had soon organised a ratepayers' association, a neighbourhood watch and an education committee, because of which Midrand Primary became the first Model C school in the country.

Naidoo went on to become a local ANC councillor and served as mayor of Midrand for her last year in office. She is disappointed by her party's decision to incorporate Midrand into

impressionnants, Midrand reste géographiquement et économiquement divisée, du fait du mur de béton de l'autoroute N1 et des sièges voyants et à la pointe de la technique de compagnies qui la bordent telles que Siemens, BMW, Vodaworld, et Midrand Virgin Activ.

A l'Ouest se trouvent des banlieues toujours en expansion de nouvelles richesses, où 70% de la population vivent dans de grandes propriétés, entourées de murs ou dans des "clusters" ou "townhouses" en développement. Vorna Valley, la première des vallées de Midrand construite dans les années 1970, est maintenant rodée et bien remplie, constituant l'habitat des travailleurs des classes moyennes et inférieures de la ville, ainsi que des commerçants et des artisans. Au Nord se trouvent Noordwyk (dont les façades sont uniformément construites en briques) et Country View ("townhouses" de style portant des noms tels que "la Hacienda"). Ces dernières sont deux des plus anciennes banlieues racialement mixtes d'Afrique du Sud, constituant à présent la porte d'entrée des nouveaux arrivants de la classe moyenne.

Au Sud Ouest se trouve la prestigieuse Kyalami estates, où toute personne qui gagne assez (mais pas nécessairement) pour se permettre l'achat d'une maison de 400 m_ dont la mise à prix commence à 1,5 millions de

der Autobahn, des N1 Freeway's, und die an ihr liegenden exhibitionistisch und futuristisch wirkenden Firmensitze von Siemens, BMW, Vodaworld, Midrand Virgin Active.

Westlich dieser Schneise liegen sich immer weiter ausdehnende, meist neureiche Wohnviertel, wo sieben Prozent der Bevölkerung auf großflächigen Grundstücken leben, in Mauer bewehrten Wohnkomplexen oder in Reihenhäusern und kleinen Wohnsiedlungen. Vorna Valley war Midrands erstes 'suburb'; in den 1970ern geplant, wirkt es heute schmuck und ordentlich. Hier haben sich Arbeiter, Handwerker und Händler der unteren Mittelschicht niedergelassen. Nördlich davon liegen Noordwyk (einförmige Backsteinfassaden) und Country View (elegante Reihenhäuser mit Namen wie La Hacienda). Beide Stadtteile gehörten zu den ersten in Südafrika, wo verschiedene Rassen zusammen wohnten. Heute siedelt sich hier die neue Mittelschicht an.

Im Südwesten liegt das herrschaftliche Kyalami Estates, ein Wohnpark, wo am liebsten jeder hinziehen möchte, der genügend verdient (und auch viele, die nicht so viel verdienen), um sich ein 400 Quadratmeter großes Wohnhaus, dessen Verputz kaum trocken ist, für wenigstens 1,5 Millionen Rand leisten zu können. Dazwischen ducken sich hier und da schmale Farmhäuser, und obwohl viele bedroht sind, halten sich ihre Bewohner auf den landwirtschaftlichen Höfen von Kyalami und Blue Hills.

Johannesburg in 2001. "Something has been lost," she said. "Our strength was that we had vision and our ears to the ground. We worked as a team. Now we're not so close-knit. Crime has gone up and nobody seems to care. We are on the edge of the city, last in line. It's very hard to accept." Country View has become just another faceless middle-class suburb.

To the east of the great divide is the Midrand town centre, Gallagher Estates and Grand Central Airport. Around this constellation are to be

Rands et dont le plâtre est à peine sec, fait des pieds et des mains pour y entrer. Entre les deux, la population au mode de vie plus rural et plus chevalin, quoique menacée, se maintient sur les terrains agricoles de Kyalami et de Blue Hills.

Country View, l'intermédiaire, était l'une des premières zones "grises" d'Afrique du Sud, déclarée comme "township" en 1990. Susie Naidoo, ainsi qu'une poignée de familles du "township" indien de Laudium, et des "townships" noirs de Tembisa et

Das in der Mitte gelegene Country View war eines der ersten so genannten grauen Gebiete Südafrikas, das 1990 von der Provinzregierung zum Township erklärt wurde. Zu den ersten Bewohnerinnen gehörte Susie Naidoo, die gemeinsam mit noch ein paar weiteren Familien aus dem indischen Township Laudium und den schwarzen Townships Tembisa und Soweto hierher kam. Das war damals die schöne, neue Welt. "Wir zogen hierher", erzählt sie, "weil wir nicht in Rassengettos leben wollten." Obwohl sie sich untereinander nicht kannten, wurden sie

Susie Naidoo, former mayor of Midrand

Susie Naidoo, ancien maire de Midrand

Susie Naidoo, frühere Bürgermeisterin von Midrand

found a depressing number of To Let and For Sale signs: even booming Midrand, it seems, has its market fluctuations. Lorraine King tells me that the marketability of these properties has been compromised "by the black townships lying some 10 km to the east", where 93 percent of Midrand's population is crammed onto seven percent of its land.

The largest of these, Ivory Park, a planned informal settlement, was established in 1991 to provide site and service accommodation as overflow for Alexandra and Tembisa. Today it houses approximately 200 000 people, most of whom live in shacks and, if they are employed, earn less than R800 per month.

Neighbouring Ebony Park, built from 1993 onwards by the South African Housing Trust, boasts 1 500 formal brick homes ranging from subsidy-standard (walls, toilet, roof) to bonded R65 000 homes, while Rabie Ridge, a former Coloured area, is slightly more upmarket. At the northern edge of this sprawling complex, 8 000 toilets stand empty in the veld, awaiting allocation, in the all-too-familiar pattern of post-1990 South African bureaucrat-style human settlement.

I spoke to a number of young people in Ivory Park about their lives and ambitions. Charles Makopo, in his early 20s, originally from Pietersburg,

Soweto, fut l'une des premières à y résider. C'était alors, à l'époque, un monde complètement nouveau à braver. "Nous sommes venus ici", dit-elle, " car nous ne voulions pas vivre dans des guettos raciaux". Bien qu'étrangers les uns aux autres, ils sont rapidement devenus une communauté aux liens très resserrés et ont rapidement monté une association d'usagers de la ville, un système de surveillance de voisinage contre le crime et un comité éducatif et grâce à cela, l'école primaire de Midrand est devenue la première école de modèle C dans le pays.

Naidoo est devenue conseiller local de l'ANC, et a officié comme maire de Midrand pendant ses dernières années d'activité. Elle est déçue par la décision de son parti d'inclure Midrand à Johannesburg en 2001. "Quelque chose s'est perdu", dit-elle. "Notre force c'était que nous étions les yeux et les oreilles de la base. Nous travaillions en équipe. Maintenant nous ne sommes pas aussi proche. Le crime a augmenté et personne ne semble s'en émouvoir. Nous sommes sur les bords de la cité, en dernière ligne. C'est très difficile à accepter". Country View est devenue une autre banlieue de classe moyenne sans visage.

A l'Est de la grande séparation qu'est l'autoroute, se trouvent le centre ville de Midrand, Gallagher estates et le grand aéroport central. On peut lire dans cette constellation, un nombre

schnell eine solidarische Gemeinschaft. Bald hatten sie eine Interessensgemeinschaft für Ratenzahler ins Leben gerufen, einen Nachbarschaftsschutz und ein Schulpflegschaftskomitee, weshalb die Grundschule von Midrand die erste der Modell-C-Schulen im Land wurde, wo schwarze Kinder eine Schule besuchen konnten, die unter eine weiße Erziehungsbehörde fiel.

Naidoo wurde später Bezirksabgeordnete des ANC und war im letzten Jahr ihrer Abgeordnetenzeit Bürgermeisterin von Midrand. Sie ist enttäuscht von der Entscheidung ihrer Partei, Midrand in Johannesburg einzugemeinden. Das war 2001. "Irgendetwas ist seither verloren gegangen", sagt sie. "Unsere Stärke war, dass wir Visionen hatten und immer wussten, was lief. Wir waren ein Team. Heute fühlen wir uns nicht mehr so eng miteinander verbunden. Die Kriminalität ist gestiegen, und keinen scheint es zu bekümmern. Jetzt leben wir am Rande der Metropole, sind die letzten in einer langen Reihe. Das ist schwer zu akzeptieren." Country View ist nur noch ein gesichtsloser Mittelklassevorort wie so viele andere.

Östlich der großen Trennungslinie liegt das Zentrum von Midrand mit Gallagher Estates und dem Grand Central Airport. Nicht zu übersehen die bedrückend große Anzahl von Schildern, auf denen "Zu vermieten" und "Zu verkaufen"

has a sparkle about him. He matriculated from Umqhele High School in Ivory Park in 1999 and sees this as his home. "I love it here", he said, laughing. "I am an indigenous Ivory Parkian. This is my home. I plan to stay for the next 40 years. Then I will buy a farm in the rural areas and retire". In contrast, Matabelo Mkhonza, in her mid-20s, baby Thando on her lap, would love to get out. "This is my mother's home, not mine. If I escape Aids, I would love to move to Pretoria or Durban and make a life for myself. I have been to those cities and they seem like nice places to live," she said.

Makopo and Mkhonza are volunteers in the Ivory Park Youth Environmental Project. Their immediate ambition is to raise funding to study tourism promotion and financial management. They are the new face of political activism in the country — responsible, Aids-aware, self-motivated, articulate, with former political allegiances absorbed in a new issue-driven politics, in this case, grassroots environmentalism.

Frontiers have always been places where people have attempted to rebuild a civilisation by establishing a restorative relationship with nature. In this sense, whether through the artificially constructed country lifestyle of Kyalami Estates or the co-operatives of Midrand Eco-City, Midrand is undoubtedly our new urban frontier.

déprimant de panneaux "à louer" ou "à vendre": il semble que même dans la Midrand en pleine expansion, le marché connaisse des fluctuations. Lorraine King me dit que la mise sur le marché de ces propriétés a été compromise par "les townships noirs qui se trouvent à environ 10 km à l'Est", où 93% de la population de Midrand s'entassent sur 7% des terres.

Le plus grand de ces "townships", Ivory Park, un bidonville planifié en tant que tel, a été établi en 1991 afin de fournir un minimum d'espace, de services et de logements pour absorber le surplus des townships d'Alexandra et de Tembisa. A ce jour, il héberge approximativement 200 000 personnes, dont la plupart vivent dans des abris de fortune et, s'ils sont employés, gagnent moins de 800 Rands par mois.

A côté d'Ebony Park, construite à partir de 1993 par la société immobilière de fiducie sud-africaine, qui se vante d'avoir construit 1500 logements en briques de standard assez basique (murs, toilettes et toit) ou des maisons mitoyennes vendues 65 000 Rands, se trouve Rabbie Ridge: une zone anciennement habitée par des métis, qui est un quartier un peu plus décent. Sur le côté nord de ce complexe tentaculaire, 8 000 toilettes vides et inutilisés sont dispersés dans la campagne, attendant d'être alloués. Ceci s'explique par les habitudes et le style bureaucratique bien trop familiers

geschrieben steht: Selbst das boomende Midrand hat anscheinend seine marktwirtschaftlichen Fluktuationen. Lorraine King erzählt, dass die Wirtschaftlichkeit dieser Objekte bedroht ist "von der Existenz der etwa 10 km weiter östlich liegenden schwarzen Townships", wo 93 Prozent von Midrands Einwohnern auf 7 Prozent seiner Grundfläche zusammengepfercht leben.

Das größte dieser Townships ist Ivory Park, eine von den Behörden geplante Siedlung, mit deren Bau 1991 begonnen wurde, um Platz und Dienstleistungen für jene Menschen zu bieten, die in den alten Townships Alexandra und Tembisa keinen Platz mehr hatten. Doch die Bewohner von Ivory Park, heute leben dort ungefähr 200.000 Menschen, haben ihre Siedlung wild und planlos weitergebaut, und die meisten fristen ihr Leben in elenden Hütten und Bretterbuden. Wenn sie überhaupt Arbeit haben, liegt ihr Einkommen unter 800 Rand im Monat.

1993 begann der südafrikanische Housing Trust das benachbarte Ebony Park mit 1.500 Backsteinhäusern zu bauen. Deren bauliche Ausstattung reicht von einfachster Grundausstattung mit Wänden, Toilette und Dach bis hin zu Häusern, die mit Hypotheken bis zu 65.000 Rand belastet sind. Rabie Ridge hingegen, früher ein Wohngebiet für Farbige, weist sich durch ein etwas gehobeneres Niveau aus. Am nördlichen Rand dieses immer weiter wachsenden Vorortbezirks stehen 8.000

View across Ivory Park in the late afternoon   Vue du Ivory Park, en fin de journée   Später Nachmittag über Ivory Park

In 1990, in response to a dangerous chemical fire at the Rhone Poulenc veterinary chemical warehouse and the threat of a hazardous waste dump at Chloorkop, on its southern border, environmental activists, led by veteran campaigner Annie Sugrue, mobilised the Midrand community, from poorest to wealthiest, around environmental safety and health. For the affluent this meant issues of security, traffic congestion, planning, and the preservation of green areas. For the poor it meant poverty eradication, job opportunities, economic growth and improved quality of life. Different agendas aside, it was a chance for the two groups to meet and talk for the first time and resulted, in 1998, in the birth of the Midrand Eco City Project.

Sugrue, the project's manager, has her work cut out for her co-ordinating the many projects which fall under its umbrella. These include an organic consumer food co-operative, a women-only eco-builders co-operative, the Iteke waste recycling project and the Ivory Park Eco Village, a showroom of ecologically sound settlement practices at the World Summit for Sustainable Development, held in Johannesburg in 2001. Sugrue's brief includes more difficult feats of persuasion, such as getting Midrand residents who live at the bottleneck of the most congested stretch of freeway

de l'Afrique du Sud par rapport aux questions de planification du peuplement humain.

J'ai parlé à un certain nombre de jeunes d'Ivory Park à propos de leur vie et de leurs ambitions. Charles Makopo, à peine 20 ans, originaire de Pietersburg s'anime lorsqu'il parle de lui-même. Bachelier de la "Umqulele High Scool" à Ivory Park en 1999, il se sent chez lui ici. "J'adore vivre ici", dit-il en riant. "Je suis un véritable habitant local d'Ivory Park ; c'est mon chez moi. Je prévoie d'y rester pour les 40 ans à venir. Ensuite je m'achèterai une ferme en zone rurale et j'y prendrai ma retraite". Au contraire, Matabelo Mkhonza, environ 25 ans, son bébé Thando sur les genoux, aimerait en sortir. "C'est la maison de ma mère, pas la mienne. Si je suis épargnée par le SIDA, j'aimerais déménager à Pretoria ou à Durban et y faire ma vie. Je suis déjà allée dans ces villes et il me semble que ce sont de chouettes endroits pour vivre", dit-elle.

Makopo et Mkhonza sont volontaires dans le projet environnemental de jeunesse d'Ivory Park. Leur ambition immédiate est de rassembler des fonds pour faire des études de promotion du tourisme et de gestion financière. Ils représentent le nouveau visage du militantisme politique du pays - responsables, conscients du SIDA, motivés, au parlé clair, dont les engagements politiques précédents ont été réinvestis dans de nouveaux sujets

Toilettenschüsseln verlassen mitten im 'veld' und warten darauf, auf die verschiedenen Siedlungen verteilt zu werden, wie sie in nur all zu gut bekannter Manier der südafrikanischen Bürokratie nach 1990 entstanden sind.

Ich spreche mit einer Reihe von jungen Leuten aus Ivory Park über ihr Leben, ihre Ziele und Wünsche. Charles Makopo ist Anfang zwanzig und kommt ursprünglich aus Pietersburg. Aber 1999 machte er seinen Schulabschluss an der Umqhele High School in Ivory Park und betrachtet das Viertel als sein Zuhause. "Es gefällt mir hier", strahlt er und lacht. "Ich bin ein eingeborener Ivory Parkianer. Dies ist mein Zuhause. Ich habe vor, die nächsten vierzig Jahre hier zu bleiben. Dann möchte ich eine Farm draußen auf dem Land kaufen und mich, wenn ich in Rente bin, dorthin zurückziehen." Matabelo Mkhonza hingegen, die Mitte zwanzig ist und Baby Thando auf dem Schoß hält, möchte gerne weg. "Meine Mutter ist hier zu Hause, nicht ich. Wenn ich nicht an Aids erkranke, würde ich gerne nach Pretoria oder Durban ziehen und dort mein eigenes Leben leben. Ich war in beiden Städten, und ich glaube, dass es sich dort gut leben lässt", sagt sie.

Makopo und Mkhonza arbeiten ehrenamtlich im Jugendumweltprojekt von Ivory Park. Zurzeit sind sie auf Geldsuche, um Tourismusförderung und Finanzmanagement studieren zu können. Sie sind das neue Gesicht des politischen

in the country to double-up car occupancy by providing zip lanes in peak-hour traffic.

Solly Ramokgano is the site manager of the Iteke waste recycling project. He was expelled from the University of Pretoria for his political activism in the early 1990s and went on to study politics and human resources through Unisa. Ramokgano joined the project last year. Iteke now employs 47 workers, admittedly at poverty relief rates (about R300 per month), but "at least that is putting food in their stomachs", he said. Robert Malele, an environmental activist since 1992 and Iteke's co-founder, dreams of expanding the recycling co-operative across Gauteng, the nation and then, he says with the typical can-do attitude of the new-city dweller, "we're going international". In the first step in that direction, Iteke will soon be opening depots in Diepsloot, Midrand and Rabie Ridge.

With community activists like Malele and Ramokgano leading the way, uninterested in the values or antics of their bourgeois former comrades across the highway, I am not surprised to learn that Ivory Park had a 93 percent rate of payment for services in the 1990s, one of the highest of any township in the country.

Midrand's affluent west and poorer east sides overlap, if it cannot be avoided, along the strip of the Old

de société: dans ce cas, la protection de l'environnement par la base.

Les espaces de peuplement frontaliers ont toujours été des endroits où les gens ont tenté de reconstruire une civilisation en établissant une relation plus forte avec la nature. Dans ce sens, que ce soit par le biais du style de vie campagnard artificiel monté de toute pièce de Kyalami estates ou par le biais des coopératives de Midrand Eco-City, Midrand constitue incontestablement notre nouvel espace frontalier urbain.

En 1990, en réponse à un dangereux feu ayant pris à l'entrepôt de produits chimiques vétérinaires de Rhône-Poulenc, ainsi qu'à la menace d'un dépôt d'ordures dangereux à Chloorkop sur sa limite sud, un groupe de militants environnementalistes, menés par Annie Sugrue, une habituée de ces campagnes, mobilisa la communauté de Midrand du plus pauvre au plus riche sur les problématiques environnementales de sécurité et de santé. Pour les nantis, cela signifiait travailler sur les questions de sécurité, de congestion de la circulation, de planification et de préservation de zones vertes. Pour les plus démunis, cela signifiait l'éradication de la pauvreté, la création d'emplois, la croissance économique et l'amélioration de la qualité de vie. Mis à part les différences d'objectifs, ce fut l'opportunité pour les deux groupes de se rencontrer et de se

Engagements in Südafrika — verantwortlich, sich der Aids-Gefahr bewusst, hoch motiviert, eloquent. War es früher die Bindung an eine politische Organisation, die sie motivierte, interessieren sie sich heute für ausgesuchte Themen in der Politik, in diesem Fall Basisarbeit in der Umweltpolitik.

Grenzgebiete waren immer Orte, wo Menschen versucht haben, Zivilisation neu zu erschaffen, indem sie mit der Natur in gesundem Einklang leben. Ob wir nun Kyalami Estates mit seinem künstlich angelegten ländlichen Lebensstil oder die Kooperativen von Midrands Öko-City nehmen, Midrand ist in diesem Sinne zweifelsohne unsere neue Grenze zwischen Stadt und Land.

Ein schweres Feuer im Lager für tiermedizinische Produkte des Pharma- und Chemiekonzerns Rhône-Poulenc und der geplante Bau einer die Umwelt gefährdenden Abfallbeseitigungsanlage im Süden von Chloorkop haben 1990 Umweltschützer auf den Plan gerufen. Unter der Führung von Annie Sugrue, einer Veteranin im Umweltschutz, mobilisierten sie Midrand und riefen Arm und Reich auf, sich für Umweltschutz und Gesundheit zu engagieren. Für die Reichen bedeutete dies Fragen von Sicherheit, Verkehrsstaus, Planung und Erhalt von Grünflächen. Für die Armen Kampf gegen Armut, um Jobmöglichkeiten, wirtschaftliches Wachstum und verbesserte

Pretoria Main Road between the Allandale and Olifantsfontein off-ramps. This is the DIY belt, boasting nine hardware and home decor stores in as many kilometres and 10 petrol stations in deference to Midrand's freeway culture. In between, imposing and ugly postmodern suburban shopping malls and mainstream furniture stores stand cheek by jowl with Big Bite Fast Foods, cash loan outlets, T Dee Hair Salon and a wealth of auto repair shops catering to the car commuters' every need. This is the

parler pour la première fois. Ce qui eut pour résultat la naissance, en 1998, du projet de Midrand Eco City.

Sugrue, la chef de projet, a dû prendre sur son temps de travail pour coordonner les nombreux projets qui en furent issus: une coopérative d'aliments biologiques gérée par les consommateurs, le projet Iteke de recyclage d'ordures, l'éco village d'Ivory Park, une exposition sur les bonnes pratiques écologiques en situation de bidonville lors du sommet mondial pour un développement durable qui a eu lieu

Lebensqualität. Abgesehen von unterschiedlichen Themen war es für die beiden Gruppen ein erster Anstoß aufeinander zuzugehen und miteinander zu reden. Das Ergebnis dieser Treffen war 1998 die Gründung des Midrand Öko-City Projektes.

Managerin Sugrue gab ihre Arbeit zugunsten der Koordinierung der vielen im Rahmen von Öko-City gestarteten Projekte auf. Unter anderem sind dies eine Kooperative für Bio-Lebensmittel, eine für biologisches Bauen nur für Frauen, das Iteke-Abfallrecyclingprojekt

Robert Malele at the Iteke Waste Recycling Centre, Ivory Park

Robert Malele du Iteke Waste Recycling Centre (Centre de Recyclage des Déchets), à Ivory Park

Robert Malele im Iteke-Abfallrecyclingprojekt in Ivory Park

indiscreet and indiscriminating, overlapping, makeshift world of Midrand, proclaimed on a billboard nearby as "A City for the new South Africa". Over the road, the Deo Gloria NG Kerk advocates love in four languages — liefde, lerato, love, thando — a quality Midranders are going to need to negotiate this contradictory, in-your-face city of the future.

At the hub of all of this stands the Boulders Shopping Centre, built on the site of the old Halfway House Hotel. Since the days of Paul Kruger, this site, with its granite boulders and underground springs, served as a watering hole for horses midway between Pretoria and Johannesburg. Now these boulders lie trapped in the mall's food court, ignominiously threaded by a mini-golf course and planted with plastic trees. Boulders Shopping Centre's first affluent consumers are now beginning to abandon the mall for the ritzy Montecasino, a Tuscan-themed casino complex, while Pep Stores, Ellerines and Chicken City move in to cater for the tastes of a blacker, less affluent clientele. Ivory Park and Tembisa have come to town.

However, to be black and living on the edge is not necessarily to be poor. Edge cities are the entry points for many into middle South Africa, providing instant access to the

à Johannesburg en 2002. La tâche de Sugrue a comporté d'autres tours de force, comme essayer de persuader les résidents de Midrand qui vivent dans la partie la plus embouteillée de l'autoroute de doubler le taux de remplissage des voitures en fournissant à ces dernières des voies spéciales pendant les heures d'embouteillage.

Solly Ramokgano est le directeur sur site du projet Iteke de recyclage d'ordures. Il a été expulsé de l'Université de Prétoria au début des années 1990 pour son activisme politique mais a continué à étudier les sciences politiques et les ressources humaines à l'Unisa. Ramokgano a adhéré au projet l'année dernière. Le projet Iteke emploie maintenant 47 travailleurs, certes à un salaire de misère (environ 300 Rands par mois), mais "au moins ça leur permet de se remplir un peu la panse", dit-il. Robert Malele, militant environnementaliste depuis 1992 et co-fondateur de Iteke, rêve de pouvoir développer la coopérative de recyclage à travers le Gauteng et dans tout le pays; puis dit-il, avec une assurance caractéristique des nouveaux habitants de la ville, "nous passerons au niveau international". L'ouverture de dépôts dans un avenir assez proche à Diepsloot, Midrand et Rabie Ridge constitue pour Iteke les premiers pas dans cette direction. Avec des militants locaux de la trempe de Malele et Ramokgano pour montrer l'exemple, de manière désintéressée, à

und ein Öko-Dorf, das Ivory Park Eco Village mit einer Ausstellung über Wohnungsbau nach ökologischen Gesichtspunkten zum Weltgipfel für nachhaltige Entwicklung 2002 in Johannesburg. Sugrue muss noch viel an Überzeugungsarbeit leisten; unter anderem will sie die an dem am meisten von Abgasen belasteten Abschnitt der Autobahn wohnenden Bewohner von Midrand dazu bringen, Fahrgemeinschaften zu bilden, die dann gesondert ausgewiesene Spuren befahren dürfen.

Solly Ramokgano leitet das Iteke-Abfallrecyclingprojekt. Wegen seiner politischen Aktivitäten wurde er Anfang der 1990er von der Universität Pretoria verwiesen. Daraufhin studierte er Politik und Human Resources an der Fernuniversität UNISA (University of South Africa). 2001 begann er im Projekt mitzuarbeiten. Heute beschäftigt Iteke 47 Arbeiter, wenn auch zugegebenermaßen zu Minimallöhnen (ca. 300 Rand monatlich), aber "das hilft zumindest, den Magen zu füllen", sagt Ramokgano. Robert Malele, Umweltschutzaktivist seit 1992 und Mitbegründer des Iteke-Projektes, träumt davon, die Recyclingkooperative auf die ganze Provinz Gauteng und danach landesweit auszudehnen. Und dann "gehen wir international", sagt er mit jener "Wir-können-alles-Haltung", die typisch ist für Menschen, die plötzlich Stadtbewohner sind. Als ein erster Schritt in diese

essence of the new South African dream — the post-1990 Pajero version of sunny skies and Chevrolet. They have become the prime destination for the new black middle-class — managers; entrepreneurs in the service, IT or distribution industries; politicians; government or parastatal bureaucrats — all anxious to stake a claim in the preferred locale of the country's nouveau riche.

Roger Chiume, a recently retired Telkom director, was one of Midrand's first black middle-class residents. My first telephone contact with him was cut short when he informed me that he was "about to tee off". In 1993, Chiume built, and still lives in, a relatively modest house, by Kyalami Estates standards, when, as he puts it, it was "still a country retreat". On his numerous business trips, he said it gave him "peace of mind" to know that his wife and two daughters were safe.

Chiume is a member of the nearby Leeukop Golf Club and said that "most black residents here play golf". But though black residents now comprise 20 percent of the Estates, it appears that suburban tastes and *modus operandi* have a similar effect on everyone: Chiume has little to do with his neighbours, white or black. When members of the Chiume family want to socialise, they return to Zondi, Soweto, where Roger grew up — or they invite their Soweto friends and relatives over

la différence de leurs anciens camarades plus aisés basés de l'autre côté de l'autoroute, je ne suis pas surprise d'apprendre qu'Ivory Park possède le taux le plus élevé de paiement d'impôts locaux, soit 93 % dans les années 90; l'un des taux le plus élevé de tous les townships du pays.

L'abondance du Midrand de l'Ouest chevauche la partie plus pauvre de l'Est de manière inévitable le long de la bande constituée par l'ancienne route de Pretoria et la section sans passerelle d'Allandale et d'Olifantsfontein. Cette zone constitue le coin dédié au bricolage, avec pas moins de neufs magasins de bricolage/quincaillerie/- aménagement de la maison, et ce sur autant de kilomètres. Parallèlement, on trouve aussi 10 stations essence qui rendent hommage à la culture autoroutière de Midrand. Entre les deux s'imposent les centres commerciaux suburbains horribles et postmodernes ainsi que les magasins de meubles. Ces derniers côtoient également les fast-foods, les bureaux d'emprunt et de prêt d'argent liquide, les salons de coiffure, les garages de réparation de voiture et divers magasins d'alimentation qui pourvoient aux besoins des travailleurs journaliers. C'est le monde indiscret, sans nuance, de bric et de broc, faisant souvent double emploi, de Midrand, ville qui se proclame sur un panneau publicitaire comme "une ville pour la nouvelle Afrique du Sud". De l'autre côté

Richtung wird Iteke bald Deponien in Diepsloot, Midrand und Rabie Ridge eröffnen.

Mit Bürgeraktivisten wie Malele und Ramokgano, die vorangehen und nicht an den Vorstellungen und Eskapaden ihrer früheren, inzwischen bourgeoisen Genossen auf der anderen Seite des Highways interessiert sind, überrascht es mich nicht, als ich höre, dass tatsächlich 93 Prozent der Bewohner von Ivory Park in den 1990ern ihre Dienstleistungsrechnungen, z.B. für Wasser und Strom, bezahlten; das Township war damit eines mit der höchsten Zahlungsmoral im Land.

Midrands reicher Westen und seine ärmeren Viertel im Osten überschneiden sich, ungewollt, entlang der Old Pretoria Main Road, zwischen den Ausfahrten Allandale und Olifantsfontein. Hier ist das Paradies für Heimwerker mit allein neun Baumärkten und Werkzeuggeschäften und 10 Tankstellen zur freien Entfaltung von Midrands Autobahnkultur. Dazwischen imposante und hässliche postmoderne Malls und Möbelgeschäfte für Jedermann neben Fast-Food-Ketten, Kreditbüros, T-Dee-Haarsalons und jede Menge Autoreparaturwerkstätten und — zubehörgeschäfte, die alle Wünsche und Bedürfnisse der Autobesitzer befriedigen. Dies ist die laute, bunt gemischte und improvisierte Welt von Midrand, "Eine Stadt für das neue Südafrika", wie es auf einer Plakatwand in der Nähe proklamiert wird. Und auf der anderen Straßenseite

**New corrugated iron houses,
Ivory Park**

Nouvelles maisons à tôles
ondulées, à Ivory Park

Neue Wellblechhäuser
in Ivory Park

to their house. "Our culture has not changed much by moving here," he said, "While we live individual, not communal, lives here in the suburbs, we still keep contact with our collective roots."

This is the contradictory space inhabited by many of South Africa's new black elite. On the one hand, middle-class values and preoccupations — individual achievement, status, nuclear family life, space, security and sport — are best satisfied within the infrastructure of the security suburb. On the other hand, a proud and essential, yet nostalgic, relationship with the culture of township life is often maintained. Somehow these contradictions are easier to live with in the anonymity of the edge city world. Likewise, assimilation into this world is somehow easier in the effrontery of the edge city than under the surveillance of old white South Africa. On the edge, the colour of one's money rapidly replaces skin colour as the currency of showy success. Acquisitiveness — 4x4 vehicles, teeny-weeny cellphones, gym-toned bodies, Deisel, Kookai, gold-plated taps, marble floors, Play Station 2s — goes hand in hand with that other must-have suburban attitude: lack of curiosity about everyone else.

Back in 1990, none of this was remotely imaginable. That was the year

de la route, L'église Deo Gloria NG prône l'amour en quatre langues — "Liefde, lerato, love, Thando" — une qualité dont les habitants de Midrand vont avoir grandement besoin pour négocier et gérer cette ville contradictoire du futur qu'est Midrand. Au centre de toute cette activité se dresse le centre commercial de Boulder, construit sur le site de l'ancien Hôtel de la Maison du Milieu. Au temps de Paul Kruger, ce site, avec ses rochers de granite et ses sources souterraines servait de base de ravitaillement en eau pour les chevaux à mi-chemin entre Pretoria et Johannesburg. Dorénavant, ces rochers sont prisonniers du quartier des restaurants du centre commercial, ignoblement posés au milieu d'un terrain de mini-golf à côté d'arbres en plastique. Les premiers consommateurs aisés du centre commercial de Boulder ont maintenant commencé à l'abandonner au profit du plus luxueux Montecasino, un gros complexe commercial bâti autour d'un casino sur le thème toscan. Parallèlement "PepStores", "Ellerines" et "Chicken city" ont fait évolué leur cuisine pour satisfaire les goûts d'une clientèle plus noire et moins riche. Ivory Park et Tembisa descendent en ville.

Néanmoins, être noir et vivre sur les marges ne signifie pas nécessairement être pauvre. Ces cités périphériques sont pour beaucoup les points d'entrée de la classe moyenne sud-africaine, en

wirbt die Deo Gloria NG Kirche für die Liebe in vier Sprachen, in Afrikaans, Tswane, Englisch und Zulu: liefde, lerato, love, thando. Midrands Bewohner werden sie brauchen, um in dieser widersprüchlichen, lärmenden Stadt der Zukunft miteinander zurechtzukommen.

Inmitten des Ganzen, dort wo sich vorher das alte Halfway House Hotel befand, erhebt sich jetzt Boulders Einkaufszentrum. Seit den Tagen von Paul Kruger diente dieser Ort mit seinen Granitfelsen und unterirdischen Wasserstellen als Pferdetränke auf halbem Weg zwischen Pretoria und Johannesburg. Nun liegt das Felsgestein säuberlich eingezäunt inmitten der Imbissmeile der Mall, lieblos bepflanzt mit Plastikbäumen, und eine Minigolfanlage windet sich hindurch. Boulders bisherige wohlhabende Kundschaft beginnt das Shopping Centre zu meiden, sie geht inzwischen lieber ins sehr viel elegantere Montecasino, einem im toskanischen Flair gehaltenen Spiel- und Kasinokomplex. Bei Boulders halten Billigtextilketten und Möbelgeschäfte wie Pep Stores und Ellerines und Hähnchengrills Einzug und folgen damit dem Geschmack einer schwärzer werdenden, weniger begüterten Klientel. Ivory Park und Tembisa haben die Stadt erreicht.

Aber schwarz sein und am Rande leben, heißt nicht unbedingt, arm sein. Städte am Rand sind für viele das Eingangstor zur südafrikanischen Mittelschicht, das Wahrwerden des neuen

Anglo American Properties laid out a walled suburb way outside the city, next to the Kyalami racetrack. Back then you could buy a 1 000-square-metre plot within its walls for R95 000 — still pricey, but nothing compared with the R450 000 it now costs to acquire the same land at Midrand's most swanky address — Kyalami Estates.

One of those who bought back then was Brian Lipschitz, then a building contractor, now manager of Kyalami Estates. "When I built my

fournissant un accès instantané à l'essence même du nouveau rêve sudafricain: la version post-1990 du Pajero bleu ciel et de la chevrolet. Elles sont devenues la destination principale pour la nouvelle classe moyenne noire — directeurs, entrepreneurs de services, des technologies de l'information, de l'industrie de distribution, politiciens, bureaucrates gouvernementaux ou para-administratifs — tous anxieux de revendiquer une place au pays des nouveaux riches.

Roger Chiume, un des directeur de

südafrikanischen Traums: die letzten Versionen eines Geländewagens à la Pajero & Co, prestigeträchtige Symbole, die zeigen, dass "man oben ist". Sie sind das vorrangige Ziel der neuen schwarzen Mittelklasse-Manager — Unternehmer, Führungskräfte der IT-Branche oder der Transportindustrie, Politiker, Bürokraten der Regierung oder halbstaatlicher Institutionen — sie alle begierig, sich ihre Position auf den von den Neureichen bevorzugten Schauplätzen zu erobern. Roger Chiume, ehemaliger Direktor bei der südafrikanischen Telefongesellschaft

Brian Lipschitz, Manager of Kyalami Estates outside the estate clubhouse

Brian Lipschitz, Agent immobilier de Kyalami Estates, devant son agente immobilière.

Der Manager von Kyalami Estates, Brian Lipschitz, vor dem Clubhaus der Anlage

house here 12 years ago," he says, "people thought I was crazy. This place was seen as too far out. Bryanston, where I came from, was seen as the edge of the city. "Today", he adds, "the best companies (Mecer, Nashua, Siemens, BMW, Vodacom), the best schools (Kyalami Prep, Beaulieu College, St Peters, Crawford College), the best shopping centres (Fourways Mall, Sandton City and Pine Slopes for its deli), the best golf courses (Kyalami, Johannesburg, Lone Hill and Leeukop country clubs) and the best gym (Midrand Virgin Active) have all moved here. You never have to go into the city any more."

Kyalami Estates is ringed by a two-metre-high, electricity topped, R7,5 million perimeter wall, with digital access control, computer-based armed reaction and 11 patrol zones. But once past this bristling electro-magnetic field, the idea abruptly changes from keeping the riff-raff out to making like Club Med. The Estates boasts 11 parks, five dams, tennis and squash courts and running, walking, reading and wine-tasting clubs. With its homes valued between R1,5 million and R14 million and a reassuringly distant view of the Johannesburg skyline, Kyalami Estates is, whether we like it or not, the model of urban living our society most aspires to for now and the foreseeable future.

Telkom qui a pris sa retraite récemment, fut l'un des premiers résidents de la classe moyenne noire de Midrand. Mon premier contact téléphonique avec lui a tourné court lorsqu'il m'a annoncé qu'il était sur le point de se "tirer". En 1993, Chiume a construit une maison relativement modeste aux normes de Kyalami Estates dans laquelle il vit encore aujourd'hui . Selon ses propres termes, c'était alors et c'est encore aujourd'hui une "maison de campagne". Lors de ses nombreux voyages d'affaires, dit-il, cela lui donnait "une certaine tranquillité d'esprit" de savoir que sa femme et ses deux filles étaient en sécurité. Chiume est membre actif du club de golf Leeukop tout proche et dit que "la plupart des résidents noirs d'ici jouent au golf". Cependant, bien que l'ensemble de la population noire atteigne maintenant 20 % du lotissement, il apparaît que la culture suburbaine et son modus operandi aient un effet similaire sur tout un chacun: Shongwe fréquente peu ses voisins, qu'ils soient blancs ou noirs. Quand les membres de la famille Chiume veulent socialiser, ils retournent à Zondi, à Soweto, où Roger a grandi. Ou bien ils invitent leurs parents et leurs amis de Soweto chez eux. "Le fait de déménager ici a peu changé à notre culture" dit-il, "bien que nous vivons ici de manière individuelle et non pas communautaire, nous continuons à garder des liens avec nos racines collectives".

Telkom und gerade pensioniert, war einer der ersten schwarzen Mittelschicht-Bewohner von Midrand. Bei meinem ersten Telefongespräch unterbrach er mich sofort, er sei gerade dabei "aufzuteen". 1993 baute sich Chiume nach Kyalami Estates-Standards ein relativ bescheidenes Haus, in dem er noch immer wohnt. Zu einer Zeit, als, wie er es nannte, die Gegend hier "noch ein ländlicher Zufluchtsort" war. Auf seinen zahlreichen Geschäftsreisen habe es ihm "Seelenfrieden" gegeben, zu wissen, dass seine Frau und die beiden Töchter dort sicher waren. Chiume ist Mitglied des nahe gelegenen Leeukop Golf Club. "Die meisten schwarzen Bewohner hier spielen Golf ", stellt er fest. Obwohl inzwischen schon 20 Prozent der Bewohner des Estates Schwarze sind, sieht es so aus, als ob die Vorlieben und Lebensweisen, wie man sie in den 'suburbs' pflegte, auf alle Bewohner abfärben: Chiume hat wenig Kontakt zu seinen Nachbarn, ganz gleich, ob schwarz oder weiß. Wenn Mitglieder der Shongwe Familie zusammenkommen möchten, fahren sie zurück nach Zondi in Soweto, wo Roger aufgewachsen ist, oder sie laden ihre Freunde und Verwandten aus Soweto zu sich nach Hause ein. "Unsere Kultur hat sich nicht sehr verändert, nur weil wir hierher gezogen sind", sagt er. "Zwar führen wir hier kein Leben in der Gemeinschaft, sondern leben für uns allen, ganz individuell, aber wir bewahren uns dennoch unsere kollektiven Wurzeln."

Voici donc l'espace contradictoire habité par bon nombre de la nouvelle élite noire sud-africaine. D'une part, les préoccupations et les valeurs de la classe moyenne — à savoir le succès individuel, le statut social, la vie de la famille nucléaire, l'espace, la sécurité et le sport — qui sont satisfaits à travers et à l'intérieur des infrastructures de la banlieue sécurisée. Et d'autre part, une relation fière, essentielle mais nostalgique, avec la culture et la vie de townships qui est souvent maintenue. D'une certaine manière, ces contradictions sont plus faciles à vivre dans l'anonymat du monde de ces citées périphériques. De même, l'intégration à ce monde est d'une certaine manière plus facile dans la nouveauté de ces cités périphériques que sous la surveillance de l'ancienne Afrique du Sud blanche. A la périphérie, la couleur de l'argent remplace rapidement celle de la peau car l'argent représente ostentatoirement le succès. La frénésie de la consommation — Véhicules 4X4, téléphones portables derniers cris, corps sculptés par la gym, Diesel, Kookai, robinets dorés, sols en marbre, playstations dernière génération — tout cela va main dans la main avec cette autre attittude suburbaine: le manque de curiosité pour autrui.

Personne n'aurait pu imaginer cela en 1990, l'année où la société "Anglo American Properties" a mis sur le marché une nouvelle banlieue entourée de murs

Dies ist der widersprüchliche Raum, in dem sich viele Vertreter der neuen schwarzen Elite Südafrikas bewegen. Auf der einen Seite die Werte und Sorgen der Mittelschicht: der Erfolg des Einzelnen, Status, das Leben in der Kleinfamilie, Platz, Sicherheit und Sport — all das wird am besten befriedigt innerhalb der sicheren Infrastruktur der neuen Wohnviertel. Auf der anderen Seite hält man noch immer voller Stolz an den Beziehungen zur Lebenskultur in den Townships fest — lebenswichtig, aber auch nostalgisch verbrämt. Irgendwie ist es wohl leichter, diese Widersprüche in der anonymen Welt der Vorortstädte zu leben. Auch ist die Assimilierung an diese Welt leichter inmitten der öden Vorstädte als unter den beobachtenden Blicken des alten weißen Südafrikas. Dort draußen am Rande ist es die Farbe des Geldes, die die Hautfarbe ersetzt und schnell zur Währung des glitzernden Erfolgs wird. Begierde — nach 4x4-Geländewagen, winzigen Handys, nach Gymnastik gedrillten Körpern, nach Deisel, Kookai, vergoldeten Wasserhähnen, Marmorfußböden und Play Station 2s — geht unweigerlich einher mit einer anderen Haltung, die Bewohnern solcher Viertel eigen ist: mangelndes Interesse an anderen.

1990 war nichts von all dem auch nur im Entferntesten vorstellbar. Es war das Jahr, als das Bauunternehmen "Anglo American Properties" weit außerhalb der Stadt ein von einer Mauer eingefasstes

en dehors de la ville, près du champ de course de Kyalami. A cette époque, on pouvait alors acheter un terrain de 1000 m_ entouré de murs pour 95 000 Rands; ce qui est assez cher, bien sûr, mais rien comparé aux 450 000 Rands qu'il faut maintenant débourser pour acquérir le même terrain dans le quartier le plus chic et le plus prétentieux de Midrand: Kyalami Estates.

Brian Lipschitz est l'un de ceux qui ont acheté dans ces années-là. Il était alors entrepreneur en construction et est maintenant directeur de Kyalami "Estates". "Quand, il y a 12 ans, j'ai construit ma maison ici", dit-il , "les gens pensaient que j'étais fou. On pensait que cet endroit était bien trop loin du centre. Bryanston, d'où je venais, était déjà considéré comme la périphérie de la cité. "Aujourd'hui", ajoute-t-il, "les sociétés les plus prestigieuses (Mercer, Nashua, Siemens, BMW, Vodacom), les meilleures écoles (l'école primaire de Kyalami, le collège Beaulieu, St Peters, le collège Crawford), les meilleurs centres commerciaux (de Fourways, de Sandton City, et de Pine Slopes pour l'épicerie fine), les meilleurs terrains de golf (clubs de Kyalami, Johannesburg, Lone Hilll et Leeukop Country) et enfin le meilleur club de gym (Midrand Virgin Active) se sont tous installés ici. Vous n'avez plus du tout besoin de vous rendre en ville."

Kyalami "estates" est cerclé par un mur haut de 2 mètres surmonté de fils

Wohnviertel nahe der Kyalami Pferderennbahn plante. Damals konnte man ein eintausend Quadratmeter großes Grundstück innerhalb der Mauern für 95.000 Rand kaufen. Das war immer noch teuer, aber kein Vergleich mit den 450.000 Rand, die es heute kostet, wenn man ein ebenso großes Stück Land in Midrands luxuriösester Adresse, in Kyalami Estates, erwirbt.

Einer von denen, die damals kauften, war Brian Lipschitz, damals Bauunternehmer, heute Manager von Kyalami Estates. "Als ich mein Haus hier vor zwölf Jahren gebaut habe", erzählt er, "haben die Leute mich für verrückt gehalten. Sie fanden das Terrain viel zu weit weg von der Stadt. Bryanston, von woher ich kam, wurde schon als das äußerste Ende der Stadt gesehen. Heute", fährt er fort, " sind die besten Unternehmen (Mecer, Nashua, Siemens, BMW, Vodacom), die besten Schulen (Kyalami Preparatory, Beaulieu College, St. Peters, Crawford College), die besten Einkaufszentren (Fourways Mall, Sandton City und Pine Slopes mit seinen Delikatessen), die besten Golfplätze (Kyalami, Johannesburg, Lone Hill und Leeukop Country Club) und das beste Fitnesszentrum (Midrand Virgin Active) hier heraus gezogen. Man muss überhaupt nicht mehr in die Stadt."

Kyalami Estates ist von einer zwei Meter hohen und 7,5 Millionen Rand teuren Mauer umgeben, die mit einem elektrisch geladenen Zaun versehen ist.

électrifiés ayant coûté 7,5 millions de Rands et est équipé d'un contrôle d'accès digital, à l'intérieur duquel une compagnie de sécurité armée et reliée à un ordinateur central patrouille dans 11 zones de surveillance. Mais une fois passé le hérissement de ce champ électro-magnétique, on passe alors brutalement de l'idée de tenir la racaille éloignée à celle d'un paradis à l'image du Club Med. La propriété se vante d'avoir 11 parcs, 5 barrages artificiels, des courts de tennis et de squash des clubs de courses et de marche à pieds, de lecture et d'œnologie. Avec des maisons qui sont évaluées entre 1,5 et 14 millions de Rands et la ligne d'horizon de Johannesburg à distance rassurante, Kyalami estates représente, que cela vous plaise ou non, le modèle et le mode de vie urbain auxquels la plupart de nos concitoyens aspirent dès à présent et dans le futur proche.

Es gibt digitale Zugangskontrolle, Computer gesteuerte Schussanlagen und elf patrouillenüberwachte Zonen. Aber hat man erst einmal diesen Angst einjagenden elektro-magnetischen Bereich hinter sich gelassen, ändert sich abrupt die Szenerie: Armut, Schmutz und Elend bleiben draußen vor den Toren, und man taucht ein wie in die Welt eines Club Med. Der riesige Wohnkomplex rühmt sich seiner elf Parkanlagen und fünf Dämme, er verfügt über Tennis- und Squashanlagen, es gibt Vereine zum Jogging und Walking, Leseclubs und Clubs zum Weinverkosten. Mit seinen Häusern, die zwischen 1, 5 und 14 Millionen Rand wert sind, und dem Blick auf die in beruhigend weiter Ferne liegende Johannesburger Skyline ist Kyalami Estates, ob es uns gefällt oder nicht, das Modell für städtisches Leben, wie es unsere Gesellschaft jetzt und in absehbarer Zukunft erstrebt.

BACK TO THE CENTRE DE RETOU

AU CENTRE ZURÜCK IN DIE STADT

When Audrey Zwambila, an energetic corporate consultant in her mid-thirties, realised that her new job with Absa Bank would mean working in Johannesburg's city centre, she was horrified. Says Zwambila, who lives in Bryanston: "I didn't want to be in town and I was very nervous about driving to work." Two years on she is "pleasantly surprised" to find that she's happy to be there and feels safe enough to recommend the central business district to her still sceptical friends.

There is just one catch: the multi-million-rand, prestige precinct housing Absa's 4 500 head office employees might as well be anywhere for all it has to do with the gritty city that surrounds it. Bounded by Commissioner, Marshall, Troye and Mooi streets, its three linked office towers contain a number of internalised atria, between them boasting an art gallery, mobile sculpture, ponds, bridges, palm trees and a miniature rain forest. They offer a comprehensive array of services. Staff can do their shopping at a Spar and a hardware store, visit the hairdresser, work out at the gym, take lunch in the staff canteen or a coffee shop fronting the street — but still within the Absa precinct. After work, taxis and buses stop outside the front door, freeway access is close by and, should there be a problem, help is on hand from the

Lorsque Audrey Zwambila, une dynamique consultante en entreprise d'environ 35 ans a réalisé que son nouvel emploi avec la banque Absa allait l'amener à travailler au centre ville de Johannesburg, elle fut horrifiée. D'après Zwambila, qui vit à Bryanston: "je ne voulais pas aller en ville et j'étais très nerveuse à l'idée de devoir de m'y rendre en voiture". Deux ans après, elle est elle-même "agréablement surprise" par le fait d'y être heureuse et de se sentir suffisamment en sécurité pour recommander le (CBD) à ses amis encore sceptiques.

Il y a juste une petite nuance : le complexe prestigieux et coûteux (plusieurs millions de Rands) qui héberge le siège d'Absa ainsi que ses 4 500 salariés aurait aussi bien pu être situé n'importe où ailleurs, car il n'a rien à voir avec le centre ville crasseux qui l'entoure. Délimité par Commissioner, Marshall, Troye et Mooi street, ses trois tours de bureaux reliées entre elles rassemble un certain nombre de fonctions internalisées, parmi lesquelles une orgueilleuse galerie d'art, des sculptures mobiles, des fontaines, des bassins, des ponts, des palmiers et une forêt tropicale miniature. Ce complexe offre une gamme complète de services en tout genre. Le personnel peut faire ses courses au supermarché Spar, et dans une quincaillerie voisine; aller chez le coiffeur, à la gym, déjeuner à la cantine du personnel ou au café qui

Als es Audrey Zwambila, einer energischen Firmenberaterin, bewusst wurde, dass ihr neuer Job bei der Absa Bank bedeutete, dass sie in Johannesburgs Innenstadt würde arbeiten müssen, war sie entsetzt. Die Mittdreißigerin wohnt in Bryanston und wollte nicht in die Stadt: "Ich hatte Angst, dorthin zur Arbeit zu fahren." Jetzt, zwei Jahre später, stellt sie "angenehm überrascht" fest, dass sie glücklich ist, hier zu sein, ja, sie fühlt sich so sicher, dass sie das Geschäftszentrum, den "Central Business District" oder CBD, sogar ihren noch immer skeptischen Freunden weiterempfiehlt.

Es gibt nur einen Haken dabei: Die millionenschwere, imposante Zentrale der Absa Bank mit ihren 4.500 Mitarbeitern könnte genauso gut woanders liegen, so wenig hat sie mit der rauen Stadt drum herum zu tun. Zwischen Commissioner-, Marshall-, Troye- und Mooi Street gelegen, beherbergen ihre drei miteinander verbundenen Bürotürme eine Reihe Glas überdachter, weiter Hallen, zwischen denen sich eine Kunstgalerie, ein mobile Skulptur, Teiche, Brücken, Palmen und ein Miniaturregenwald befinden. Ein umfassendes Angebot an Serviceleistungen steht dem Personal zur Verfügung. Ihre Einkäufe können die Mitarbeiter bei 'Spar' tätigen, ein Haushaltswarengeschäft ist vorhanden, sie können zum Friseur gehen, sich in einem Fitnessclub entspannen, im Personalrestaurant zu Mittag essen und

Absa-sponsored satellite police station, also within the precinct.

All of which is why Zwambila loves it. "Absa has created a self-sufficient environment that I never have to leave." Yet though she enthuses that it is wonderful "when you realise you can walk down the street and not be mugged", she admits to having ventured outside Absa's patrolled, designer-perfect world just once — to attend a meeting in the Carlton Centre, a block away.

Zwambila's relationship to her work environment perfectly captures the contradictions of the Johannesburg CBD (Central Business District). For what has "grown on her" is not Johannesburg, but the reassurance of knowing that her corporate world is just the same as it would be anywhere else in the city — Rivonia, Sandton — a secured, self-sufficient cocoon that she never has to leave, thereby avoiding altogether the chaotic, threatening, multicultural muddle around it.

Absa, whose decision to stay in the city in the mid-1990s was applauded for its optimism and investment in the decaying centre, is not alone in building on the idea of elegant isolation in the midst of unpredictable streets. In Sandton, banking group Nedcor's new R850 million head office complex adopts a remarkably similar approach. Here too, boasts Derek van den Bergh,

donne sur la rue mais qui restent néanmoins sur le domaine d'Absa. Après le travail, les taxis et les bus s'arrêtent juste devant la porte d'entrée ; l'entrée de l'autoroute est toute proche et s'il devait y avoir le moindre problème, du secours viendrait rapidement du poste de police sponsorisé d'Absa et se trouvant aussi sur son domaine. C'est pourquoi Zwambila apprécie autant l'endroit. "Absa a su créer un environnement auto-suffisant d'où je n'ai pas besoin de sortir". Cependant, bien qu'elle s'emballe et trouve merveilleuse l'idée de "pouvoir marcher dans la rue et de ne pas se faire agresser", elle admet qu'elle ne s'est aventurée qu'une fois en dehors du monde parfait et surveillé d'Absa, et ce pour participer à une réunion au Carlton Center qui se trouve à deux pas.

La relation de Zwambila à son environnement de travail illustre parfaitement les contradictions du CBD de Johannesburg. Car ce qui a "grandi en elle" ce n'est pas Johannesburg, mais l'assurance de savoir que son entreprise-monde est exactement la même que s'il elle s'était trouvée n'importe où ailleurs dans l'agglomération — Rivonia, Sandton — c'est-à-dire un cocon sécurisé et auto-suffisant qu'elle n'est jamais dans l'obligation de quitter, et de ce fait lui permet d'éviter le désordre chaotique, multiculturel et menaçant qui l'entoure.

Absa, dont la décision de rester au

ihren Espresso im Coffee Shop nehmen, der zur Straße geht - und das alles innerhalb des Areals der Bank. Nach der Arbeit können sie Taxis und Busse direkt vor dem Haupteingang bekommen, die Auffahrt zur Schnellstraße ist nicht weit, und sollte es irgendein Problem geben, findet man sofort Hilfe auf der von der Bank gesponserten Polizeiwache innerhalb des Gebäudes.

Und daher liebt es Zwambila. "Absa hat eine autarke Umgebung geschaffen, aus der ich nie hinaus muss." Aber obwohl sie davon schwärmt, wie toll es ist, "wenn du merkst, du kannst die Straße hinuntergehen und wirst nicht überfallen", gibt sie zu, dass sie sich nur einmal aus Absas überwachter, designer-perfekten Welt hinausgewagt hat - zu einer Besprechung ins Carlton Centre einen Block weiter. Zwambilas Verhältnis zu der Umgebung, in der sie arbeitet, verdeutlicht die Widersprüche, die in Johannesburgs Geschäftszentrum zu Tage treten. Denn was ihr ans Herz gewachsen ist, ist nicht Johannesburg, sondern die Beruhigung zu wissen, dass ihre Firmenwelt genau so gut in einem anderen Stadtteil liegen könnte, z.B. in Rivonia oder Sandton, und ein abgesicherter, autarker Kokon ist, den sie nie verlassen muss. Und dass sie auf diese Weise das ganze chaotische, bedrohliche und multikulturelle Durcheinander draußen vermeiden kann.

Die Entscheidung der Absa Bank Mitte der 1990er, in der Innenstadt zu bleiben

Inside the ABSA North Tower atrium   Intérieur de l'atrium de la Tour Nord d'ABSA.   Im Innenhof des Nordturms der Absa Bank

general manager of Nedcor's Property Services, "staff don't have to venture out". All they need — library, restaurant, convenience store, travel agent, bank, crèche — can be found on its secured internal street.

The CBD's remaining corporates — and their panorama is not insignificant, featuring four of the country's largest banks, the mining houses, Old Mutual, Sanlam, BHP Billiton and Transnet, to name a few — have, quite simply, dug in. They have staked out their turf and carved up the city into patrolled, flag-festooned, designer-paved, rubbish-binned corporate enclaves known as Community Improvement Districts. Their contribution to urban renewal is amply rewarded by the Central Johannesburg Partnership (CJP), the irresistibly acronymed Bongo (Business-Orientated Non-Governmental Organisation) dedicated to servicing them. The CJP provides additional cleaning and security, while Business Against Crime's state-of-the-art, ISO 9000-compliant surveillance system keeps its cameras trained on these buildings around the clock.

Simulating their suburban counterparts, these new monoliths have absorbed and privatised all the paraphernalia that usually make a city buzz — coffee shops, magazine stands, bookstalls, stationers, chemists, hairdressers. For those inside, the city has ceased to exist; for

centre ville au milieu des années 1990 a été largement applaudie et saluée pour son optimisme et ses investissements dans le centre décadent, n'est pas seule à adhérer à l'idée d'un isolement élégant au milieu de rues imprévisibles. A Sandton, le groupe financier Nedcor a adopté une approche similaire pour son nouveau complexe de 850 millions de Rands qui lui tient lieu de siège. Dans ce cas aussi, Derek Van den Bergh, directeur général des services sur la propriété de Nedcor se vante du fait que "les membres du personnel n'ont pas besoin de s'aventurer au dehors". Tout ce dont ils ont besoin - bibliothèque, restaurant, superette, agence de voyage, crèche, banque - se trouve dans les rues intérieures sécurisées.

Les entreprises qui restent dans le CBD - et elles ne sont pas insignifiantes, puisqu'il s'agit des quatre plus grandes banques du pays, des entrepises de l'industrie minière, d'Old Mutual, de la Sanlam, de Billiton et de Transnet pour n'en nommer que quelques-unes - ont tout simplement creusé le filon.

Elles ont jalonné le terrain et modelé la ville de façon à fabriquer des enclaves de sociétés surveillées au drapeau festonné, au pavement bien dessiné, et aux ordures bien entassées dans les poubelles. C'est ce que l'on nomme le quartier des améliorations communautaires. Leur contribution au renouveau urbain est largement récompensée par le Partenariat pour le

und in eine verfallende Stadt zu investieren, wurde wegen ihres Optimismus begrüßt. Mit seiner Idee der eleganten Isolierung inmitten einer unberechenbaren Umgebung steht das Institut nicht alleine da. In Sandton geht die Bankengruppe Nedcor mit ihrer neuen 850 Millionen Rand teuren Zentrale (100 ZAR = ca. 13 EUR) einen ganz ähnlichen Weg. Auch hier, erläutert Verwaltungsdirektor Derek van den Bergh stolz, "muss das Personal nicht hinaus auf die Straße." Alles, was die Mitarbeiter brauchen, Bücherei, Restaurant, ein Geschäft, Reisebüro, Bank, Kinderkrippe, gibt es auf den sicheren und gesicherten Binnenstraßen.

Auch die anderen im Zentrum gebliebenen Unternehmen (und es sind nicht die unbedeutendsten; allein vier der größten Banken sind hier vertreten, die Minengesellschaften, Old Mutual, Sanlam, Billiton and Transnet, um nur ein paar wenige zu nennen) sind hier inzwischen fest verwurzelt. Sie haben ihr Gelände abgesteckt und die Stadt in patrouillenüberwachte, mit Flaggen verzierte, designer-gepflasterte und mit Abfallbehältern ausgestattete firmeneigene Enklaven eingeteilt, die unter dem Begriff "Community Improvement Districts" oder Gemeindesanierungsgebiet bekannt sind. Ihr Beitrag zur Stadterneuerung wird großzügig von der "Central Johannesburg Partnership" (CJP) belohnt, einer Business-orientierten Nichtregierungsorganisation, kurz Bongo

those outside, the city is a pretty desperate place.

For beyond these corporate cocoons lies a denuded, rather sad world of former retail space now shut up in concrete, demolished buildings, open parking lots, vacant office space and slow street trade, bearing witness to the vacuum created by these new investment "islands".

In the revamped Gandhi (alias Van der Byl) Square, the three plastic tables of the Traffic Square Café stand forlornly empty. I come across one rowdy, packed Brazilian Coffee Shop, one internet cafe and a single branch of CNA stationers (a national chain), but, for the rest, what remains is a succession of loan sharks, wholesale hawker outlets, public phone shops and fast food stores announced with clumsy drawings of steaming chickens.

They serve the city's poor. But for the in-betweeners — those neither cushioned by the corporate "malls" nor at the bottom of the economic pile — the inner-city is an awkward place to be. They are the independent entrepreneurs, service providers and their clients who have taken up the C- and D-grade office space in the abandoned shadows of the A-grade office acreage which is still a hard sell. They count among their numbers mostly black accountants, doctors, engineers, hairdressers, photographers and small manufacturers.

Centre de Johannesburg (CJP) ainsi que par les organisations non-gouvernementales oeuvrant dans le domaine des affaires (Acronyme Bongo : Business Orientated Non Governmental organisation) dont l'objectif est de servir ces grosses sociétés. Le Partenariat pour le Centre de Johannesburg (CJP) fournit de surcroît un service de nettoyage et de sécurité , alors que le système de surveillance ultra-moderne ISO 9000 de l'organisation "entreprises contre le crime" laisse tourner ses caméras sur ces immeubles 24 heures sur 24.

Stimulant leurs homologues suburbains, ces nouveaux complexes monolithiques ont absorbé et privatisé tout l'attirail et le bazar qui fait habituellement l'animation d'une ville — les cafés, les kiosques à journaux, les librairies, les papeteries, les pharmacies, les coiffeurs. Pour ceux qui sont à l'intérieur, la ville a cessé d'exister; pour ceux qui sont à l'extérieur, la ville est devenue un endroit désespérant. Car au-delà de ces entreprises encocoonées, s'étend un monde dénudé et plutôt triste d'anciens espaces de vente maintenant fermés, d'immeubles de bétons à moitié démolis, d'espaces de parking à ciel ouvert, d'espaces de bureaux vides et d'un commerce de rue tournant au ralenti, autant de lourds témoins du vide laissé par ces nouveaux "îlots" d'investissement.

genannt. CJP kümmert sich zusätzlich um Reinigung und Sicherheit, während das moderne ISO-9000-Überwachungssystem von "Business Against Crime" ("Unternehmen gegen Verbrechen") seine Kameras rund um die Uhr auf deren Gebäude halten.

Diese neuen Monolithen der Wirtschaft haben es ihren Pendants in den Außenbezirken der Stadt abgeguckt und sich alles einverleibt und angeeignet, was für gewöhnlich großstädtisches Treiben ausmacht — Cafés, Zeitungskioske, Buchläden, Schreibwarenläden, Drogerien, Apotheken, Friseurgeschäfte. Für die, die drinnen sind in diesen großen Komplexen, existiert die City nicht; für die, die draußen sind, ist sie ein ziemlich elender Ort. Denn jenseits der Firmenkokons liegt eine nackte, traurige Welt mit geschlossenen Geschäften, zerstörten Gebäuden, offenen Parkflächen, leeren Büroräumen und einem lauen Straßenhandel, die das Vakuum offenbaren, die diese neuen Investment-Inseln geschaffen haben.

Auf dem aufpolierten Gandhi (alias Van der Byl) Platz stehen die drei Plastiktische des Traffic Square Café hoffnungslos leer herum. Ich komme an einem voll besetzten Brazilian Coffee Shop vorbei, an einem Internet Café und einer Filiale von CNA, einer südafrikanischen Papier- und Schreibwarenkette. Der ganze Rest sind Kredithaie, Straßenhändler, Shops zum Telefonieren und Fast-Food-Läden, die mit plumpen Zeichnungen von dampfenden

Dressmaker Zilla Mabala is one such entrepreneur. She occupies about 60 square metres in the relatively well-maintained, four-storeyed, Art Deco Cambridge House on Troye Street, just two blocks north of the Absa precinct. She is one of between 500 and 600 clothing manufacturers in the recently proclaimed Fashion District making everything from wedding dresses and Mandela shirts to ethnic uniforms for casino employees and customised G-strings for the city's strippers. They are clustered around the Johannesburg

Sur la place Gandhi récemment rénovée (anciennnement Van Der Byl), les trois tables en plastique du café Traffic de la place restent désespérément vides. Je passe devant un café brésilien bondé et animé, un café internet et l'unique papeterie CNA (une chaîne nationale), mais tout le reste n'est qu'une succession de petits escrocs prêteurs d'argent, de divers colporteurs au détail, de petites échoppes de téléphonie, ou de magasins de restauration rapide annoncés par

Hühnchen die Aufmerksamkeit auf sich zu lenken versuchen.

Sie bedienen die Armen der Stadt. Aber für die, die dazwischen liegen, also für die, die weder gut gepolstert in einer "Firmen-Mall" sitzen noch am untersten Ende der Einkommensskala stehen, für die ist die Innenstadt ein unangenehmer Ort. Es sind die unabhängigen Unternehmer, Dienstleister und deren Kunden, die die zweit- und drittklassigen Büros im Schatten der noblen Geschäftsräume der Toplage übernommen haben. Zu dieser Gruppe

A typical pavement scene in the Fashion District of Johannesburg's city centre

Scène typique d'une rue piétonne, dans le Quartier de la Mode, au centre ville de Johannesburg

Typische Straßenszene im Fashion District in der Innenstadt Johannesburgs

School girls and a CJP security guard in Gandhi Square

Ecolières et garde de l'agence de sécurité CJP, à Ghandi Square

Schülerinnen und Wachmann der Central Johannesburg Partnership auf dem Gandhi Square

Sewing Centre in Pritchard Street, a one-stop shop for the micro garment industry.

Mabala makes what is, for her, a good living. She is able to pay her R400 a month rent and her daily transport to and from her home in Alexandra, feed herself and her family and employ a Congolese assistant. However, she does not particularly enjoy working in town. "My customers are word of mouth," she says. "They complain about coming to town because they are afraid of the crime on the streets." Mabala does not venture out much herself. She cooks her own lunch and heads for home before it gets dark. Her sentiments are echoed by Liaqat Ali Jatt, the Pakistani owner of Paradise Cash and Carry nearby, who complains bitterly about the theft from his roller-shutter-doored shop and the lack of response from the police. Mabala and Jatt's turf is clearly not a high-impact zone in Business Against Crime's surveillance of the city.

Xolela Mangcu, urban planner and director of the Steve Biko Foundation, can see two skylines from his office in Braamfontein — Johannesburg's and Sandton's. Mangcu, like many of the new black middle class, has no sense of belonging in or being a citizen of Johannesburg.

"I live in Sandton, play in Rosebank, and go home to Ginsburg, in the Eastern Cape," he says. "While I

quelques maladroits dessins de poulet fumant.

Ils sont au service de la ville des pauvres. Mais pour ceux qui se situent entre les deux — ceux qui ne sont ni protégés par le monde de l'entreprise, ni au bas de l'échelle économique — le cœur du centre-ville est devenu un endroit inadapté. Parmi ceux-ci, figurent les entrepreneurs indépendants, fournisseurs de services et leurs clients qui occupent désormais les espaces de bureaux de standard inférieur à l'ombre des espaces de bureaux high-tech qui restent très difficiles à vendre. La plupart sont des comptables, des docteurs, des ingénieurs, des coiffeurs, des photographes et de petits producteurs de biens divers.

Zilla Mabala, couturière, fait partie de ces entrepreneurs. Elle occupe environ 60 m_ dans un immeuble art déco de quatre étages plutôt bien entretenu , le "Cambridge House" dans la Troye Street, à deux immeubles seulement au Nord du domaine d'Absa. Elle est l'une des 500 à 600 couturiers-designers de l'industrie du vêtement installée dans ce quartier proclamé récemment Quartier de la Mode. Leur production s'étend de la robe de mariée aux chemises de Mandela en passant par les uniformes ethniques pour les employés de casino et par les strings réalisés sur commande pour les spectacles de strip-tease de la ville. Ils sont enfermés dans le centre de la couture de Johannesburg situé dans

gehören schwarze Buchhalter, Ärzte, Ingenieure, Friseure, Fotografen, Inhaber kleiner Produktionsbetriebe.

Und auch Zilla Mabala. Sie ist Schneiderin mit ungefähr 60 Quadratmeter Arbeitsfläche in dem relativ gepflegten vierstöckigen Art Deco-Cambridge-Haus in Troye Street, nur zwei Quadrate weiter nördlich von der Zentrale der Absa Bank. 500 bis 600 Schneidereien arbeiten in diesem erst kürzlich zum Fashion District erklärten Viertel. Sie nähen alles — vom Hochzeitskleid und Mandela T-Shirt bis zu Berufsuniformen im Ethnolook für die Kasinoangestellten und maßgeschneiderte String-Tangas für Johannesburgs Stripper und Stripperinnen. Sie alle haben sich um das Nähzentrum in Pritchard Street niedergelassen, einem Kaufhaus speziell für die Kleintextilbranche.

Mabala lebt für ihre Verhältnisse gut. Sie kann jeden Monat die 400 Rand für ihre Miete aufbringen sowie das Fahrgeld für die tägliche Fahrt hin und zurück nach Alexandra, wo sie wohnt. Das Geld reicht, um sich und ihre Familie zu ernähren und eine Angestellte aus dem Kongo zu beschäftigen. Dennoch arbeitet sie nicht besonders gern in der Stadt. "Meine Kunden sagen mir ganz offen, dass sie nicht gern in die Stadt kommen, weil sie Angst haben, auf der Straße überfallen zu werden." Mabala selbst geht nicht viel raus. Sie kocht sich ihr eigenes Mittagessen und versucht nach Hause zu

still speak of Jozi, it has lost its identity for me."

For Mangcu, one of the problems is that "official Johannesburg language is directed at investors". (Here one assumes he is referring to mantras like Mayor Amos Masondo's latest "African World Class City"). "It is not connected to everyday life and so does not inspire the collective identity that will make Jozi vibe again."

Mangcu has put his finger on it. What is missing from Johannesburg is its being identified by its citizens as a central and important figure in their landscape, as somewhere they choose to go, to play, to work or to live. Instead, a disdain for the urban (and love of the suburbs), a deep distrust of the heterogeneous and a horror of middle age — all qualities epitomised by the Johannesburg city centre — seem to characterise the collective psyche. The words, the sentiments, the images, the Johannesburg with which most people identify and to which they aspire are the homogeneous shopping malls or "Tuscan" villas which proliferate in the northern suburbs, or in the culturally rich townships of their youth. Somehow Newtown's always becoming yet never belonging culture — theatres, museums, galleries and music venues — cannot quite counter their urban antipathy. It is going to take more than the fancy French lighting

Pritchard Street, un magasin où il faut absolument s'arrêter si l'on est dans la micro industrie du tissu.

Mabala gagne, d'après elle, bien sa vie. Elle est en mesure de payer son loyer de 400 Rands par mois, son transport quotidien pour aller et revenir d'Alexandra où se trouve sa maison, se nourrir ainsi que sa famille et employer un assistant congolais. Cependant, elle n'apprécie pas pariculièrement de travailler en ville. "Mes clients proviennent du bouche à oreille", dit-elle. "Ils se plaignent de devoir venir en ville car ils ont peur des crimes de la rue". Mabala ne s'y aventure d'ailleurs guère elle-même. Elle prépare son propre déjeuner et se dépêche de rentrer à la maison avant qu'il ne fasse sombre. Sa position renvoie à celle de Liaqat Ali Jatt, le pakistanais propriétaire du "Paradis du Prêt à Emporter" tout proche. Ce dernier se plaint amèrement du vol commis dans magasin en dépit du rideau métallique qui le fermait, et de l'inaction de la police. Le champ d'action de Mabala et de Jatt n'est pas, à l'évidence, une zone à fort impact pour l'organisation "Entreprises Contre le Crime", sensée surveiller le centre ville.

Xolela Mangcu, urbaniste et directeur de la fondation Steve Biko, peut apercevoir deux lignes d'horizon de son bureau à Braamfontein — celle de Johannesburg et celle de Sandton. Mangcu, comme bien des noirs de la nouvelle classe moyenne, n'a aucun

kommen, bevor es dunkel wird. Nicht anders geht es ihrem pakistanischen Ladennachbarn Liaqat Ali Jatt, Inhaber des Kleidergeschäfts "Paradise Cash and Carry", der sich bitter beklagt wegen des Diebstahls in seinem mit einem Metallrollgitter versehenen Geschäft und der mangelnden Reaktion der Polizei. Die Gegend, wo Mabala und Jatt ihre Läden haben, ist eindeutig keine vorrangig wichtige Zone für "Business Against Crime".

Xolela Mangcu, Stadtplaner und Direktor der Steve-Biko-Stiftung erblickt von seinem Büro in Braamfontein zwei Skylines, die von Johannesburg und die von Sandton. Mangcu, wie viele Vertreter der neuen schwarzen Mittelschicht, liegt nichts daran, Johannesburger zu sein. "Ich lebe in Sandton, verbringe meine Freizeit in Rosebank, und mein Zuhause ist Ginsberg im östlichen Kap", sagt er. "Zwar sage ich noch immer 'Jozi' für Johannesburg, aber es hat für mich seinen Charakter verloren."

Eines der Probleme, so Mangcu, sei, dass "die offizielle Sprache, mit der Johannesburg spricht, sich an Investoren richtet" (und es ist zu vermuten, dass sich Mangcu hier auf die Slogans des Regierenden Bürgermeisters Amos Masondo bezieht wie der erst kürzlich verkündete von der "African World Class City"). "Diese Sprache hat nichts mit dem alltäglichen Leben zu tun und schafft daher keine kollektive Identität, die Jozi wieder zum Leben erwecken würde."

and strange midget-sized busts littering Mary Fitzgerald Square (which has just undergone a R4,5 million makeover) to change things. Meanwhile, Johannesburg's prevailing image remains one of a diseased and dirty city.

Johannesburg's first "Supermayor", Amos Masondo, has done little since he took office in 2001 to inspire another picture. Known as a trustworthy but dull party man, Masondo is hardly Johannesburg's answer to New York's Giuliani or Dakar's Diop. Many residents have never heard of him.

He declared the inner city one of his "six most urgent priorities" at his inauguration. Ever since, he has droned on about its contradictions, its chronic decay and, at the same time, its good infrastructure and "extraordinary economic and social potential". While all this is true, his rhetoric conveys no more of a sense of the city than as a problem to be solved. One never gets an image of the city as a place to be — somewhere one would choose to bring up children, walk your dogs, eat out, go to the movies, shop, make a living.

Indeed, Masondo's own transport programmes raise the idea of the city as a place to come and go from rather than to inhabit. These include plans to serve the 800 000 daily commuters and 400 000 annual shoppers moving

sentiment d'appartenance ou de citoyenneté par rapport à la ville de Johannesburg. "Je vis à Sandton, je me divertis à Rosebank, et retrouve mes origines à Ginsburg, dans la région du Cape Est," dit-il, "Bien que je parle encore de Jozi, elle a perdu son identité pour moi".

Pour Mangcu, l'un des problèmes est que "la langue officielle de Johannesburg s'adresse d'abord aux investisseurs". (On peut supposer qu'il fait référence ici à des expressions telles que celle employée par le maire Amos Masondo "une ville africaine de classe mondiale"). "Rien de tout cela n'est connecté à la vie quotidienne et en conséquence, n'alimente pas l'identité collective qui redonnera de la vie à Jozi".

Mangcu a mis le doigt là où ça fait mal. Car ce qui manque à la ville de Johannesburg, c'est d'être identifiée par ses citoyens comme une figure importante et centrale de leur paysage, comme un endroit où ils choisissent d'aller, de sortir, de travailler ou de vivre. Au contraire, on découvre un dédain envers l'urbanité (et un amour pour les banlieues), une profonde méfiance envers l'hétérogénéité et envers l'horreur du Moyen Age — toutes des caractéristiques incarnées par le centre-ville de Johannesburg -qui semblent marquer les représentations collectives. Les mots, les sentiments, les images de Johannesburg auxquelles la plupart des gens s'identifient et ce vers quoi ils

Mangcu legt den Finger in die Wunde. Das Problem ist, dass Johannesburgs Bürger die Stadt nicht als den Mittelpunkt ihres Lebens betrachten. Als einen Ort, wo sie gerne hingehen, die Freizeit genießen, arbeiten und leben. Stattdessen scheint Verachtung für die Stadt (und Liebe zu den 'suburbs') die kollektive Psyche zu bestimmen. Außerdem tiefes Misstrauen gegenüber allem Heterogenen und Horror vor der Generation der mittleren Jahrgänge - beides kennzeichnend für Johannesburgs Zentrum. Die Sprache, das Gefühl, das Image, jenes Johannesburg, mit dem sich die meisten Menschen identifizieren und das sie sich ersehnen, sind die homogenen, immergleichen Malls und Einkaufszentren und die Villen im mediterran-toskanischen Flair, wie sie im Norden der Stadt aus dem Boden gestampft werden, oder die kulturell reichen und lebendigen Townships ihrer Jugend. Die Theater, Museen, Galerien und Musikveranstaltungen im Stadtteil Newtown, die zwar immer irgendwie stimmig sind, aber nie richtig greifen, schaffen es nicht, dass die Menschen ihre Antipathie gegen die Stadt fallen lassen. Um die Dinge zu ändern, braucht es mehr als die fantastische Beleuchtung eines französischen Designers oder seltsame kleine Holzbüsten auf dem Mary Fitzgerald Platz (der gerade für 4,5 Millionen Rand saniert wurde). Solange aber bleibt das vorherrschende Bild von Johannesburg das einer kranken und

through the city with more and better taxi ranks, freeway off-ramps and informal markets. While such improvements may make commuting easier and even counter the prevailing image of the inner city as a wild, barely traversable, Escape from New York nightmare, what makes most major cities in the world interesting is not those who move in and out of it, but those who live in it: that in the shadows of big business and high finance, ordinary people earning a range of incomes do ordinary things and love it.

Aside from lacking the personal charisma to engage public imagination, Mayor Masondo has delegated responsibility for overseeing the city's transformation to Sol Cowan, Councillor for the Inner City on the Mayoral Committee, and Graeme Reid, CEO of the Johannesburg Development Agency (JDA). Cowan is wild and unpredictable, given to frequent tongue-lashings of big business for deserting the city. Reid is a solid former NGO man, who hates the limelight. Together they head up the bunch of suit-and-tied, middle-class, middle-aged white men leading the inner city regeneration drive. They include an ex-lawyer, an ex-builder, an ex-engineer, an ex-trade unionist, an ex-shrink and an ex-accountant, who have given up their day jobs, so to speak, to tackle the city's problems.

aspirent sont incarnés par les centre commerciaux bien homogènes et par les villas "toscanes" qui prolifèrent dans les banlieues nord, ou dans les townships culturellement riches de leur jeunesse. D'une certaine manière, la culture toujours en devenir de Newton, mais jamais re-appropriée — théâtres, musées, galeries et scènes de musique — ne peut guère contrer leur antipathie urbaine. Il faudra bien plus que l'éclairage fantaisiste français et les étranges bustes miniatures éparpillés sur la place Mary Fitzgerald (qui vient juste de subir un ré-aménagement de 4,5 millions de Rands) pour changer les choses. Parallèlement, l'image dominante de Johannesburg reste celle d'une ville malade et sale. Le premier "super maire" de Johannesburg, Amos Masondo, a fait bien peu depuis qu'il a pris le pouvoir en 2001 pour donner une autre image de la ville. Reconnu à la fois comme un homme sérieux mais aussi comme un homme de parti bien terne, Masondo n'est pas vraiment ce que Johannesburg pourrait attendre en comparaison à Giuliani, son homologue new-yorkais ou à Diop son homologue Dakarois. Beaucoup de résidents n'ont jamais entendu parler de lui. Il déclara que le centre ville était l'une des "six priorités les plus urgentes" lors de son discours de prise de fonction. Depuis, il a parlé avec monotonie des contradictions de la ville, de sa décadence chronique et en même

dreckigen Stadt.

Johannesburgs erster Regierender "Super"-Bürgermeister Amos Masondo hat wenig getan, um diese Bild zu korrigieren, seit er 2001 das Amt übernahm. Bekannt als zuverlässiger, aber blasser Parteimensch, ist Masondo kaum Johannesburgs Antwort auf New Yorks Giuliani oder Dakars Diop. Viele Bewohner haben noch nie von ihm gehört.

Bei seiner Amtsübernahme erklärte er die Innenstadt zu einer seiner "sechs vorrangig zu lösenden Problempunkte". Seither hat er immer wieder dieselben Widersprüche heruntergeleiert: der chronische Verfall einerseits und die gute Infrastruktur und das "außergewöhnliche wirtschaftliche und soziale Potential" andererseits. Das stimmt zwar, aber für Masondo ist die Stadt nichts anderes als ein Problemfall, der der Lösung bedarf. Nie entsteht das Bild einer Stadt, in der man seine Kinder aufwachsen sehen möchte, wo man einkaufen, arbeiten, den Hund ausführen, essen oder ins Kino gehen, kurz - leben möchte.

Und auch Masondos Programme für den innerstädtischen Verkehr vermitteln das Gefühl, dass die Stadt ein Ort ist, in den man hinein und aus dem man wieder hinausfährt, aber nicht ein Ort zum Wohnen. So will man die 800.000 Pendler pro Tag und die 400.000 Käufer, die jährlich die Innenstadt besuchen, mit mehr und besseren Taxihalteplätzen, zusätzlichen Autobahnauffahrten und weiteren ungeregelten, informellen Märkten

While one can only commend their missionary zeal, none among them has the personality, authority (or the colour?) the city needs right now.

Arguably the last person to fight for the city with the requisite ambition was Ian Davidson, the last Democratic Party Chairperson of the Johannesburg Management Committee. In the early 1990s, Davidson adopted an "ugly but energetic" New York precinct-based approach to the city centre, to counter moves within his own party favouring suburban Sandton as the future city's

temps de l'excellence de son infrastructure et de "son extraordinaire potentiel économique et social". Bien que tout cela soit vrai, sa rhétorique contribue à laisser penser que la ville a effectivement un problème à résoudre . On ne perçoit guère l'image d'une ville où il faut être — un endroit où l'on voudrait élever ses enfants, promener son chien, sortir au restaurant, aller au cinéma, faire du shopping, en bref, un endroit où l'on voudrait vivre.

En effet, le propre plan de transport de Masondo donne une idée de la ville

versorgen. Mag sein, dass diese Verbesserungen den Pendlern das Leben erleichtern und dem vorherrschenden Image entgegenwirken, dass das Johannesburger Zentrum ein wilder, kaum durchquerbarer Albtraum sei. Doch was die meisten großen Städte in der Welt interessant macht, sind nicht die Menschen, die kommen und gehen, sondern die, die in ihr wohnen: dass im Schatten von Großunternehmen und Bankinstituten ganz normale Leute ihr Leben leben, ganz normale Dinge tun und die Stadt lieben.

Neil Fraser of the Central Johannesburg Partnership (left) and Graeme Reid of the Johannesburg Development Agency (right)

Neil Fraser du Partenariat Central de Johannesburg (à gauche) et Graeme Reid de l'Agence de Développement de Johannesburg (à droite)

Neil Fraser von der Central Johannesburg Partnership (links) und Graeme Reid von der Johannesburg Development Agency (rechts)

The Mary Fitzgerald Square, centrepiece of the Newtown Cultural Precinct, after its makeover

Le Mary Fitzgerald Square, place principale du Newtown Cultural Precinct, après sa rénovation

Der Mary Fitzgerald Square, Mittelpunkt des Newtown Cultural Precinct, nach der Sanierung

heart. He brought the Gauteng Legislature and administrations to the Johannesburg city centre through a deal with ANC provincial strongman Paul Mashatile in the corridors of CODESA (Congress for a Democratic South Africa, the national forum through which the terms of South Africa's transition to democracy was negotiated between 1992 and 1994), and set about positioning the inner city as an international business centre. Newtown, a cultural precinct on the site of a disused inner city power station, Ellis Park, the sports precinct on the eastern edge of the central business district, and the disastrous (from the start) Civic Spine, a plan to revamp the City Hall precinct, were part of that vision. They would form the cultural bedrock and provide the ambiance — hotels, restaurants, conference venues, concert halls, museums, sporting events — that international business expected.

Davidson lost the war. His vision was scuppered, largely by its moment in history which rendered it automatically illegitimate to the city's new leaders, but also for its failure to anticipate the influx of poor and unemployed, looking to survive economic adjustments beyond their control.

Instead, Sandton caught the imagination of the post-1994 ruling elite, the business community, and

comme d'un lieu de transit plutôt que comme un endroit où l'on habite. Cela passe notamment par des projets pour fournir aux 800 000 banlieusards qui font quotidiennement le trajet jusqu'en ville et aux 400 000 clients annuels qui se déplacent dans la ville, plus de stations de taxi-minibus, plus d'entrées et de sorties d'autoroutes et plus de marchés informels. Bien sûr, de telles améliorations peuvent rendre les trajets quotidiens plus faciles et même contrer l'image dominante d'un centre ville sauvage, difficilement traversable ; elles ne permettent pas de s'échapper du cauchemar new-yorkais. Car ce qui rend la plupart des agglomérations mondiales intéressantes, ce ne sont pas ceux qui y entrent et qui en sortent, mais ceux qui y vivent: les gens ordinaires avec différents revenus qui, à l'ombre des grosses entreprises et de la haute finance, font des choses ordinaires et aiment ça.

Au-delà de son manque de charisme personnel qui permettrait de susciter l'imagination et l'enthousiasme du public, Masondo, le maire, a délégué la responsabilité du suivi de la transformation de la ville à Sol Cowan, conseiller pour le Centre-ville au conseil municipal et à Graeme Reid, directeur général de l'Agence de Développement de Johannesburg. Cowan est un personnage sauvage et imprévisible comme le montrent ses fréquents coups de gueule contre les entreprises qui

Abgesehen davon, dass es ihm am persönlichen Charisma fehlt, um der Öffentlichkeit Visionen zu vermitteln, hat Bürgermeister Masondo die Verantwortung für die Sanierung und Entwicklung der Stadt auch noch an Sol Cowan, Abgeordneter des Innenstadtbezirks im Bürgermeisterkomitee, und an Graeme Reid, Generaldirektor der Johannesburger Entwicklungsorganisation, ("Johannesburg Development Agency", JDA) delegiert. Cowan ist leicht erregbar, sein Verhalten unvorhersehbar, und er neigt dazu, die großen Firmen zu beschimpfen, weil sie die Stadt verließen. Reid war früher ein vertrauenswürdiger Mitarbeiter einer Nichtregierungsorganisation, der nicht gern im Rampenlicht steht. Gemeinsam leiten sie die Gruppe der weißen Männer mittleren Alters, Vertreter der Mittelschicht, ordentlich in Anzug und Krawatte, die das Unternehmen Innenstadtsanierung vorantreiben. Zu dieser Gruppe gehören ein ehemaliger Rechtsanwalt, ein ehemaliger Baumeister, ein ehemaliger Ingenieur, ein ehemaliger Gewerkschaftler, ein ehemaliger Psychotherapeut und ein ehemaliger Wirtschaftsprüfer, die ihre eigentliche Arbeit quasi aufgegeben haben, um sich um die Probleme der Stadt zu kümmern. Ihr missionarischer Eifer ist zu loben, doch keiner von ihnen besitzt die Persönlichkeit und Autorität (oder die Farbe?), die die Stadt jetzt braucht.

Der Letzte, der womöglich mit echtem Ehrgeiz für die Innenstadt gekämpft hat,

most of the city's people.

Yet, despite this official failure to re-present the city, and despite the absence of Mangcu's "language of the ordinary", downtown Johannesburg is not without people, however marginal, who love it. Dennis Maseko, a 20-something national lottery draw officer from Barberton, now lives in Carr Gardens, a recently completed three-storey rental housing complex with 145 units, built by the Johannesburg Housing Company (JHC). "I would not move out unless I need something bigger", he says. "I find living here convenient, quiet (in comparison with the townships), and safe." Maseko's work is an easy taxi ride away in Auckland Park; he does his shopping at the Oriental Plaza, gyms in town and "sometimes goes to the Market Theatre".

Maseko is one of a new breed of small but regular income earners — taxi drivers, hairdressers, cleaners, factory workers, small entrepreneurs — who are proud to call the inner city home, courtesy of the JHC. Adopting a "low cost does not mean low quality" approach and effective management, it has, since the mid-1990s, built or refurbished 10 inner-city buildings, housing almost 3 000 people. In doing so, it has challenged the perception of the inner city as a Wild West shootout between intransigent landlords and rabid tenant committees and

désertent le centre ville. Reid, quant à lui, est un ancien membre d'ONG solide, qui déteste les feux des projecteurs. Ensemble, ils dirigent la poignée de col-blancs de la classe moyenne, âgés de 40 à 50 ans, tous des Blancs, qui pilotent le renouveau du centre-ville. Parmi eux, on trouve un ex-juriste, un ex-constructeur immobilier, un ex-ingénieur, un ex-syndicaliste, un ex-psychiatre et un ex-comptable, qui ont tous soi-disant abandonné leur profession pour gérer les problèmes de la cité. Bien que leur zèle soit louable, aucun d'entre eux n'a la personnalité, l'autorité (ou la couleur ?) dont la ville a en fait besoin.

On pourrait soutenir que la dernière personne à avoir lutté pour la ville avec suffisamment d'ambition fut Ian Davidson le dernier président appartenant au parti démocrate du conseil de gestion de Johannesburg. Au début des années 90, Davidson avait adopté une approche "bien laide mais dynamique" comparable à celle adoptée pour le centre ville de New York. Et ceci afin de contrer les pressions à l'intérieur même de son parti pour favoriser la banlieue de Sandton comme le cœur futur de l'agglomération. Il avait fait déménager les instances législatives et administratives de la Province du Gauteng au centre ville de Johannesburg grâce à un accord avec l'homme fort de l'ANC dans le Gauteng, Paul Mashatile; accord négocié dans les

war Ian Davidson, Mitglied der Demokratischen Partei und der letzte Vorsitzende im Johannesburger Management-Komitee. In den frühen 1990ern entwickelte Davidson ein "hässliches, aber dynamisches" Konzept à la New York, das auf dem Bau großer Geschäftskomplexe basierte, und steuerte damit Tendenzen in seiner eigenen Partei entgegen, nach denen das suburbane Sandton das zukünftige Herz der City sein sollte. Es gelang ihm, die gesetzgebenden Körperschaften und die Verwaltung der Provinz Gauteng in die Johannesburger Innenstadt zu bringen — Ein Abkommen mit dem starken Mann des ANC in Gauteng, Paul Mashatile, in den Korridoren von CODESA (dem Kongress für ein demokratisches Südafrika, das nationale Forum, auf dem die Bedingungen für Südafrikas Übergang zur Demokratie zwischen 1992 und 1994 ausgehandelt wurden) machte es möglich. Außerdem war er es, der damit begann, die Innenstadt als internationales Geschäftszentrum zu lancieren. Zu seiner Vision gehörten der Stadtteil Newtown mit einer Kulturmeile auf dem Gelände eines stillgelegten innerstädtischen Elektrizitätswerks, Ellis Park mit einem Sportgelände am östlichen Rand des Geschäftszentrums und das (von Beginn an) fürchterliche Civic Spine, ein Sanierungsgebiet rund um das Rathaus. Sie sollten sozusagen die kulturelle Grundlage bilden und mit Hotels, Restaurants, Konferenzmöglichkeiten,

transformed it into an attractive residential location. John Ndebele, JHC's property services manager, said that a recent survey of their buildings had shown that 56 percent of tenants saw the inner city as their preferred residential location, and 61 percent saw it as their permanent home.

There are others who have put their money where their mouth is. Rees Mann, third generation inner-city garment trader, ex-city councillor and former vice president of the International Youth Chamber of Commerce, is passionate about the city. "I am an urban person", he says. "I grew up in Rosettenville, still live in the south and have worked in the city my whole life. I hate suburbs. I love this place". Mann is the linchpin of the emerging Fashion District, bounded by Von Wielligh, Market, Kerk and End streets, where his facilities include machine repairs, a pleating service, a bridal boutique and a fashion school accredited by City and Guilds of London.

Sitting on a fake leopard skin-covered chair in his Fashion Café, a variation on the internet cafe, where garment manufacturers pore over fashion magazines, he said he welcomed the transformation the city has undergone since 1994. "It has not died," he said. "Just become something different, more African, more vibrant." Mann's energies are

couloirs du Congrès pour une Afrique du Sud Démocratique (CODESA), le forum national où la transition vers la démocratie a été négociée entre 1992 et 1994. Il avait aussi commencé à positionner avec énergie le centre-ville en tant que centre d'affaires international. Faisaient également partie de cette vision, Newtown, le quartier culturel à construire sur l'emplacement d'une station énergétique en désaffection, Ellis Park le quartier dédié au sport entourant le stade à l'est du quartier central des affaires, ainsi que le désastreux (depuis le début) "Civic Spine", un plan visant à rénover le quartier de la Mairie. Ces projets avaient pour but de former le lit culturel de la ville et d'y apporter une certaine ambiance — hôtels, restaurants, salles de conférences et de concerts, musées et événements sportifs — devant attirer le monde international des affaires.

Mais Davidson a perdu la guerre. Sa vision a été largement sabotée, rendue automatiquement illégitime à partir du moment où la cité a vu arriver de nouveaux dirigeants; En raison de son échec à anticiper l'afflux des pauvres et des chômeurs cherchant à survivre aux ajustements économiques échappant à leur contrôle.

Au contraire, Sandton a su capter l'imagination de l'élite dirigeante post-1994, la communauté des affaires et du commerce ainsi que la plupart des habitants de la ville.

Konzerthallen, Museen und Sportveranstaltungen für die Atmosphäre sorgen, die das internationale Business erwartete.

Davidson verlor den Kampf. Seine Vision erledigte sich, hauptsächlich durch den geschichtsträchtigen Zeitpunkt, in den sein Plan fiel, so dass er für die neuen Führer der Stadt automatisch unannehmbar wurde. Aber auch, weil er nicht den Zustrom von Armen und Arbeitslosen vorherzusagen in der Lage war, die, angesichts der neuen wirtschaftlichen Gegebenheiten, auf die sie keinen Einfluss hatten, ums Überleben kämpften. Stattdessen war es Sandton, das die Phantasie der nach 1994 regierenden Elite, der Geschäftsleute und fast aller Bewohner der Stadt erregte.

Doch obwohl es den Verantwortlichen nicht gelang, der City ein neues Gesicht zu geben, und Xolela Mangcu das Fehlen der "gewöhnlichen Alltagssprache" bemängelt, wohnen im Zentrum, in "downtown" Johannesburg, Menschen, und mögen sie auch eine Randgruppe sein, denen es dort gefällt. Dennis Maseko stammt aus Barberton und arbeitet bei der Nationallotterie. Er ist Mitte zwanzig und lebt heute in Carr Gardens, einem vor kurzem fertig gestellten dreistöckigen Mietshaus der "Johannesburg Housing Company" (JHC) mit insgesamt 145 Wohnungen. "Solange ich keine größere Wohnung brauche, möchte ich von hier nicht wegziehen", sagt er. "Ich finde es ganz bequem hier,

going into turning the north-eastern quadrant of the city into what he terms "the hub of a Pan African Fashion industry", marketing itself to the tastes of black America.

Despite these optimistic voices, they remain in the minority and, to date, largely unheard. While those in power still reluctantly reside downtown — in the ugly Metropolitan Centre, home to the City of Johannesburg's vast centralised administrative machine; in and around the old City Hall, which houses the Gauteng Legislature and the offices and administrations of the Gauteng Provincial Government; and in the many judicial, financial and other public sector institutions located downtown — for most people, Sandton's suburban enclaves and fake urbanity have supplanted Davidson's gritty aging city, Masondo's commuter interchange and Mann's vibrant, African streets as the glamorous, safe, homogeneous centre of our new democratic imagination.

Cependant, en dépit de cet échec officiel à représenter la ville et à lui redonner une bonne image, et en dépit de l'absence de ce que Mangcu appelle "le langage des gens ordinaires", le centre-ville de Johannesburg a néanmoins ses partisans et ses amoureux, aussi marginaux soient-ils. Dennis Maseko, un salarié de la loterie nationale, âgé d'une vingtaine d'année, habite maintenant à Carr Gardens, un complexe immobilier de 145 appartements en location, bâti sur 3 étages par la Société Immobilière de Johannesburg. "Je ne déménagerais pour rien au monde, à moins d'avoir besoin de quelque chose de plus grand", dit-il. "Je trouve que vivre ici est pratique, calme (en comparaison avec les townships) et sûr". Maseko travaille à Auckland Park, une courte distance en taxi-minibus de son logement ; il fait ses courses à Oriental Plaza, va à son club de sport en ville, et "se rend parfois au Market Theater".

Maseko appartient à la nouvelle génération de noirs à revenus modestes mais réguliers — conducteurs de taxi-minibus, coiffeurs, travailleurs à la chaîne, petits entrepreneurs — qui sont fiers d'appeler le centre ville leur "chez eux", grâce à la Société Immobilière de Johannesburg. En adoptant une approche de "bas loyers, ce qui ne signifie pas basse qualité" et une gestion rigoureuse, cette instance a construit ou rénové depuis le milieu des années 90

das Leben hier ist im Vergleich zu den Townships ruhig und sicher." Masekos Arbeitsplatz in Auckland Park ist leicht mit dem Sammeltaxi zu erreichen, seine Einkäufe erledigt er im Oriental Plaza, Sport treibt er in der Stadt, und "manchmal gehe ich ins Market Theatre".

Maseko gehört zu der neuen Generation von Geldverdienern, die über ein kleines, aber immerhin regelmäßiges Einkommen verfügen. Zu ihnen gehören auch Taxifahrer, Friseurinnen und Friseure, Reinigungspersonal, Fabrikarbeiter, Kleinunternehmer. Stolz bezeichnen sie das Stadtzentrum als ihr Zuhause, "Johannesburg Housing Company" sei Dank. Mit dem Anspruch, dass "niedrige Kosten nicht schlechte Qualität bedeuten muss ", und einem effizienten Management hat das Unternehmen seit Mitte der neunziger Jahre zehn innerstädtische Wohnkomplexe gebaut oder saniert, in denen rund 3.000 Menschen wohnen. Auf diese Weise trat es der Vorstellung entgegen, dass die Innenstadt ein Wildwestschauplatz sei, wo sich unnachgiebige Hausbesitzer und wütende Mieterkomitees bekriegten, sondern verwandelte sie in ein angenehmes Wohnviertel. John Ndebele, Verwaltungsdirektor der JHC, berichtet von einer kürzlich in ihren Häusern durchgeführten Studie, nach der 56 Prozent der Mieter die Innenstadt als bevorzugte Wohngegend bezeichnen und 61 Prozent sie sogar als ihr dauerndes Zuhause.

dix immeubles en centre ville, permettant à presque 3 000 personnes d'accéder à un logement. Ce faisant, elle a remis en question l'image d'un centre-ville sauvage où des fusillades éclatent à chaque coin de rue entre propriétaires intransigeants et locataires enragés et l'a transformé en lieu de résidence attractif. John Ndebele, le directeur des services de la propriété déclara qu'un récent sondage sur leurs immeubles avait montré que 56 % des locataires voyaient le centre ville comme leur lieu de résidence préféré, et que 61 % y

Und noch andere machen Nägel mit Köpfen. Rees Mann, Bekleidungskaufmann in dritter Generation in der City, früherer Stadtabgeordneter und ehemaliger Vizepräsident der Internationalen Jugendhandelskammer, ist begeistert vom Leben im Zentrum. "Ich bin ein Stadtmensch, ich wuchs in Rosettenville auf, lebe noch immer im Süden und habe mein ganzes Leben lang in der Stadt gearbeitet. Ich hasse die 'suburbs'. Und ich liebe diesen Ort hier." Mann ist die Hauptperson im prosperierenden Fashion District zwischen

Dennis Maseko in Carr Gardens rental housing complex

Dennis Maseko dans le complexe d'habitations à louer, Carr Gardens

Dennis Maseko zu Hause in Carr Gardens, einem kürzlich fertig gestellten Mietshaus

voyaient leur habitat permanent .

D'autres sont passés à l'acte en y investissant leur argent. Ainsi, Rees Mann, issu de la troisième génération de marchands de tissus de centre-ville, ex-conseiller municipal et ancien président de la Chambre de Commerce International des Jeunes, est un passionné de la ville. "Je suis un urbain", dit-il. "J'ai grandi à Rosettenville, je continue encore aujourd'hui à vivre dans le sud et j'ai toujours travaillé au centre ville. Je déteste les banlieues. J'adore cet endroit." Mann est le moteur du Quartier émergeant de la Mode délimité par Von Wielligh, Market, Kerk et End Street, dans une entreprise qui comprend des machines de réparation, des machines à plisser le tissu, une boutique de la mariée et une école de mode accréditée par le syndicat de confection de Londres.

Assis sur une chaise recouverte d'une fausse peau de léopard dans son "café de la mode", une variante du café internet, où les fabricants de tissus feuillètent les magazines de mode, il dit qu'il voit d'un bon œil les transformations que la ville a subies depuis 1994. "Le centre ville n'est pas mort", dit-il. "Il est juste devenu un lieu différent, plus africain, plus vibrant".

Mann est en train de mettre toute son énergie à essayer de transformer le quart nord-est de la ville en ce qu'il appelle lui-même le "pivot de l'industrie de la mode panafricaine" pour se vendre

Von Wielligh-, Market-, Kerk- und End Street. Er bietet Nähmaschinenreparaturen, einen Plissee- und Faltendienst, eine Boutique für Brautkleider sowie eine von dem führenden Londoner Institut für Berufliche Bildung "City and Guilds" anerkannte Modeschule.

Während wir reden, sitzt Rees Mann auf einem mit falschem Leopardenfell bedeckten Stuhl in seinem "Fashion Café", das irgendwie an ein Internet Café erinnert, nur dass hier Schneiderinnen und Schneider Modemagazine studieren. Er begrüße die Veränderungen, die seit 1994 in der Innenstadt stattfanden, sagt er. "Sie ist nicht tot, sie ist nur anders geworden. Afrikanischer, vibrierender." Mann möchte seine ganze Energie darauf verwenden, den nord-östlichen Teil der City zum, wie er es nennt, "Zentrum der panafrikanischen Modeindustrie" zu machen und mit den dort produzierten Produkten sogar das schwarze Amerika zu gewinnen.

Doch diese optimistischen Stimmen bleiben in der Minderheit und verhallen bis heute weithin ungehört. So arbeiten die, die an der Macht sind, nur höchst ungern 'downtown' im Zentrum — im hässlichen Metropolitan Centre, dem Herzstück von Johannesburgs ausgedehnter zentralisierter Verwaltungsmaschinerie; in und um das alte Rathaus, wo inzwischen Gautengs Legislative sowie die Büros und Verwaltung von Gautengs Provinzregierung untergebracht sind; und

conformément aux goût de l'Amérique noire.

Ces quelques voix optimistes restent minoritaires et à ce jour largement inaudibles. Alors que ceux qui sont au pouvoir refusent de résider au centre ville - dans l'horrible centre ville qui héberge dans les locaux de l'ancienne Mairie la vaste machine administrative de la Municipalité de Johannesburg, ainsi que les bâtiments des instances législatives et les bureaux de l'administration de la Province du Gauteng; et les diverses institutions judiciaires, financières et du secteur public -. Car, pour une vaste majorité, l'enclave de la banlieue de Sandton et sa fausse urbanité ont supplanté la ville vieillissante et poussiéreuse de Davidson, celle des banlieusards en transit de Masondo, et celle des rues africaines vibrantes de Mann. Sandton représente dorénavant le centre glamour, sûr et homogène de notre nouvelle imagination démocratique.

in den vielen Verwaltungsbehörden und Institutionen der öffentlichen Hand. Gleichzeitig hat sich das suburbane Sandton, die Enklave mit seiner falschen Urbanität bei den allermeisten Leuten gegen Davidsons raue, alternde City, Masondos Pendlerstadt und Manns vibrierende afrikanische Straßen durchgesetzt. Der einst weiße Stadtteil bildet heute das glamouröse, sichere, homogene Zentrum unserer neuen Vorstellungen von Demokratie.

JOBURG GOES GLOBAL JOBURG 5

3

INTERNATIONALISE TOTAL GLOBAL

Johannesburg's Executive Mayor Amos Masondo was distracted. It was 3pm on a Friday afternoon in mid-December. He had double-booked me with the launch of the first Peoples' Centre to open in the city, and he had yet to prepare his speech for the occasion. To his relief, I agreed to drop our interview and tag along to the Peoples' Centre launch instead.

Johannesburg's Region 4 covers a large area from Randpark Ridge in the north to Riverlea in the south and Greenside in the east to Florida Lake in the west. Its 216 000 residents are solidly lower-middle to middle class. Its People's Centre is intended to be an easy-access point of contact between local government and residents, a place where locals may lodge complaints about anything from overcharged service accounts to missing manhole covers and expect prompt help from friendly officials. It is somewhat incongruously located in the swish Diners Club Building at the top of the SABC ridge in Auckland Park.

The launch was a multicultural medley, the room decorated with beaded African dolls, basketware and animal skin rugs. Bare-chested drummers announced the proceedings, while Lawrence Boya, former civic activist and now Region 4's director, urged his staff to "leave their comfort zones behind and serve their customers with passion". Excited

Le maire de Johannesburg, Amos Masondo était préoccupé. C'était un vendredi après midi de la mi-décembre à 3 heures. Il avait pris deux rendez-vous en même temps: l'un avec moi et l'autre pour l'inauguration du premier "Centre du Citoyen" qui allait ouvrir dans l'agglomération, et dont il devait préparer le discours. A son grand soulagement, j'ai accepté d'annuler notre entretien et d'assister à la place à l'inauguration du Centre du Citoyen. La région 4 de Johannesburg couvre un large territoire qui s'étend de Randpark Ridge au Nord, à Riverlea au Sud en passant par Greenside à l'Est et paer le lac Florida à l'Ouest. Ses 216 000 résidents font partie de la classe moyenne ou se situent tout juste en dessous. Son Centre du Citoyen a pour but de constituer un point d'accès et de contact facile entre le gouvernement local et les résidents; un endroit où les habitants pourraient se plaindre sur tous les sujets qui les concernent, les factures trop élevées, les plaques d'égoûts manquantes, etc., et où ils pourraient trouver une aide rapide grâce à l'aide de fonctionnaires bienveillants. Juste une petite incongruité due au fait que le club soit situé dans le bâtiment du Swiss Diners Clubtout en haut de la crête de SABC, la société de radio et de télévision sud-africaine à Auckland Park.

L'inauguration se révéla une sorte de méli-mélo multiculturel, avec une salle décorée de poupées africaines en

Johannesburgs Regierender Bürgermeister Amos Masondo war irritiert. Es war drei Uhr, Freitagnachmittag Mitte Dezember. Er hatte versehentlich einen Gesprächstermin mit mir auf dieselbe Uhrzeit gelegt, wo die Eröffnungsfeierlichkeiten für das erste Bürgerzentrum der Stadt stattfinden sollten — und seine Rede zu diesem Anlass musste er auch noch vorbereiten. Er war erleichtert, als ich damit einverstanden war, unser Interview fallen zu lassen, stattdessen folgte ich ihm zur Eröffnung des Bürgerzentrums.

Johannesburgs 4. Verwaltungsbezirk, Region 4, erstreckt sich über ein großes Gebiet von Randpark Ridge im Norden bis nach Riverlea im Süden und von Greenside im Osten bis Florida Lake im Westen. Seine 216.000 Bewohner gehören durchweg zur Mittel- und unteren Mittelschicht. Das Bürgerzentrum soll Anlaufstelle zwischen Bezirksregierung und Bürger werden, ein für jedermann und jede Frau zugänglicher Ort, wo die Bewohner Beschwerden einlegen und alles vorbringen können, was sie bedrückt, von der überzogenen Dienstleistungsabrechnung bis zum fehlenden Gullydeckel. Und sie können schnelle Hilfe von freundlichen Beamten erwarten. Das neue Bürgerzentrum liegt in Auckland Park, auf derselben Anhöhe und ganz in der Nähe des südafrikanischen Rundfunks SABC, und ist ein wenig unpassend im schicken Gebäude des

employees in oversized blue t-shirts proclaimed their commitment to "Batho Pele" (service excellence). Presiding over all this was Johannesburg's favourite 11-official-languages-in-one-sentence struggle poet, Don Mattera, who lives in the area. At the same time, a rather sweet photographic exhibition of Region 4's people — children doing ballet at the local hall, pensioners at a fête, teenagers having fun at a public pool — made the tribal themes seem a little remote.

However, they made a lot of sense when Masondo invoked his "Johannesburg as World Class African City" slogan. Clearly the drum rolls and African masks were designed to connote "African" to Region 4's rather "Un-African" people. These ethno-nostalgic accessories were local interpretations of Masondo's global thinking.

But two months later, Supermayor Masondo dropped the "African" from his mantra entirely. The newly honed Joburg 2030 Vision has Johannesburg aspiring directly to "World Class City" status. According to this plan, by 2030, international corporates will have been enticed out of their cushy New York, London or Tokyo offices into safe, middle-income, wide-bandwidth Johannesburg. Our economy will lie firmly in a globally competitive service sector (trade, finance and business,

perles, de paniers artisanaux et de tapis en peaux de bêtes. Des joueurs de tambours aux torses nus annonçaient les différentes phases de la cérémonie, tandis que Lawrence Boya, ancien militant municipal et maintenant directeur de la Région 4, incitait son personnel à "aller au devant de leur bureau ou de la vitre, à quitter cette zone de confort pour servir avec passion leurs concitoyens". Les employés, quand à eux très excités dans leurs tee-shirts bleus trop grands pour eux, proclamaient leur engagement à "Batho Pele" (excellence de service). Cette cérémonie était présidé par un résident local, Don Mattera le poète favori de la lutte de Johannesburg, un homme capable de résumer les 11 langues officielles en une phrase. Au même moment avait lieu une exposition assez sympathique de photographies des habitants de la Région 4 -des enfants en train de danser dans la salle municipale, une fête de retraités, des jeunes en train de s'amuser dans une piscine publique - ceci rendant le thème africain un peu lointain et déplacé.

Cependant, tout cela a repris de son sens lorsque Masondo a lancé son slogan "Johannesburg comme cité africaine de classe mondiale". A l'évidence, les roulements de tambours et les masques africains étaient là pour donner à la Région 4 une note "africaine" alors que ses habitants sont plutôt "non-africains". Ces accessoires

Diners Club untergebracht.

Die Eröffnungsveranstaltung war ein multikulturelles Potpourri, der Raum mit perlenbesetzten afrikanischen Puppen, Korbwaren und Tierfellen dekoriert. Trommler mit bloßen Oberkörpern verkündeten die Abfolge des Programms, und Lawrence Boya, früher Bürgeraktivist und heute Verwaltungsdirektor von Region 4, rief seine Mitarbeiter auf, "die alten bequemen Pfade zu verlassen und von nun an den Kunden mit Leidenschaft zu dienen". Begeisterte Angestellte in übergroßen blauen T-Shirts erklärten sich der Aktion "Batho Pele" ("Die Menschen zuerst") verpflichtet. Die Veranstaltung stand unter der Leitung von Don Mattera, Johannesburgs hoch geachtetem "Poet der Befreiungsbewegung", dem "11-offizielle-Sprachen-in-einem-Satz-Dichter", der in diesem Stadtteil wohnt. Allerdings drängte eine etwas süßliche Fotoausstellung von Menschen aus Region 4 — Kinder beim Ballett in einer Halle, Ruheständler bei einem Fest, Teenager, die Spaß in der Schule haben - die ethnischen Themen ein wenig ins Abseits.

Dabei waren sie durchaus angebracht, als Masondo beschwörend von Johannesburg als "World Class African City", als afrikanische Stadt der Weltklasse, sprach. Trommeln ertönten, und afrikanische Masken suggerierten eine Verbindung des Wörtchens "afrikanisch" mit den eher "unafrikanischen" Bewohnern von Region

information and communication technology) and the city's poor will have migrated to "lower cost centres" to where the manufacturing sector will have relocated (Butterworth or Malelane, perhaps?). Johannesburg's citizens, we are told, will be living a lifestyle closer to that of a citizen of San Francisco, London or Tokyo than of the unofficial capital of a developing country.

I asked Sandy Lowitt, the feisty young economist behind the Gauteng Economic Development Strategy and drafter of Johannesburg's vision, about her choice of comparative cities. "I believe we should demand more of ourselves, not less", she said. "Each of those cities fundamentally reinvented themselves in 30 years. They are the benchmarks against which we should measure our success".

Jenny Robinson, an equally feisty ex-Durban geographer, now resident at the Open University in Milton Keynes in England, disagreed. She found such comparisons "actively unhelpful", for they usually employ "limited or only partial representations of other cities", forgetting that those outcomes are the result of many, only partially known, decisions.

Councillor Kenny Fihla, the city's head of finance, strategy and economic development, on the other hand, was of the opinion that the city needed to "learn from best practice

ethno-nostalgiques constituaient les interprétations locales de la pensée internationale de Masondo.

Deux mois plus tard, le terme "africain" avait complètement disparu du discours de monsieur Masondo. La nouvelle version appelée "Joburg Vision 2030" aspire directement au statut de "ville de classe mondiale". Selon ce projet, d'ici 2030, les entreprises multinationales seront attirées hors de leurs confortables bureaux de New York, Londres ou de Tokyo pour venir s'établir dans une Johannesburg sécurisée, à revenus moyens, et à large bande passante. Notre économie s'appuierait alors fermement sur un secteur tertiaire compétitif au point de vue international (commerce, finance, affaires, technologies de l'information et de la communication) et les pauvres du centre ville auraient migré vers des "centres meilleurs marché" où le secteur de la production se serait également relocalisé (Peut-être à Butterworths ou à Malelane ?). On nous dit aussi que les citoyens de Johannesburg auront un style de vie plus proche de celui de San Francisco, de Londres ou de Tokyo que celui d'une capitale non officielle d'un pays en voie de développement.

J'ai demandé à Sandy Lowitt, la jeune économiste pleine d'entrain qui est derrière la stratégie de développement économique du Gauteng et à l'origine de cette vision de Johannesburg, de justifier son choix à propos des villes de

4. Diese ethno-nostalgischen Accessoires waren die Interpretation von Masondos globalem Denken auf lokaler Ebene.

Doch zwei Monate später streicht der Regierende "Super"-Bürgermeister das "afrikanisch" aus seinen Beschwörungsformeln. Die neu aufgelegte "Joburg 2030 Vision" möchte Johannesburg gleich zu einer "World Class City", einer Stadt der Weltklasse, machen. Nach diesem Plan werden im Jahre 2030 internationale Firmen aus ihren bequemen New Yorker, Londoner oder Tokioter Büros ins sichere, weltoffene, wenn auch nur Mittelklasse-Johannesburg gelockt worden sein. Unsere Wirtschaft wird fest verankert sein in einem global wettbewerbsfähigen Dienstleistungssektor (Handel, Business und Finanzen, Informations- und Kommunikationstechnologie), und die Armen der Stadt werden in Viertel mit niedrigem Lebensstandard abgewandert sein, wohin sich dann auch der Produktionsbereich verlagert haben wird (nach Butterworth oder Malelane vielleicht?). Johannesburgs Bürger, so wird uns gesagt, werden dann einen Lebensstil haben, der eher dem eines Bürgers von San Francisco, London oder Tokio gleicht als dem eines Bewohners der inoffiziellen Hauptstadt eines Entwicklungslandes.

Ich frage Sandy Lowitt, die dynamische junge Wirtschaftswissenschaftlerin, die hinter dem Strategiepapier für die wirtschaftliche

anywhere in the world, be it Mexico City, Sydney or wherever. That is what will make us world class," he said,

Masondo's World Class Vision is nothing if not bold. It is not new though. It has simply put flesh on the bones and updated a very similar plan hatched in the early 1990s by the last Democratic Party-led Johannesburg City Council, to claim a place for Johannesburg in the A-team of cities worldwide.

Ian Davidson, DP leader in the Johannesburg City Council at the time,

comparaison. "Je crois que nous devons être plus exigeants avec nous-mêmes", dit-elle. "Chacune de ces villes s'est littéralement réinventée en 30 ans. Elles constituent donc les points de repères par rapport auxquels nous devons mesurer notre succès." Quant Jenny Robinson, ex-géographe de Durban tout aussi pleine d'entrain, résidant actuellement à l'Université de Milton Keynes en Angleterre, réfute cette vision. Elle pense que de telles comparaisons sont "improductives", car "elles n'utilisent que des représentations

Entwicklung Gautengs steht und auch die Vision für Johannesburg entworfen hat, nach ihrer Auswahl der Vergleichsstädte. "Ich glaube, wir sollten mehr von uns fordern, nicht weniger", sagt sie. "Alle diese Städte sanierten sich von Grund auf innerhalb von dreißig Jahren. Sie sind die Messlatte, an der wir unseren Erfolg messen sollten".

Jenny Robinson, eine nicht weniger energische Geografin aus Durban, die heute an der Open University in Milton Keynes in England ist, widerspricht. Sie fände solche Vergleiche "kontraproduktiv",

Mayor Amos Masondo

Le maire, Amos Masondo

Amos Masondo, Regierender Bürgermeister

told me: "The vision for Johannesburg then was as a global, international city in the first instance, not an African one." It was to function as an international business centre, supported by the culture, sports facilities and lifestyles to which the international business elite was accustomed (hence Newtown, Ellis Park and the Civic Theatre). He continued nostalgically: "That vision has not yet been replaced. If I had had five more years, I could have made it a reality."

To understand Johannesburg's ambitions now, we need to go back to 1986. The townships were in flames, its once invincible economy was failing and its 100th anniversary celebrations had gone off like a damp squib. Only a loyal few had come to celebrate a century of white dominance and brush aside increasingly irrepressible black claims to the city. Johannesburg, which had once boasted of being the British Empire's "great gold centre", if not a New York, then (at least) a Chicago or (at worst) a St Louis of Africa, was realising that its "golden heart" had been tarnished, possibly for good. Its leaders started to speak of the city as needing an economic and an image makeover.

The first attempt at its reinvention was contained in a glossy black booklet and went under the name of "Urban Renaissance". Put out shortly

partielles ou limitées des autres villes", tout en oubliant que ces réalisations sont issues de nombreuses décisions certes, mais seulement partiellement connues.

Au contraire, le conseiller Kenny Fihla, le directeur des finances et du développement stratégique et économique de la ville était plutôt d'avis que la ville avait besoin "de puiser les bonnes pratiques partout dans le monde, que celles-ci soient de Mexico, Sydney ou de n'importe quelle autre ville. C'est ce qui fera de nous une ville de classe mondiale", dit-il.

Cette vision n'est rien, si ce n'est qu'elle est très téméraire. Elle n'est cependant pas nouvelle. Elle a seulement étoffé et actualisé un projet très similaire qui a pris naissance au début des années 90 au sein de la dernière municipalité menée par le Parti Démocratique. Ce projet plaçait Johannesburg parmi les villes gagnantes les plus dynamiques de la planète.

Ian Davidson, le leader du Parti Démocratique au conseil municipal de Johannesburg à cette ópoque mc dit : "La vision pour Johannesburg alors était tout d'abord celle d'une cité internationale, globale et pas du tout africaine". Elle devait fonctionner comme un centre d'affaires international, soutenue par les infrastructures culturelles, sportives auxquelles l'élite internationale des entreprises est habituée; Ce qui explique Newtown, Ellis

denn dabei griffe man immer nur auf "begrenzte oder Teilbereiche anderer Städte" zurück und übersähe, dass das, was sich dort entwickelt hat, die Folge von vielen, zum Teil nur unzureichend bekannten Entscheidungen sei.

Der Abgeordnete Kenny Fihla, zuständig für das Finanz-, Strategie- und Wirtschaftsentwicklungsamt, meint hingegen, dass die Stadt "von den besten Strategien weltweit lernen muss, sei es von Mexiko-Stadt, Sydney oder von woher auch immer. Das wird aus uns Weltklasse machen."

Masondos Weltklasse-Vision ist ausgesprochen kühn. Aber sie ist nicht neu. Sie ist lediglich die angereicherte und aktualisierte Version eines vergleichbaren Planes, der zu Beginn der 1990er Jahre von dem letzten Johannesburger Stadtrat noch unter Führung der Demokratischen Partei (DP) entworfen worden war. Johannesburg sollte einen Platz unter den Topstädten dieser Welt bekommen.

Ian Davidson, zu jener Zeit Vorsitzender der DP im Johannesburger Stadtrat, erzählt: "Die Vision für Johannesburg damals war in erster Linie die einer globalen, internationalen Stadt, nicht die einer afrikanischen." Sie sollte internationales Businesszentrum werden mit kulturellen Aktivitäten, Sportstätten und einem Lebensstil, wie ihn die Elite der internationalen Geschäftswelt gewöhnt war (daher auch Newtown, Ellis Park und das Civic Theatre). Und ein wenig

after the centenary celebrations by the planner of the city's freeways and former mayor, Eddy Magid (only Johannesburg would entrust the awakening of the city to a road engineer), the city was portrayed as a landscape of square grids, bare of anything but a few towering office blocks, symbols of a prosperous future. It suggested that this future could be engineered, on the same basis that rocketed the city onto the front pages of international architectural magazines in the apartheid building boom of the 1960s. If a Carlton Centre, designed by Skidmore Owings and Merrill of New York, at 200 metres, the highest reinforced-concrete building in the world, and a Standard Bank, work of German architect Helmut Hentrich, technological wonder with its floor slabs ingeniously cantilevered from its central core, could have been built then, why not now?

Unfortunately for the city fathers, this image failed to capture the imagination of either citizens or investors. By the early 1990s it was gathering dust on the shelves of the city planning department, and Davidson launched his rescue plan for the flagging city. His initiative consolidated around the image of Johannesburg as "Gateway to Africa". It was argued that its superior infrastructure, locational advantage

Park et le Civic Theatre)". Et il poursuit, un brin nostalgique: "cette vision n'a pas encore été remplacée. Si j'avais eu cinq ans de plus à ma disposition, j'aurais pu en faire une réalité".

Pour comprendre les ambitions actuelles, il faut revenir en 1986. Les townships étaient en flammes et son économie, qui fut un temps invincible, était en train de vaciller. Les festivités du 100ème anniversaire avaient pris l'allure d'une affaire complètement ratée: une poignée seulement de fidèles étaient venue célébrer un siècle de domination blanche et repousser les demandes de la part des Noirs de plus en plus pressantes pour le centre-ville. Johannesburg, qui se vantait un temps d'être le "magnifique centre de l'or" de l'empire britannique, si elle n'était pas New York, équivalait au moins à Chicago et au pire à Saint Louis d'Afrique, était en train de réaliser que son "cœur d'or" se ternissait peut-être pour de bon. Ses dirigeants ont alors commencé à entrevoir la nécessité de reconsidérer l'image et l'économie de la ville.

La première tentative en ce sens fut mise noir sur blanc dans un petit livret à couverture noire et brillante intitulé "renaissance urbaine". Publié peu après les célébrations du centenaire d'Eddy Magid, le concepteur du plan autoroutier de la ville et de son maire (seule Johannesburg pouvait confier la naissance et le développement de la ville à un ingénieur du génie civil), la ville y

wehmütig fährt er fort: "Diese Vision ist noch durch nichts ersetzt worden. Wenn ich noch einmal fünf Jahre gehabt hätte, hätte ich sie realisieren können."

Um Johannesburgs heutige ehrgeizige Pläne zu verstehen, müssen wir ins Jahr 1986 zurückgehen. Die Townships standen in Flammen, seine einst unschlagbare Wirtschaft steuerte auf die Pleite zu, und die Feierlichkeiten zum 100. Geburtstag verpufften wie eine nasse Feuerwerksrakete. Nur ein paar wenige Getreue waren gekommen, um ein Jahrhundert weißer Vorherrschaft zu feiern, und fegten die ständig lauter werdenden, kaum noch zu unterdrückenden Forderungen der Schwarzen beiseite. Johannesburg, das sich einst rühmte, das "große Goldzentrum" des britischen Empires zu sein, wenn nicht gar ein New York, dann doch ein Chicago oder wenigstens ein St. Louis von Afrika, musste feststellen, dass sein "goldenes Herz" an Glanz verloren hat, und das wahrscheinlich für immer. Die Regierenden im Rathaus begannen davon zu sprechen, dass die Stadt eine wirtschaftliche Erneuerung und eine Imageaufbesserung brauche.

Der erste Entwurf zur Wiederbelebung der Stadt war in einem glänzenden schwarzen Büchlein enthalten und lief unter dem Namen "Städtische Renaissance". Er wurde bald nach den Hundertjahrfeierlichkeiten von dem Planer der Stadtautobahnen und früheren Bürgermeister Eddy Magid (nur

Pavement hairdressing in the Johannesburg city centre

Coiffure pratiquée sur une rue piétonne au centre ville de Johannesburg

Friseursalon "Johannesburg city centre"

and mature financial sector made it the obvious launch pad for investors and South African utilities (Eskom, Transnet) to tap the vast, under-exploited resources of the Dark Continent beyond its borders. (In comparison, 2030 also speaks of the "export opportunities" available to utility companies on the subcontinent and constructs Africa as the primary market). Johannesburg could and should exploit its position and become the "Tokyo or New York of Africa".

Davidson's plan set the pattern for things to come. A new breed of official, the "super bureaucrat" took over the running of City Hall. Extremely expensive, accountable only to themselves, they were hired to turn the city into the cutting edge "world city showroom" its politicians dreamed of. The portly Colin Wright, Executive Director of Trade and Industry, set himself up in Afro-chic quarters in the Sanlam building in the Johannesburg city centre, spurning the drabness of the civic centre for his promotional activities. From here, when he was not in Davos, Switzerland, assuming to represent the entire nation at the World Economic Forum, he wined and dined visiting trade delegations from Atlanta, New York and Birmingham.

Then there was the wily Danie Malan, Executive Director of Sport, who masterminded Johannesburg's failed Olympic bid and the even larger

était décrite comme un paysage formé d'un carroyage serré, relativement déserte mis à part quelques tours de bureaux, symbôles d'un futur prospère. Il fut suggéré que l'ingénierie de ce futur pouvait être réalisé de la même manière que pendant la période d'explosion architecturale de l'Apartheid des années 1960 qui vit la ville projetée sur les couvertures de magazines d'architecture internationaux. Si le Carlton Centre, dessiné par les architectes new-yorkais Skidmore Owings et Merril qui, en atteignant 200 m, est le plus haut immeuble en béton armé dans le monde; et l'immeuble de la Standard Bank de l'architecte allemand Helmut Hentrich, véritable merveille technologique avec des dalles de plancher en porte à faux par rapport à son centre, ont pu à l'époque être construits, alors pourquoi pas aujourd'hui ?

Malheureusement pour les pères de la cité, cette image n'a pas su capter ni l'imagination des citoyens, ni celle des investisseurs. Au début des années 1990, elle traînait sur les étagères poussiéreuses du bureau de la planification de la ville, et c'est alors que Davidson lança son projet pour sauver la ville en déclin. Il consolida son initiative autour de l'image d'un Johannesburg "portail vers l'Afrique". La maturité du secteur financier, la supériorité de son infrastructure liée aux avantages locaux ont été mis en avant pour démontrer

Johannesburg vertraut das Erwachen der Stadt einem Straßeningenieur an) entworfen. Die Stadt stellte sich darin als eine in Planquadrate gerasterte Landschaft dar, bar jeglicher Objekte ausgenommen einiger Bürowolkenkratzer, Symbole einer prosperierenden Zukunft. Der Plan suggerierte, dass diese Zukunft auf denselben Voraussetzungen aufbauen könne, wie sie in den 1960ern bestanden, als der Apartheid-Bauboom die Stadt auf die Titelseiten internationaler Architekturzeitschriften katapultierte. Wenn damals in Johannesburg von den New Yorker Architekten Skidmore Owings und Merril ein Carlton Centre gebaut werden konnte, das mit seinen 200 Metern das höchste Stahlbetongebäude der Welt war, und eine Standard Bank, Werk des deutschen Architekten Helmut Hentrich, das mit seinen vom Gebäudekern abgehängten freitragenden Deckenscheiben einem technischen Wunder gleichkommt, warum dann nicht auch heute?

Aber diese Idee begeisterte weder Bürger noch Investoren - bedauerlich für die Stadtväter. Anfang der 1990er verstaubte der Plan in den Regalen des Stadtplanungsamts, und Davidson startete seinen Rettungsplan für die angeschlagene Stadt. Seine Initiative konzentrierte sich auf Johannesburg als "Gateway to Africa", als Einfallstor nach Afrika.

Ihre herausragende Infrastruktur, ihr Standortvorteil und ihr solider

financial liability, the underutilised Johannesburg athletics stadium. Maverick art activist Christopher Till was made Executive Director of Arts and Culture, inaugurated the controversial Johannesburg Biennale and annual Arts Alive festival, and turned an imploded power station into Africa's very own cultural theme park — the Newtown Cultural Precinct.

It was Ian Simons's job as Executive Director of Strategic Projects to lure the private sector into co-sponsoring flagship projects, emulating those pursued by other "successful" cities in the world. They included a R200 million rail link between Yeoville and downtown, a R300 million convention centre in the inner city, and a R100 million commercial theme park, Jewel City. Many of these are starting to see the light of day, albeit in mutated form (the Shilowa Express, a proposed high-speed rail link between Johannesburg, Pretoria and the Johannesburg international airport, the Sandton Convention Centre in the heart of the city's new financial district and, persistently, Jewel City on Johannesburg's east side).

The only black member of the squad, Nicky Padayachee, a medical doctor in his former life, was hired as Town Clerk to keep the regular bureaucrats in line, a task he accomplished with much fluster and to varying effect.

l'intérêt comme rampe de lancement pour les investisseurs et pour le secteur des commodités sud-africaines (Eskom, Transnet) par rapport à la conquête des ressources énormes et sous exploitées du continent noir. (En comparaison, le projet 2030 parle "d'opportunités à l'exportation" sur le continent pour les entreprises de services et désigne l'Afrique comme le premier marché). Johannesburg peut et doit exploiter sa position et devenir le "Tokyo ou le New York de l'Afrique".

Le plan de Davidson pose les bases pour l'avenir. Une nouvelle génération de fonctionnaires, "les supers bureaucrates", ont pris les rênes de la mairie. Extrêmement dépensiers, responsables seulement devant eux-mêmes, ils ont été embauchés pour faire de la ville "la vitrine mondiale" dont rêvent les politiques. Colin Wright, le directeur général bien en chair du bureau de l'industrie et du commerce s'est installé dans les quartiers afro-chics du centre ville de Johannesburg, dans l'immeuble de la Sanlam, repoussant avec mépris la grisaille du Civic Theater pour ses activités promotionnelles. Quand il n'est pas à Davos en Suisse, prétendant représenter la Nation toute entière au Forum Mondial de l'Economie, il offre à dîner et à boire aux délégations commerciales venues d'Atlanta, de New York et de Birmingham.

Il y a ensuite l'astucieux Danie Malan,

Finanzsektor, so hieß es, mache die Stadt zum natürlichen Sprungbrett für Investoren und südafrikanische Dienstleistungsunternehmen (Eskom, Transnet), um die riesigen und noch kaum genutzten Ressourcen des Dunklen Kontinents jenseits der Grenzen zu erschließen. (Zum Vergleich - auch die "Joburg 2030 Vision" spricht von Exportmöglichkeiten, die sich Unternehmern auf dem Subkontinent eröffneten, und sieht Afrika als den vorrangigen Absatzmarkt.) Johannesburg könnte und sollte seine Position nutzen und das "Tokio oder New York Afrikas" werden.

Davidsons Plan war Modell für die Zukunft. Eine neue Generation von Beamten, die "Superbürokraten", übernahm die Führung im Rathaus. Sehr teuer, nur sich selbst verantwortlich, hatte man sie eingestellt, damit sie die Stadt zu dem führenden "World City Showroom" machten, von dem die Politiker träumten. Der korpulente Colin Wright, Leitender Direktor für Handel und Industrie, verschmähte die tristen städtischen Büros und richtete sich im schicken Afrostil im Sanlam Building in der City ein, von wo aus er seine Promotiontätigkeit anging. Wenn er nicht gerade im Schweizer Davos weilte und das ganze Land beim Weltwirtschaftsforum vertrat, bewirtete er hier großzügig ihn besuchende Handelsdelegationen aus Atlanta, New York und Birmingham.

Dann war da der clevere Danie Malan,

Curiously enough, this team was surprisingly successful. In 1991, Johannesburg was proclaimed the fourth of the top-10 growth cities in the world and, by 1994, thanks, I suspect, to serious lobbying by Wright, it was voted among the world's top-50 cities by *Fortune* magazine. The city seemed well on its way to realising its dream.

But none of this impressed the new metropolitan and local councillors elected in 1995 to supersede those of the apartheid era. Budgets for strategic projects were slashed. The key architects of the old Johannesburg were fired (Wright, Simons) or demoted (Till), with Malan and Padayachee using their wiles to secure themselves places in the new administration. A Reconstruction and Development Programme (RDP) office was set up, in line with national redistributive objectives, and councillors set their sights on delivering a better life for all. This was presided over by the African National Congress's (ANC's) local Executive Committee Chairperson, enigmatic lawyer Colin Matjila, and the Rasputin-like Ivor Isaacs.

Matjila's team was a motley, incompatible crew. There was his right-hand man, Isaacs, whose heady ambition included a scheme to transform Alexandra into a "Jukskei Marina", and who is now working with Matjila on the development of 24 000 low-cost houses at Cosmos City in the

le directeur général du bureau des Sports qui a dirigé le projet visant à attirer à Johannesburg les jeux Olympiques, projet qui a échoué de même que la sous-utilisation du stade athlétique de Johannesburg dont les conséquences financières sont bien plus graves. Christopher Till, l'ancien militant-dissident de l'art, nommé directeur général des arts et de la culture, a inauguré la biennale controversée "d'arts vivants" et a transformé une ancienne station d'énergie en parc à thème culturel version Afrique — le quartier culturel de Newtown.

Ce fut la tâche de Ian Simon, directeur général des projets stratégiques, que de convaincre le secteur privé de co-financer ces projets phares, entrant en compétition avec ceux des autres villes à succès du monde. Cela inclus un projet de 200 millions de Rands de liaison par le rail entre Yeoville et le centre ville, un centre de congrès de 300 millions de Rands, toujours au centre-ville, et un parc commercial à thème, la "cité des bijoux". Beaucoup de ces projets ont commencé à voir le jour, quoique sous des formes légèrement différentes: le Shilowa express, le train à grande vitesse reliant Johannesburg, Pretoria et l'aéroport international de Johannesburg; le centre de congrès de Sandton, au cœur du nouveau quartier financier de la ville, et enfin, la cité des bijoux à l'Est de Johannesburg.

Leitender Direktor für Sport, der hinter Johannesburgs gescheiterter Olympiabewerbung und der finanziell noch weitaus größeren Schuldenlast für das kaum genutzte Johannesburger Stadion steckte. Der unabhängige Kunstaktivist Christopher Till wurde Leitender Direktor für Kunst und Kultur; er eröffnete die umstrittene Johannesburg Biennale, rief das jährliche Arts Alive Festival ins Leben und verwandelte ein implodiertes Kraftwerk in einen afrikanischen Kulturthemenpark, das "Newtown Cultural Precinct".

Ian Simons Aufgabe als Leitender Direktor für Strategische Projekte war es, die Privatindustrie als Co-Sponsor für herausragende Vorhaben zu gewinnen, die sich an Projekten in anderen "erfolgreichen" Städten der Welt messen ließen oder sie gar übertrafen. Pläne dieser Art waren die 200 Millionen Rand (100 ZAR = ca. 13 EUR) teure Bahnverbindung zwischen Yeoville und dem Zentrum, ein Kongresszentrum für 300 Millionen Rand in der City und Jewel City, ein kommerzieller Themenpark für 100 Millionen Rand. Viele dieser Vorhaben sind dabei, aus der Taufe gehoben zu werden, wenn auch in veränderter Form. (Der Shilowa Express, ein geplanter Hochgeschwindigkeitszug, soll Johannesburg, Pretoria und Johannesburgs internationalen Flughafen, das Sandton Kongresszentrum im neuen Finanzviertel und, nach wie vor, Jewel City in Johannesburgs Osten miteinander verbinden.)

Randburg area. There was Norman Prins, a former squatter leader, whose politics were far more about positioning himself than getting anything done; Prins is now a capacity development officer in informal settlements for the United Nations. There was Eugene Robson, then in charge of the city's coffers, who went on to become CEO of Krugersdorp. Finally, there were Patrick Flusk and Sizakele Nkosi, struggle activists from Riverlea and Alexandra respectively, and myself, plucked from the virtual

Le seul membre noir de cette équipe, Nicky Padayachee, ancien médecin, a été embauché pour aider les fonctionnaires à maintenir le cap, une tâche qu'il a accomplie de manière assez trouble et avec des résultats variables.

Assez curieusement, cette équipe s'est révélée gagnante. En 1991, Johannesburg s'est vue proclamer quatrième sur les 10 citées en croissance dans le monde, et en 1994, grâce, je présume, au fort lobbying de Wright, elle a été portée sur la liste des

Das einzige schwarze Mitglied der Gruppe war Nicky Padayachee. Dem früheren Arzt kam nun als Stadtdirektor die Aufgabe zu, die ganz normalen Beamten auf diese Linie einzuschwören, eine Aufgabe, die er aufgeregt und mit wechselndem Erfolg erfüllte.

Es mag seltsam klingen, aber dieses Team war überraschend erfolgreich. 1991 stand Johannesburg an vierter Stelle der ersten zehn am schnellsten wachsenden Städte der Welt, und 1994 setzte die Businesszeitschrift 'Fortune' — wie ich vermute, dank der fleißigen Lobbyarbeit

A client being assisted at the Peoples' Centre in Johannesburg's Region 4

Client recevant de l'assistance au People's Center, Johannesburg, Région 4

Der Kunde ist König im Bürgerzentrum von Johannesburgs Region 4

reality of academia to head up housing, urbanisation and environmental management.

We were dominated, according to 2030 apologist Rashid Seedat (now Director of the Corporate Planning Unit in the Johannesburg City Council), by a "small brickmaking" conception of local economic development. We put on overalls and led clean-up campaigns, sat night after night in informal settlements negotiating people around their poverty, built clinics, campaigned for Masakhane (a political campaign to persuade those who had boycotted local authority service charges in the 1980s to begin paying) and set up art competitions at primary schools to discover what children wanted the city to be. All of which, Seedat later said, was gravely misplaced. "A global city like Johannesburg", he said, mouthing World Bank jargon, "needs a different sense of local economic development, based on the sexy stuff of competitiveness and economic growth."

By 1997, the city was bankrupt. The Greater Johannesburg Metropolitan Council was unable to pay its electricity bill of R300 million. This was due, in large part, to it having lost its revenue base to its substructures in terms of the Local Government Transition Act of 1993, which made them legally autonomous

premières 50 villes par le magazine Fortune. La ville semblait alors en passe de réaliser son rêve.

Mais rien de tout cela n'a réussi à impressionner la nouvelle municipalité et les nouveaux conseillers locaux élus en 1995 pour succéder à l'équipe de l'ère de l'apartheid. Les budgets pour les projets dits stratégiques ont été coupés. Les architectes clés de l'ancienne Johannesburg ont été renvoyés (Wright, Simons) ou rétrogradé (Till) ; alors que d'autres comme Malan et Padayachee ont usé de toutes les ruses pour se faire une place dans la nouvelle administration. Un bureau a été monté pour le "Programme de Reconstruction et de Développement", en cohérence avec les objectifs de redistribution nationale. Les conseillers se sont fixés pour nouvel objectif de donner à tous la possibilité d'une vie meilleure. Tout cela fut orchestré par le président du comité local de l'ANC (African National Congress), par l'énigmatique juriste Colin Matjila et par le très raspoutinien Ivor Isaacs.

L'équipe hétéroclite de Matjila s'est révélée relativement incompatible. Il y avait tout d'abord Isaacs, l'homme de main dont la grande ambition comportait un projet visant à transformer Alexandra en une "marina au bord de la Juskei", et qui est maintenant en train de travailler avec Matjila sur le développement de 24 000 logements à prix modérés à "Cosmos city" dans le quartier de

von Wright - die Stadt auf die Liste der 50 Top-Städte der Welt.

Aber all das beeindruckte die neu gewählten Stadt- und Bezirksabgeordneten nicht, die 1995 die Vorgänger aus der Apartheid-Ära ablösten. Gelder für strategische Projekte wurden gestrichen. Die wichtigsten Architekten des alten Johannesburg wurden gefeuert (Wright, Simons) oder strafversetzt (Till), lediglich Malan und Padayachee gelang es, sich geschickt einen Platz in der neuen Verwaltung zu sichern. Ein Wiederaufbau- und Entwicklungsprogramm ("RDP"), das die neuen nationalen Ziele widerspiegelte, wurde ins Leben gerufen, und die Abgeordneten mühten sich um ein besseres Leben für alle. Die Leitung des Programms hatten der Vorsitzende des örtlichen Executive Committee's des ANC, der undurchsichtige Rechtsanwalt Colin Matjila, und der Rasputin-gleiche Ivor Isaacs.

Matjillas Team war eine bunt gemischte Gruppe, die eigentlich kaum zusammenpasste. Da war Matjillas rechte Hand, Isaacs, der von der Idee besessen war, den kleinen, extrem verschmutzten Juksei Fluss, der träge durch die Elendsviertel von Alexandra fließt, in eine noble, mit Yachten belebte "Juksei Marina" zu verwandeln. Heute arbeitet er mit Matjila am Bau von 24.000 Niedrigkostenhäusern in Cosmos City in Randburg. Dann war da Norman Prins, früher tonangebend in der illegalen

local authorities. While still being responsible for buying and transferring bulk water and electricity to them, the metro relied on them to pay for these services from locally raised revenue. Co-operation between the two levels was non-existent.

Political heavyweight and Matjila's arch-competitor, Kenny Fihla took advantage of this crisis to outmanoeuvre his rival (who then disappeared into the obscurity of black empowerment) and took up the position of Chairperson of the "Committee of 10". This body, later expanded to 15, was decreed by the Gauteng Province to negotiate Johannesburg out of its mess. The ANC tightened its political belt and ousted members who challenged the official line that a radical new approach to governing the city was needed.

Ketso Gordhan, the city's first real diva, managerialist supremo, alias City Manager, took over in 1998. His two-year brief was to oversee the move to a unicity, a metropolitan authority with a single tax base, and to restructure its administration by breaking it up into a number of business entities, responsible to that authority as their 100 percent shareholder, for delivering services. Where not directly privatised, the public sector was to begin acting like a private company.

What this has meant in practice is that employees who were using metro

Randburg. Il y avait aussi Norman Prins, un ancien leader de squatters dont la politique consistait plus à se positionner lui-même qu'à réaliser quoique ce soit. Il est maintenant agent de développement pour les Nations Unies sur le dossiers des camps informels. Eugene Robson, quant à lui, était en charge des finances de la ville, puis est devenu président directeur général de Krugersdorp. Enfin, il y avait aussi Patrick Flusk et Sizakele Nkozi, respectivement de Riverlea et d'Alexandra, d'anciens opposants au régime et tirés hors de la réalité virtuelle du monde académique pour se pencher sur la gestion des problèmes de logement, d'urbanisation et d'environnement.

Nous étions dominés, selon l'apologiste de 2030 Rashid Seedat, (maintenant directeur de l'unité de planification pour les entreprises de la municipalité) par une conception de "petits-pas" de développement économique local. Nous avons mis nos tenues de travail et avons mené des campagnes de ramassage pour la propreté, nous nous sommes réunis nuits après nuits dans les camps de peuplement informels pour essayer de discuter avec les gens sur les questions de pauvreté, de construction d'hôpitaux, de la campagne de Masakhane (une campagne politique pour persuader ceux qui avaient boycoté les factures des autorités locales dans les années 80 de commencer à repayer). Nous avons

Siedlungsbewegung, dem es mehr darum ging, sich selbst politisch zu positionieren als etwas zu bewegen. Heute ist er für die Vereinten Nationen als "capacity development officer" in unreguliert entstandenen Siedlungen tätig. Dann gab es noch Eugene Robson, damals Stadtkämmerer, der später Generaldirektor von Krugersdorp wurde. Und schließlich waren da noch Patrick Flusk und Sizakele Nkosi, kämpferische Aktivsten aus Riverlea bzw. Alexandra, und ich selbst, die ich aus dem Elfenbeinturm der akademischen Welt herausgerissen wurde, damit ich mich um Wohnungsbau, Urbanisierung und Umwelt kümmerte.

Wie Rashid Seedat, Apologet der "Joburg 2030 Vision" (heute Direktor der Corporate Planning Unit im Johannesburger Stadtrat), monierte, hatten wir uns einem Planungskonzept unterzuordnen, das wirtschaftliche Entwicklung auf unterster Ebene wollte. Wir zogen uns Overalls an und leiteten Putzkampagnen, saßen Nacht für Nacht in Elendssiedlungen und sprachen mit den Leuten über ihre Armut, wir bauten Gesundheitszentren, führten "Masakhane"-Aktionen durch (um diejenigen, die in den 1980ern die Zahlung städtischer Dienstleistungsabrechnungen boykottierten, dazu zu bewegen, sie jetzt zu bezahlen) und organisierten Kunstwettbewerbe an Grundschulen, um herauszufinden, wie Kinder sich ihre Stadt

The Johannesburg Athletics Stadium from Troyeville

Le Johannesburg Athletics Stadium (Stade Athlétique de Johannesburg) de Troyeville

Das Johannesburg Stadion, von Troyeville aus gesehen

transport to do their monthly shopping or travel to funerals elsewhere in the country, who assumed that pay day meant half day and who regularly took time off to take spouses to work or children to school are now subjected to various motivational gimmicks like "employee of the month" or "best idea" awards. A lot of clever branding has re-imaged Metro Solid Waste into Pikitup and Metro Electricity into City Power, while Johannesburg Water remains

Johannesburg Water, with a new consumer-friendly news bulletin, *The Watering Hole*. It is difficult to assess what else has actually been achieved.

At the same time the city commissioned a longer term plan to re-engineer Johannesburg into an "African World Class City". Before it could be released, Gordhan's contract was up and Johannesburg's first Supermayor, Masondo, was sworn in. Gordhan left for First Rand Bank, performance bonus of nearly R500 000 in pocket, having "been successful in carrying out his mandate to fix the institution", according to Fihla, by then Chairperson of the Transformation Lekgotla which was running the city. Masondo inherited the task of fixing the city. 2030 is his manifesto for doing so.

Trevor Ngwenya, a former Soweto ANC Councillor, now an Alternative Information and Development Centre

également mis en place des concours artistiques dans les écoles primaires pour découvrir ce que les enfants voulaient que leur ville soit.

Sedaat dira plus tard de tout cela que était fort déplacé. "Une cité globale comme Johannesburg", dit-il, reprenant le jargon de la banque mondiale, "a besoin d'un sens différent du développement économique local, basé sur les concepts suffisamment sexy de la compétitivité et de la croissance économique".

En 1997, la ville était en faillite. Le Conseil d'agglomération de Johannesburg fut dans l'incapacité de payer sa facture d'électricité de 300 millions de Rands. Cela s'explique en grande part par la perte de son revenu basé sur certaines structures que la loi de 1993 sur la transition vers un gouvernement local a légalement transformé en autorités locales autonomes. Tout en étant responsable de l'achat et du transfert d'eau et d'électricité à ces autorités, la municipalité pensait que ces dernières payeraient ces services avec le revenu collecté localement. Or, la coopération entre les deux niveaux était non existante.

Le poids lourd politique et le rival numéro un de Matjila, Kenny Fihla a profité de la crise pour évincer son rival (qui par la suite a disparu dans l'obscurité du "Black empowerment") et a pris le poste du "comité des 10".

wünschten. Alles das, so Seedat später, sei völlig fehl am Platz gewesen. "Eine globale Stadt wie Johannesburg", sagt er im Weltbankjargon, "braucht eine ganz andere wirtschaftliche Entwicklung. Und sie muss sich dabei auf die aggressiven Elemente von Wettbewerb und Wirtschaftswachstum stützen."

1997 war die Stadt bankrott. Die Stadtverwaltung von Groß-Johannesburg, Greater Johannesburg Metropolitan Council, konnte ihre Stromrechnung in Höhe von 300 Millionen Rand nicht mehr bezahlen. Die Hauptursache dafür war, dass die Stadt, gemäß dem "Local Government Transition Act" von 1993, ihre Einkommensbasis an die Bezirke verloren hatte; der "Transition Act" gewährte den Bezirksbehörden einen rechtlich autonomen Status. Während die Stadt verpflichtet war, Wasser und Strom zu kaufen — und zu bezahlen — und die einzelnen Stadtviertel damit zu beliefern, war sie auf die Bezirke angewiesen, dass diese die Gebühren bei den Kunden eintrieben. Eine Kooperation zwischen diesen zwei Ebenen aber gab es nicht.

Das politische Schwergewicht und Matjilas Erzrivale Kenny Fihla profitierte von dieser Krise und stach seinen Rivalen aus (der daraufhin in der undurchschaubaren Masse von "black empowerment"-Aktivitäten verschwand) und übernahm den Vorsitz des "Komitees der 10". Diese Institution, die später auf 15 Mitglieder erweitert wurde, war von der Provinz Gauteng beauftragt worden,

(AIDC) activist, was kicked out of the ANC as a result of his objections to Gordhan's plan. "Back in 1997", he said, "at the time of the financial crisis, our leaders started telling us that we had to dream new dreams. The old ones of a better life for all were not good enough. We were told to dream of becoming a World Class city". Ngwenya saw this as part of the same tendency to forget the past that saw "comrades going for crash courses in economics and voice training in the United States" after the election. "The RDP was this country's last collective manifesto," he said, "after that, the community began to be seen as the enemy."

Our city fathers disagree. By 2030, they tell us, Johannesburg will be one of the world's great cities. Forget comparisons with Durban or Cape Town, even Buenos Aires or Istanbul — we will all be enjoying the lives of the rich and famous, or at least middle-income citizens of London and New York (I'm not sure where the Bronx fits in to this). All our citizens will have found formal-sector employment, except the informal operators who will operate as such "by choice". They will be important, we are told, in "maintaining the African essence of our City". Africa — once central to our identity formation — will have been reduced to a quaint, exotic icon of a distant land.

Cette assemblée, qui s'est plus tard agrandie à 15, s'est vu confier par la Province du Gauteng la mission de tirer Johannesburg de ces disfonctionnements. L'ANC a resserré son emprise politique et a évincé tous les membres qui remettaient en cause la ligne officielle selon laquelle une nouvelle approche plus radicale de gestion de la ville était nécessaire.

Ketso Gordhan, la première vraie star de la ville, gestionnaire suprême, alias "city manager" a pris ses fonctions en 1998. Sa tâche pendant deux ans fut d'une part de surveiller la transition vers l'unité, c'est-à-dire une autorité métropolitaine disposant d'une base unique d'impôts locaux, et d'autre part de restructurer son administration en la divisant en un certain nombre d'entités commerciales correspondant à différents services, mais responsable devant l'autorité métropolitaine ; cette dernière étant actionnaire à 100 % de chacune des entités. Ainsi, bien que non privatisé directement, le secteur public a commencé à agir comme une société privée.

En pratique, cela signifie que les salariés qui utilisaient les véhicules de services municipaux pour faire leurs courses hebdomadaires ou pour se rendre à des funérailles quelque part dans le pays, qui supposaient que le jour de paye équivalait à une demi-journée et qui prenaient régulièrement sur leur temps de travail pour amener

Johannesburg aus seinem Chaos zu führen. Der ANC schnallte seinen politischen Gürtel enger und warf die Mitglieder hinaus, die sich der offiziellen Linie widersetzten, dass nämlich ein radikal neuer Ansatz notwendig sei, um die Stadt zu regieren.

1998 übernahm Ketso Gordhan, ein erster wirklicher Star und Supermanager, als City Manager die Leitung. Seine Aufgabe in den folgenden zwei Jahren war es, eine oberste Behörde zu schaffen, in der die städtischen Gelder zusammenfließen sollten, und die Verwaltung neu zu strukturieren. Diese sollte in mehrere Dienstleistungseinheiten untergliedert werden, die der neuen Behörde als deren 100%-iger Shareholder verantwortlich wären. Wo nicht sofort privatisiert wurde, sollte der öffentliche Sektor nach privatgesellschaftlichen Gesichtspunkten zu arbeiten beginnen.

Dies bedeutete in der Praxis, dass Angestellte, die mit Dienstfahrzeugen ihre monatlichen Einkäufe tätigten oder zu Beerdigungen aufs Land fuhren, die glaubten, dass Zahltag halber Arbeitstag bedeutete und die regelmäßig ihre Ehefrauen zur Arbeit und die Kinder zur Schule brachten, jetzt mit diversen Knüllern wie "Angestellter des Monats" oder "Preis für die beste Idee" auf Trab gebracht werden. Eine clevere Namensumtauschaktion hat die städtische Müllabfuhr in "Pikitup" ("Heb's auf") umgetauft und die städtischen Stromwerke in City Power. Nur

leurs épouses au travail ou leurs enfants à l'école sont maintenant soumis à diverses carottes motivationnelles du type récompense pour "l'employé du mois" ou "la meilleure idée". Un grand nombre d'idées ont permis, dans ce cadre, de renommer l'entreprise d'enlèvement des ordures en "pikitup" (contraction acronyme de "to pick it up" c'est-à-dire enlever, ramasser) et l'entreprise municipale d'électricité en "city power" (c'est-à-dire ville énergie), tandis que l'entreprise de distribution d'eau est restée "Johannesburg Water"

Johannesburg Wasser bleibt Johannesburg Wasser und gibt ein neues kundenfreundliches Nachrichtenbulletin heraus, "The Water Hole" ("Das Wasserloch"). Es lässt sich kaum aufzählen, was sonst noch alles erreicht wurde. Gleichzeitig erteilte die Stadt den Auftrag zum Entwurf eines langfristigen Konzepts, das Johannesburg wieder zu einer "African World Class City" machen sollte. Bevor der Plan an die Öffentlichkeit kam, war Gordhans Vertrag abgelaufen, und Johannesburgs erster Super-Bürgermeister Masondo wurde im Amt

The Johannesburg Stock Exchange and the Deutsche Bank buildings, Sandton

Immeuble de la Johannesburg Stock Exchange et la Deutsche Bank, Sandton

Die Johannesburg Börse und das Gebäude der Deutschen Bank in Sandton

mais dispose désormais d'un nouveau bulletin d'information destiné au consommateur, "le trou à arroser". Il est difficile d'évaluer les autres réalisations efficaces qui ont pu avoir lieu.

Dans le même temps, la ville a commandé un plan à long terme afin, de manière quasi scientifique, de transformer Johannesburg en "une cité africaine de classe mondiale". Avant la sortie de ce plan, Gordhan était en fin de contrat et le premier "super maire" de Johannesburg, Masondo, avait pris ses fonctions. Gordhan est parti pour la banque First Rand, avec une prime de performance d'environ 500 000 Rands en poche, pour "avoir réussi au cours de son mandat à remettre sur pied l'institution avec succès", selon Fihla, alors Président de la "transformation Lekgotla" qui était alors chargé de la politique de la ville. Masondo a hérité de cette tâche. 2030 constitue son manifeste pour ce faire.

Trevor Ngwenya, ancien conseiller ANC de Soweto, maintenant militant d'un Centre Alternatif d'Information et de Développement, a été renvoyé de l'ANC du fait de son opposition au plan de Gordhan. "En 1997", dit-il, "au temps de la crise financière, nos dirigeants ont commencé à nous dire que nous devions avoir de nouveaux rêves. Rêver à une vie meilleure, c'était du déjà vu. On nous a dit de rêver à devenir une ville de classe mondiale". Selon Ngwenya cela relève de la même

vereidigt. Gordhan wechselte zur First Rand Bank mit einem Leistungsbonus von fast 500.000 Rand in der Tasche; er habe, so Fihla, zu der Zeit Vorsitzender der "Transformation Lekgotla", der Versammlung, der damals die Leitung der Stadt oblag, "erfolgreich sein Mandat erfüllt und die Institution neu geordnet". Masondo erbte die Aufgabe, die Stadt neu zu ordnen. Sein Manifest ist die "Joburg 2030 Vision".

Trevor Ngwenya, ehemaliger ANC-Abgeordneter und heute Mitarbeiter am Alternativen Informations- und Entwicklungszentrum (AIDC), war wegen seiner Einwände gegen Gordhans Pläne aus der Partei ausgeschlossen worden. "Damals, 1997", sagt er, "während der Finanzkrise erzählten uns unsere Führer, wir sollten neue Träume träumen. Die alten Träume von einem besseren Leben für alle seien nicht gut genug, wir sollten von einer Stadt der Weltklasse träumen." Ngwenya sieht darin die allgemeine Tendenz, die Vergangenheit zu vergessen, so wie damals nach den Wahlen, als "Genossen in die USA gingen, um dort Crashkurse in Wirtschaft und Stimmtraining zu absolvieren". "Das Wiederaufbau- und Entwicklungsprogramm ("RDP") war das letzte gemeinsame Manifest dieses Landes", sagte er, "danach fing man an, die menschliche Gemeinschaft als den Feind zu betrachten."

Unsere Stadtväter sind anderer Meinung. Im Jahr 2030, sagen sie uns,

tendance à oublier le passé qui a vu des "camarades aller suivre des cours intensifs d'économie et de travail de la voix aux Etats-Unis" après les élections. "Le Programme de Reconstruction et de Développement fut le dernier manifeste collectif en date de ce pays", dit-il, "Par la suite, la communauté locale a commencé à être considérée comme une ennemie".

Les pères de la cité ne sont pas d'accords. D'ici 2030, nous disent-ils, Johannesburg sera l'une des villes les plus fantastiques du monde. Oubliées les comparaison avec Durban ou la ville du Cap, ou même Buenos Aires ou Istanbul — nous serons tous en mesure de vivre la vie des riches et des célèbres, ou du moins celle des citoyens à revenus moyens de Londres ou de New York (je ne sais pas trop où le Bronx se situe dans cette vision). Tous nos citoyens auront trouvé un emploi dans le secteur formel, à l'exception des opérateurs informels qui agiront de la sorte "par choix". Ils seront alors importants, nous dit-on, pour "maintenir l'essence africaine de notre ville". L'Afrique — qui fut un temps centrale à la formation de notre identité — sera alors réduite à une icône pittoresque et exotique d'une terre lointaine.

wird Johannesburg eine der großartigsten Städte der Welt sein. Vergessen Sie Durban oder Kapstadt, selbst Buenos Aires oder Istanbul — wir werden alle das Leben der Reichen und Berühmten leben oder doch zumindest das der Mittelschicht von London und New York (ich bin mir nicht sicher, wie die Bronx da hineinpasst). Alle unsere Bürger werden reguläre Arbeit gefunden haben — mit Ausnahme der anderen, die eben keine geregelte Arbeit "wollen". Diese werden, so sagt man uns, einen bedeutenden Beitrag leisten, "um das Afrikanische unserer Stadt zu bewahren". Afrika — einst Mittelpunkt unserer Identitätsbildung — wird dann nur noch eine malerisch-exotische Ikone eines fernen Landes sein.

ON THE ROAD SUR LA

4

UTE AUF DER STRASSE

man David, known to his friends and neighbours as "Mannetjies", lives on Beacon Road, Kliptown, Soweto, in a ramshackle, run-down brick house. A round, gregarious man in his late thirties, David moved into the house he calls home in 1970 with his mother, who was a live-in domestic worker for the Indian family who lived there and ran a butchery from the premises. When they moved out, they left the house to David and his mother.

As a child, he remembers doing odd jobs in the shop while his friends, the family's children, went to school. He has still never had any formal education. "I don't speak any language," he told me. "I just communicate." David left his formal job in 1999 to become a volunteer community worker, which he finances from the spaza shop which currently occupies the same space as his living room.

Here couches and TVs are all muddled up with fridges, loaves of bread and an endless stream of people at the door. He is slowly transforming the room next door into a proper, shiny-tiled, glass-countered café which, he said, is intended as an example to the community.

"We blacks think that business is a few tomatoes and an orange crate. I want people to see that if I can do this", he said, pointing to the shop in

man David, connu de ses amis et voisins sous le nom de "Mannetjies", vit dans Beacon Road, dans le quartier de Kliptown à Soweto, dans une maison de briques minuscule et délabrée. David, cet homme un peu rond et à l'esprit grégaire qui va vers la quarantaine, s'est installé dans la maison qu'il nomme son chez soi en 1970 avec sa mère, employée de maison à domicile pour une famille indienne qui vivait là et qui tenait une boucherie sur la propriété. A leur déménagement, ils laissèrent la maison à David et à sa mère.

De son enfance, il se souvient d'effectuer des travaux domestiques divers, pendant que ses amis, les enfants de la famille, allaient à l'école. A ce jour, il n'a toujours pas reçu d'éducation à proprement parler. "Je ne parle aucune langue" m'a-t-il dit. "Je me contente de communiquer". David quitta son emploi formel en 1999 pour devenir animateur socio-culturel volontaire, activité qu'il finance grâce au magasin de matériel d'occasion qui occupe pour le moment le même espace que son salon. Ici, les canapés et les postes de télévision se mêlent aux réfrigérateurs, aux miches de pain et à une file interminable de personnes qui se tient à la porte. Il transforme lentement la pièce d'à côté en un véritable café, aux carrelages brillants et au comptoir de verre, et qui, dit-il, devrait servir d'exemple pour la communauté. "Nous,

man David, ein rundlicher, geselliger Mann Ende dreißig, den seine Freunde und Nachbarn nur als "Mannetjies" kennen, lebt in Beacon Road, Kliptown, Soweto, in einem schäbigen, heruntergekommenen Backsteinhaus. David zog 1970 mit seiner Mutter in das Haus, das er sein Zuhause nennt. Sie hatte bei der indischen Familie, die hier wohnte und nebenan eine Fleischerei besaß, eine Stelle als Hausangestellte bekommen. Als die Familie auszog, überließ sie das Haus David und seiner Mutter.

Als Kind, so erinnert er sich, musste er im Laden mitarbeiten, während seine Freunde, die Kinder der Familie, zur Schule gehen konnten. Er hatte nie eine richtige Schulausbildung. "Ich spreche keine andere Sprache", sagt er, "ich mache mich irgendwie verständlich." 1999 gab David seine Arbeit auf und wurde freiwilliger Sozialarbeiter. Er lebt von seinem "Spaza Shop", einem Kramladen, der ihm zugleich Wohnzimmer ist und in dem er so ziemlich alles verkauft, was man im täglichen Leben braucht. Teile von Couchgarnituren und Fernseher stehen neben Kühlschränken, auf denen sich Brot stapelt, und an der Türe staut sich eine endlose Schlange von Leuten. Er ist gerade dabei, aus dem angrenzenden Raum ein richtiges Café zu machen, mit glänzenden Bodenfließen und einer Glastheke. Das soll, wie er sagt, für die anderen auch ein Vorbild sein: "Wir

the making behind him, "they can too."

This is typical of a new breed of entrepreneurial working-class people aspiring to a better life, but not wanting to get out of the township. "I have no interest in duplicating white people's lives," said David. "I like to live where I can greet people noisily in the street and have a presence in my community." As we talk, his attractive, curlered wife, Daphne, and their toddler leave the house for the morning parade up Beacon Road to Freedom Square. The historic site where, in 1955, the ANC's Freedom Charter, upon which our present constitution is based, was signed is now the market where Daphne Mann does her shopping.

Kliptown came into existence in 1904 when the Johannesburg Town Council identified it as the place to dump residents of the former "Coolie Location", after it had been razed to the ground by pneumonic plague that year. Known as the Klipspruit Camp, it housed 3 100 people — 1 600 Indians, 142 Coloureds and 1 358 Blacks, divided into racially separated tent towns. People were allowed to leave only when they could prove that they had a "proper residence" to go to back in Johannesburg.

By the 1950s brick houses with front stoeps had replaced the tents. Many of these still stand, albeit precariously, along the roads and

les Noirs, nous pensons que pour faire des affaires, quelques tomates et un cageot d'oranges suffisent. Je veux que les gens voient que si je peux faire ça", dit il, en montrant du doigt le magasin en construction derrière lui, "ils peuvent en faire autant".

Ce discours est typique d'une nouvelle classe d'ouvriers à l'esprit entrepreneur qui aspirent à une vie meilleure, mais qui ne veulent pas quitter le township. "Je n'ai aucune envie de copier la vie des Blancs", dit David. "J'aime vivre là où je peux saluer bruyamment les gens dans la rue et où ma présence peut être reconnue par la communauté." Pendant que nous discutons, Daphne, la tête pleine de bigoudis, sa jolie femme au physique avantageux, quitte la maison en compagnie de leur enfant pour la promenade matinale en direction du haut de Beacon Road jusqu'à Freedom Square. Le lieu historique où, en 1955, la Charte de la Liberté de l'ANC, sur laquelle notre constitution actuelle est basée, a été signée, est désormais le marché où Daphne Mann fait ses courses. Kliptown vit le jour en 1904, lorsque la Mairie de Johannesburg identifia le lieu pour y amasser les résidents de l'ancienne "Coolie Location", après qu'elle ait été totalement détruite par la peste pneumonique cette même année. Connu sous le nom de "Klipspruit Camp", il abritait 3 100 personnes —

Schwarze glauben, dass ein paar Tomaten und eine Kiste mit Orangen ein Geschäft sei. Ich möchte, dass die Leute begreifen, dass, wenn ich das kann", und er deutet hinter sich auf die Umbauarbeitn, "sie das auch können."

Diese Haltung ist typisch für eine neue Generation von Arbeitern, die unternehmerisch zu denken beginnt, endlich besser leben möchte, aber dabei nicht aus dem Township hinaus will. "Ich habe keine Lust, das Leben der Weißen zu kopieren", sagt David. "Ich möchte dort leben, wo ich Leute laut auf der Straße begrüßen kann und meinen Platz in der Gemeinschaft habe." Während wir miteinander sprechen, verlässt seine attraktive Frau Daphne, mit Lockenwicklern im Haar und der Tochter an der Hand, das Haus und wandert die Beacon Road hinauf Richtung Freedom Square. Der historische Ort, wo 1955 die Friedenscharta des ANC, die Grundlage unserer heutigen Verfassung, verabschiedet wurde, ist heute ein Marktplatz, wo Daphne ihre Einkäufe erledigt.

Kliptown entstand 1904. Der Johannesburger Stadtrat hatte das Gelände ausgewählt, um dort Bewohner der früheren "Coolie Location" unterzubringen, die nach einem Ausbruch von Lungenpest abgerissen und eingeebnet wurde. Die neue Siedlung, in der 3.100 Menschen — 1.600 Inder, 142 Farbige und 1.358 Schwarze — nach Rassen getrennt in Zeltstädten hausten,

scattered between the shack sprawl along the Klipspruit River. New Look (its various sections now more politically correctly named Chris Hani and Charter Square), the squatter camp that snaked its way along the Klipspruit River, had already begun to grow.

Back then, Aunt Eve Makoka, now in her 70s, was Kliptown's resident nurse. "Kliptown was a very multicultural place," she recalled. "Along Railway Road, Mr Harrison, a white man, lived with his Basotho wife. Next door to him were Indians, and next door to that, a Coloured family. We all lived together very peacefully."

In 1955, this highly creolised community living in Soweto's backyard became host to the Congress of the People when it met on a dusty soccer field at the northern end of the town, to sign the ANC's popular liberation manifesto. Makoka recalls closing her clinic early that week to attend the Freedom Charter celebrations. "But what I recall most vividly," she said, "was that we were prevented by the Congress from eating potatoes. Any hawkers selling potatoes had their stalls smashed. The reason was that prisoners in Bethal were being forced to plant potatoes and were dying in the heat."

Today Freedom Square is a bustling marketplace where taxis weave between clothes, chickens, fruit and

1600 Indiens, 142 Métis et 1 358 Noirs, divisés selon des camps de tentes racialement séparés. Les habitants n'étaient autorisés à quitter le lieu que lorsqu'ils pouvaient prouver qu'ils disposaient d'un "véritable lieu de résidence" où se rendre de retour à Johannesburg.

Vers les années 1950, les maisons de briques aux façades qui donnent sur la rue ont remplacé les tentes. Beaucoup d'entre elles se tiennent toujours là, bien qu'assez précairement, le long des rues, éparpillées entre les cabanes qui s'étalent le long de Rivière Klipspruit. "New Look" (ses différents quartiers se nomment désormais, pour être plus politiquement correct, "Chris Hani" et "Charter Square"), le camp de squatters qui commença à s'installer en sinuant le long de la Klipspruit, avait déjà commencé à s'étendre. De retour dans ces années, Tante Eve Makoka, maintenant âgée d'environ 70 ans, était l'infirmière de Kliptown. "Kliptown était un endroit très multiracial" se rappelle-t-elle. "Le long de Railway Road, M. Harrison, un Blanc, vivait avec sa femme, une Basotho. A côté de chez lui vivaient des Indiens, et à côté d'eux, une famille de Métis. Nous vivions tous ensembles parfaitement en paix."

En 1955, cette communauté fortement créolisée qui vivait dans les arrière-cours de Soweto accueillit le Congress of People lors de sa réunion sur un terrain de football poussiéreux à l'extrémité nord

wurde unter dem Namen "Klipspruit Camp" bekannt. Die Menschen durften das Camp nur dann verlassen, wenn sie in Johannesburg eine "richtige Wohnung" nachweisen konnten.

Um 1950 wurden die Zelte durch Backsteinhäuser mit Veranden an der Vorderseite ersetzt. Viele dieser Häuser stehen noch immer, wenn auch inzwischen recht baufällig, verstreut zwischen dem Bretterbudengewimmel am Klipspruit River. Damals entstand schon "New Look", ein Slumviertel, das sich entlang der Windungen des Flusses erstreckte (heute werden seine verschiedenen Bezirke politisch korrekter "Chris Hani" und "Charter Square" genannt). Zu der Zeit arbeitete Aunt Eve Makoka als Krankenschwester in der Siedlung. "Kliptown war ein richtig multikultureller Ort", erinnert sich die alte Dame, die inzwischen Mitte siebzig ist. "An der Railway Road wohnte Mr. Harrison, ein Weißer, mit seiner Frau, eine Basotho. Nebenan lebten Inder, und dann kam eine farbige Familie. Wir lebten alle ganz friedlich miteinander."

1955 war diese bunt gemischte Gemeinde in Sowetos Hinterhof Gastgeber des "Congress of the People". Der Volkskongress versammelte sich auf einem staubigen Fußballfeld im Norden des Stadtteils, um das populäre Befreiungsmanifest des ANC, die Friedenscharta, zu verabschieden. In dieser Woche, erzählt Makoka, schloss sie ihre Krankenstation früh, um an der

vegetables (including potatoes), motor car scrap, shoe doctors and stalls offering radio and TV repairs. Its edges are lined by rickety stalls, a soft-drink depot, a building material yard and wholesale warehouses owned by Indian shopkeepers who, throughout the apartheid period, were the only race group formally permitted to trade in the area.

Kliptown is not a place with any real boundaries. It extends outwards centrifugally from the intersection of Union and Beacon roads, fusing with

de la ville, pour signer le manifeste de libération populaire de l'ANC. Makoka se souvient avoir fermé sa clinique tôt cette semaine pour assister aux célébrations de la Charte de la Liberté. "Mais ce dont je me souviens avec le plus de précisions", dit-elle, "ce fut lorsque le Congrès nous empêcha de manger des pommes de terre. Tout colporteur qui vendait des pommes de terre voyait son étalage réduit à néant. La raison en était que les prisonniers de Bethal étaient forcés à planter des pommes de terre et mourraient sous la chaleur."

Veranstaltung teilzunehmen. "Aber an was ich mich besonders erinnere, ist, dass man uns auf dem Kongress sagte, wir sollten keine Kartoffeln essen. Jedem Straßenhändler, der Kartoffeln verkaufte, wurde sein Stand demoliert. Die Begründung war, dass Gefangene, die man in Bethal zwang, Kartoffeln zu setzen, in der Hitze wegstarben."

Der Platz der Freiheit ist heute eine quirlige Marktgegend, wo sich Taxis durch Kleider, Hühner, Obst und Gemüse (einschließlich Kartoffeln) schlängeln, vorbei an Ständen, in denen Schuhe

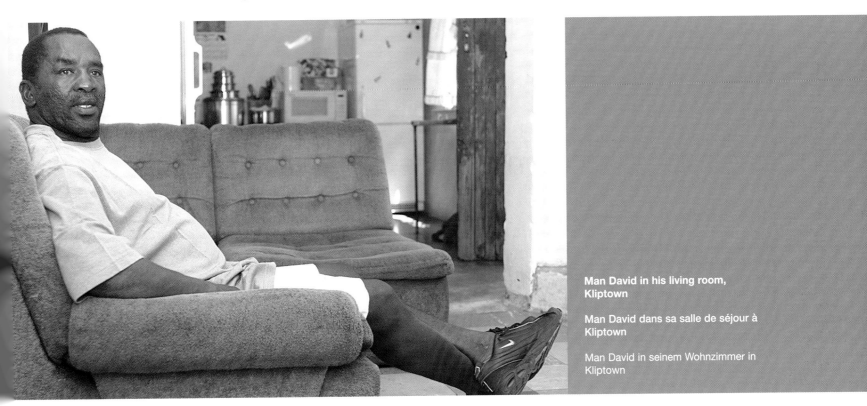

Man David in his living room, Kliptown

Man David dans sa salle de séjour à Kliptown

Man David in seinem Wohnzimmer in Kliptown

Union Road, Kliptown   Union Road, à Kliptown   Die Union Road in Kliptown

Pimville to the north, Eldorado Park to the east and Dhlamini to the west. To the south it merges indistinguishably with the endless shack sprawl continuing down the Klipspruit River.

It has been largely overlooked by government resources since 1994. Instead, its residents have begun to take responsibility for its maintenance and development.

Gene Duiker, the slight, arthritic director of the Kliptown, Our Town Development Trust, proudly showed me around the photographic exhibition put together by residents, funded by the French development agency, CRIAA, on display in the local community centre. This former transportation depot has been resourcefully converted into a nursery school, meeting rooms and an exhibition space. Graffiti on its walls proclaims that to do art and karate is better than to do crime. "We are working on signing a lease with the City Council for this building," he said. "Then we will be able to raise money to renovate it."

Shebeens, churches, clinics, crèches, many of them informal, are scattered throughout the township. Bob Nameng, Makoka's son, the local Rastafarian and self-appointed youth club co-ordinator, organises soccer and basketball matches, beauty pageants, clean-up campaigns and talent contests for the neighbourhood's

Aujourd'hui, Freedom Square est un marché plein de vie où les taxis se faufilent entre les vêtements, les poulets, les fruits et les légumes (dont des pommes de terre), les pièces détachées de voitures, les cordonniers et des étalages proposant réparation de postes de radio et de télévision. Ses bordures sont délimitées par des étales branlants, un dépôt de boissons non-alcoolisées, une cour remplie de matériaux de construction et des entrepôts de vente en gros dont les propriétaires sont des marchands indiens qui, durant l'apartheid, constituaient le seul groupe racial officiellement autorisé à faire commerce dans le quartier.

Kliptown n'est pas un quartier possédant de véritables frontières. Il s'étend vers l'extérieur de manière centrifuge depuis l'intersection de Union et de Beacon roads, fusionnant avec les quartiers de Pimville au Nord, d'Eldorado Park à l'Est et de Dhlamini à l'Ouest. Au sud, il se mêle de manière imprécise à l'étendue de cabanes sans fin qui se poursuit le long de la Klipspruit.

Depuis 1994, le gouvernement l'avait quasiment oublié de ses allocations. Pour résoudre les problèmes, ses résidents ont commencé à prendre la responsabilité de son entretien et de son développement. Gene Duiker, directeur frêle et arthritique de Kliptown, Our Town Development Trust, me fit visiter avec fierté l'exposition de photographies

geflickt, Autoteile verkauft oder Radio- und Fernsehgeräte repariert werden. Rundherum säumen wacklige Verkaufsstände das Gebiet, dazwischen liegen ein Getränkemarkt, ein Hof mit Baumaterialien und Geschäfte mit Kleidern und Haushaltswaren. Diese gehören Indern, denen es zu Apartheidzeiten als einzigen offiziell erlaubt war, in diesem Stadtteil Handel zu treiben.

Kliptown ist kein in sich geschlossener Ort. Von der Kreuzung Union- und Beacon Road dehnt es sich gleichsam zentrifugal aus, vermischt sich mit Pimville im Norden, Eldorado Park im Osten und Dhlamini im Westen. Im Süden verschmilzt es übergangslos mit den windigen Baracken und Bretterbuden, die sich scheinbar endlos am Klipspruit River aneinander reihen.

Nach 1994 wurde Kliptown von der Regierung schmählich vernachlässigt. Stattdessen fingen seine Bewohner an, sich selbst um den Erhalt und die Entwicklung ihres Viertels zu kümmern. Gene Duiker, der schmale, unter Arthritis leidende Direktor des "Kliptown, Our Town Development Trust" zeigt mir stolz die Fotoausstellung im Gemeindezentrum, die die Bewohner mit finanzieller Unterstützung der französischen Entwicklungshilforganisation CRIAA zusammengestellt haben. Mit viel Geschick wurden in diesem ehemaligen Depot der Verkehrsbetriebe eine Krankenschwesternschule, Versammlungsräume und der

youth. His mother's house doubles as both home and soccer club. He and David, the Kliptown, Our Town youth co-ordinator, know each other well. Together they plan youth activities, one on each side of the railway track which runs down the west side of Freedom Square. David and his friends have turned the old family butchery adjoining his house into an auditorium, raked seats and all. Here he shows "soap operas and American action movies" for R2 and, every so often, hosts a "Talk Show" where Kliptown's youth are invited to say what they feel and think about anything they please. Drugs, Aids and crime are most often on the agenda.

But now, considerable funds have been earmarked for Kliptown's development.

The provincial government is committed to upgrading its housing and local government is preparing to host an international competition for the design of Freedom Square. As these necessary improvements happen, will all the little practices of "making do" that Kliptown's residents have developed to survive and that are integral to their culture be respected and maintained?

Its way of life exemplifies the multilayered communal experience the majority of white South Africans have cut themselves off from. People have little money and even less faith in the

montée par les résidents et financée par l'Agence de Développement Française, le CRIAA, exposition que l'on peut visiter au centre communautaire local. Cet ancien dépôt de transport avait été converti de manière ingénieuse en école maternelle, salles de réunion et espace d'exposition. Les graffitis sur ses murs proclament qu'il vaut mieux faire de l'art et du karaté que d'être un criminel. "Nous essayons de signer un bail avec le Conseil Municipal pour ce bâtiment," dit-il. "Ensuite, nous pourrons lever des fonds pour le rénover."

Les débits de boisson, les églises, les cliniques, les crèches, beaucoup étant informels, sont éparpillés dans le township. Bob Nameng, le fils de Makoka, le Rastafari local qui a pris sur lui la responsabilité de coordinateur du club de jeunes, organise des matchs de football et de basket-ball, des concours de beauté, des campagnes de nettoyage et des concours de talents pour les jeunes du voisinage. Le domicile de sa mère lui sert à la fois de maison et de club de football. Lui et David, le coordinateur jeunesse du Kliptown, Our Town, se connaissent bien. Ils programment ensemble les activités des jeunes, chacun d'un côté de la voie ferrée qui longe le côté Est de Freedom Square. David et ses amis ont transformé l'ancienne boucherie familiale adjacente à sa maison en un auditorium, avec des rangées de sièges inclinées et tout ce qu'il faut pour en faire un

Ausstellungsraum untergebracht. Graffiti an den Wänden zeigen, dass Kunst und Karate besser ist als Verbrechen. "Wir bemühen uns jetzt darum, vom Stadtrat einen Pachtvertrag für dieses Gebäude zu bekommen", sagt Duiker. "Dann können wir Geld sammeln und es renovieren."

Überall im Township gibt es die traditionellen 'shebeens' oder Bierhallen, Kirchen, Krankenstationen, Kinderkrippen, viele entstanden einfach so, inoffiziell. Bob Nameng, der Sohn von Eve Makoka, ist der Rastafari des Viertels und selbsternannter Jugendclubkoordinator. Er organisiert für die Jugendlichen in der Nachbarschaft Fußball- und Basketballspiele, Putzkampagnen, Schönheits- und Talentwettbewerbe. Das Haus seiner Mutter ist sowohl sein Heim als auch das des Fußballclubs. Er und David, der die Jugendarbeit von "Kliptown, Our Town" leitet, kennen sich gut. Gemeinsam planen sie Aktionen für die Jugendlichen, jeder auf einer Seite der Eisenbahnlinie, die westlich des Freedom Square vorbeiläuft. David und seine Freunde haben den alten, ans Haus angrenzenden Fleischerladen in einen Vorführraum verwandelt und Stühle, und was man sonst noch so dafür braucht, zusammengesammelt. Hier zeigt er "Soaps und amerikanische Action-Filme" für zwei Rand und organisiert manchmal "Talk Shows". Dann ist Kliptowns Jugend eingeladen, zu sagen, was sie fühlt und denkt, über alles, was ihr gefällt. Drogen, Aids und Verbrechen sind die Themen,

post-apartheid system. Most are unemployed. During the day, they walk the streets, talking, gambling, shopping; they meet outside Lucky's Shoe Repairs or the sangoma's shop to gossip; they wash or rebuild cars at Bob's Place with pickings from the local scrapyard.

Life is lived on the street as much as possible. Houses like the Davids' that front the promenading main street are prized observation spots from where one can greet and meet acquaintances and do deals. The typical Kliptown front stoep doubles as a living-room, complete with sofas and orange crate seating and is within hailing distance of neighbours. The living-room is a hair salon, a grocery shop and an advice centre. Homework, committee meetings and soccer spectating take place around the kitchen table. Hospitality is a celebration of the neighbourhood "superfamily", given and received with no formality. Guests simply arrive and participate in whatever is going on at the time — cooking, eating, repairing the door lock, throwing a screed, peering under the scrap car's bonnet.

These socio-spatial practices contrast dramatically with those of the middle class, with its monofunctional spaces and demanding rituals of hospitality — invitations, doorbells, hallways, cloakrooms, formal dining rooms. For the South African middle

véritable auditorium. Là, il projette "des feuilletons et des films d'action américains" pour 2 Rands et, de temps à autres, organise un "Talk Show" où les jeunes de Kliptown sont invités à prendre la parole sur ce qu'ils ressentent et pensent sur les questions qu'ils décident d'aborder. Les drogues, le Sida et le crime sont les sujets qui reviennent le plus souvent au programme.

Mais aujourd'hui, des fonds considérables ont été alloués au développement de Kliptown. Le gouvernement provincial s'est engagé à améliorer ses logements et le gouvernement local se prépare à accueillir une compétition international consacrée à la conception de Freedom Square. Au fur et à mesure que ces améliorations nécessaires se produisent, est-ce que les petit pratiques de "faire aller" développées par les résidents de Kliptown pour survivre et qui font partie intégrante de leur culture seront respectées et conservées ?

Ses modes de vie font un exemple de l'expérience communale à différents niveaux, expérience dont la majorité des Sud-Africains blancs se sont isolés. Les gens n'ont que peu d'argent, et encore moins confiance en le système post-apartheid. La plupart d'entre eux sont sans emploi. Pendant la journée, ils déambulent dans les rues, discutent, jouent, font leurs courses ; ils se retrouvent à l'extérieur de la cordonnerie de Lucky ou du magasin du sangoma

die am häufigsten auf der Tagesordnung stehen.

Inzwischen aber wurden beträchtliche Gelder für die Entwicklung des Viertels bereitgestellt. Die Provinzregierung wurde beauftragt, die Wohnverhältnisse zu verbessern, und die Bezirksregierung bereitet eine internationale Ausschreibung zur Neuplanung des Freedom Square vor. So notwendig diese Maßnahmen auch sind, wird man die vielen kleinen Selbsthilfeinitiativen, die Kliptowns Bewohner ins Leben gerufen haben, um zu überleben, und die integraler Bestandteil ihrer Kultur sind, respektieren und beibehalten?

Dieser Lebensstil steht beispielhaft für die vielschichtige Erfahrung in einer solchen Gemeinschaft, eine Erfahrung, von der sich die Mehrheit der weißen Südafrikaner ausgeschlossen hat. Die Menschen haben wenig Geld und noch weniger Vertrauen in das Post-Apartheidsystem. Die meisten haben keine Arbeit. Tagsüber gammeln sie auf den Straßen herum, machen Glücksspiele, gehen einkaufen; sie treffen sich vor Luckys Schuhreparaturwerkstatt oder vor dem Sangoma-Laden, in dem sie Amulette und allerlei Zaubertränke und Tinkturen bekommen. Sie waschen Autos bei Bob's Place und reparieren sie mit Autoteilen vom Schrottplatz.

Meist spielt sich das Leben auf der Straße ab. Häuser wie das von David, die auf die Hauptstraße schauen, wo alles vorbei flaniert, sind beliebte

View across Charter Square
informal settlement,
Kliptown

Vue du Charter Square, lieu
d'habitations informelles, à
Kliptown

Blick über Charter Square,
eine Barackensiedlung in
Kliptown

class, the home is an autonomous family domain into which guests are selectively and ceremoniously introduced. The private world of the home and the public world of work or leisure are distinct and separate. For the working class, these overlap and merge — inside and outside, public and private, family and community, work and home — are extensions of the same. "In Kliptown," David told me, "we all know one another. We all live in one yard."

It is this attitude to and use of space which is transforming the roads, streets and pavements of Johannesburg since apartheid loosened its grip on the city, reinstating them, not as thoroughfares, but as common ground for public life.

Johannesburg boasts about 9 000 km of road. First came the haphazard and hastily constructed trails which connected the city's gold diggings to one another. These were soon overlaid by an orderly, domesticating grid of city and suburban streets, scrupulously managed by by-laws and health inspectors.

During apartheid, roads became symbols of oppression and sites of resistance. Forced removals, the movement of troops and armoured vehicles, marches, road-blocks, running street battles: the culture of the street was a highly politicised one.

pour discuter ; ils lavent ou réparent leurs voitures à Bob's Place avec des pièces récupérées à la décharge locale de voitures.

La vie se déroule autant que possible à l'extérieur. Les maisons, comme celles de David, qui bordent la rue principale où les gens se promènent sont des lieux d'observations prisés d'où l'on peut saluer du monde et retrouver ses connaissances et faire des affaires. Le devant de la maison typique de Kliptown fait également office de salon, avec des canapés et des cageots d'oranges en guise de sièges, et se trouve à portée de voix des voisins. Le salon est un salon de coiffure, une épicerie et un centre de conseils. Les devoirs à la maison, les réunions du comité et le visionnage des match de football se déroulent autour de la table de la cuisine. L'hospitalité est une célébration de la "superfamille" que constitue le voisinage, et est donnée et reçue sans formalités. Les invités viennent simplement et participent aux évènements qui se déroulent au moment où ils arrivent — on fait la cuisine, on mange, on répare le verrou de la porte, on fait un laïus, on jette un coup d'œil sous le capot de la voiture.

Ces pratiques socio-spatiales contrastent considérablement avec celles de la classe moyenne, avec ses espaces monofonctionnels qui demandent des rituels d'hospitalité précis — invitations, sonnettes, allées,

Beobachtungsplätze. Hier kann man alle Welt vorübergehen sehen, Freunde und Bekannte grüßen und den ein oder anderen Handel abschließen. Die typische Kliptowner Veranda, die 'front stoep', dient als Wohnraum mit Sofas und Orangenkisten zum Sitzen und liegt in Rufweite zum Nachbarhaus. Der Wohnraum ist auch Friseursalon, Lebensmittelgeschäft und Anlaufstelle für alle, die einen Rat brauchen. Hausaufgaben, Treffen von Komitees, Fußball schauen — alles findet rund um den Küchentisch statt. Die nachbarschaftliche Großfamilie zelebriert Gastfreundschaft, die man ohne große Formalitäten gibt und sich nimmt. Besucher kommen einfach so und nehmen an allem teil, was gerade abläuft - Kochen, Essen, Türschloss reparieren, Reden schwingen, und natürlich guckt man auch gemeinsam unter die Motorhaube des Schrottautos.

Die sozio-räumlichen Gewohnheiten dieser Menschen unterscheiden sich dramatisch von denen der Mittelschicht mit ihren monofunktionalen Räumen und obligatorischen Ritualen der Gastfreundschaft — Einladungen, Türglocken, Eingangshallen, Garderoben, das Esszimmer. Für die südafrikanische Mittelschicht ist das Heim eine autonome Familiendomäne, in die Gäste selektiv und zeremonienreich eingeführt werden. Die private Welt des Heims und die öffentliche Welt der Arbeit und Freizeit sind unterschiedliche Dinge und werden

As apartheid ended and the road was liberated, it became, for many, synonymous with anxiety. It brought strangers into our midst and those strangers were distrusted, feared and often armed and dangerous. A new landscape of razor wire, electric fencing, motorised gates, road closures, sentries and security patrols turned the road into a paramilitary zone.

Simultaneously, it was claimed by a myriad small-time traders, domestic workers and informal institutions, as a site of conviviality, livelihood and leisure, as extensions of their homes. Its liberation brought new freedom of movement between rural and urban areas and new migration across national boundaries.

The road became a paradoxical symbol of fear, mobility and freedom.

Magnes Mabaso was a domestic worker in Killarney until 1998 when, as she puts it, her "old lady died". "But I much prefer my new job," she said of the life she invented to replace domestic work. She sits, day in and day out, on the corner of Riviera and Main selling peanuts, cigarettes and sweets to commuters and passing pedestrians. She makes R30 to R40 per day, from which she contributes to supporting all four of her adult children. An ironing-board covered in plastic serves as her stall, newspapers on the ground as her carpet. She and

salles de bains d'invités, salles à manger formelles. Pour la classe moyenne sud-africaine, la maison est un domaine familial autonome dans lequel les invités sont introduits de manière sélective et cérémonieuse. Le monde privé de la maison et le monde publique du travail ou des loisirs sont distincts et séparés. Pour la classe ouvrière, ces mondes se recoupent et se mélangent — l'intérieur et l'extérieur, le public et le privé, la famille et la communauté, le travail et la maison - et sont des extensions d'une seule et même chose. "A Kliptown", m'a dit David, "nous nous connaissons tous. Nous habitons tous dans la même cour".

C'est cette attitude vis-à-vis de l'espace, et l'utilisation de cet espace, qui transforme les routes, les rues et les trottoirs de Johannesburg depuis que l'apartheid a perdu son emprise sur la ville, les réinstaurant, non pas en tant que voies publiques mais en tant qu'espace commun pour la vie publique. Johannesburg compte environ 9 000km de route. Surgirent premièrement des voies construites au hasard et à la hâte, qui connectaient les mines de la ville de l'or les unes aux autres. Celles-ci furent rapidement remplacées par une grille de rues ordonnées et organisées dans la ville et dans les banlieues, scrupuleusement gérées par des règlements et des inspecteurs de la santé. Pendant l'apartheid, les routes devinrent des symboles de l'oppression

auseinander gehalten. In der Arbeiterklasse greifen sie ineinander über und verschmelzen miteinander — innen und außen, öffentlich und privat, Familie und Gemeinschaft, Arbeit und Zuhause, das sind nur verschiedene Ausformungen derselben Sache. "In Kliptown", sagt David, "kennen wir uns alle. Wir leben alle in einem großen Hof."

Diese Einstellung zum Raum — und die Art, ihn zu nutzen — hat die Straßen und Bürgersteige von Johannesburg verändert, nachdem die Apartheid ihren harten Zugriff auf die Stadt gelöst hat. Sie sind nicht einfach mehr reine Durchgangsstrecken, sondern wurden wieder zum gemeinschaftlichen Grund für öffentliches Leben. Johannesburg verfügt über 9.000 Kilometer Straße. Zuerst waren es die praktisch von selbst entstandenen und eilig gebauten Pisten, die die Goldminen der Stadt untereinander verbanden. Doch bald wurden diese durch ein Raster von ordentlichen städtischen und vorstädtischen Straßen ersetzt, über die Straßenämter und Gesundheitsinspektoren peinlich genau wachten. Zu Apartheidzeiten wurde die Straße zum Symbol für Unterdrückung und ein Ort des Widerstands. Beschlagnahmungen, Truppenbewegungen und gepanzerte Fahrzeuge, Demonstrationsmärsche, Straßenblockaden und heftige Straßenkämpfe: die Kultur der Straße war im höchsten Maße politisiert.

her friends sit, at sundowner time, on orange crates eating raw peanuts and drinking water from yoghurt containers. "Now I can sit and talk to my friends while I work," she explained, as she sold a cigarette for R1 to a man about to catch his taxi. Next to her, a man offering shoe repairs played cards with his mates, while, across the street, vegetable sellers looked after each other's children.

A few blocks away, Francois Morgan stands at the intersection of Houghton Drive and Harrow Road with his begging-board, as he has done each day for the past six years. One of 11 children, Morgan grew up in an orphanage. Though he is a registered construction carpenter and plumber, he can no longer find a job, a situation he attributes to affirmative action. Instead, he entertains passing motorists with his brilliantly ironic cardboards which parody middle-class life, with appeals like "Holiday house needs fixing", "Poodles need grooming" or www.poorbrother.com", and which earn him R60 to R80 per day. He told me, with a twinkle in his eye, that he "dreams up what to tune the people" each day as he walks to work from where he lives, in a shack behind the house of a black family in Berea.

Gladys Kubayi is in her late 40s and lives in Chiawelo, Soweto. Each year since 1994, she has spent the summer

et des lieux de résistance. Les émigrations forcées, le déplacement des troupes de l'armée et des véhicules blindés, les marches, les barrages de route, les luttes de rue continuelles : la culture de la rue était une culture hautement politisée. A l'approche de la fin de l'apartheid et à mesure que la rue se libérait, cet espace devint, pour beaucoup, synonyme d'anxiété. Cela amenait des étrangers parmi nous et l'on ne faisait pas confiance à ces étrangers, ils engendraient la crainte et étaient souvent armés et dangereux. Un nouveau paysage constitué de barbelés ornés de lames de rasoir, de clôtures électriques, de portails électriques, de rues fermées, de sentinelles et de patrouilles de sécurité firent de la route une zone paramilitaire.

Simultanément, elle fut réclamée par une myriade de petits commerçants, d'employés à domicile et d'institutions informelles comme lieu de convivialité, de vie et de loisir, et comme extension du domicile. Sa libération engendra une nouvelle liberté de mouvement entre les zones rurales et les zones urbaines et de nouvelles migrations en provenance des pays limitrophes. La route devint un symbole paradoxal de peur, de mobilité et de liberté.

Magnes Mabaso était employée de maison à Killarney jusqu'en 1998 lorsque, comme elle le dit, "sa vieille mère mourut". "Mais je préfère de beaucoup mon nouveau travail" dit-elle

Als die Apartheid zu Ende war und die Straße befreit, wurde sie für viele zum Synonym für Angst. Sie brachte Fremde in unsere Gemeinschaft, und diesen Fremden misstraute man und fürchtete sie, oft waren sie bewaffnet und gefährlich. Eine neue Landschaft mit Bandstacheldraht, Elektrozäunen und automatisch schließenden Eingangtoren, Straßensperren, Wachposten und Sicherheitspatrouillen verwandelten die Straße in eine paramilitärische Zone.

Gleichzeitig besetzten Myriaden von fliegenden Händlern, Hausangestellten und Einrichtungen, die keiner Behörde unterliegen, die Straße und machten aus ihr, gleichsam in Fortsetzung ihrer Wohnungen, einen Ort der Geselligkeit, des Broterwerbs und der Freizeit. Die Befreiung der Straße brachte neue Bewegungsfreiheit zwischen Stadt und Land und neue Wanderbewegungen über die nationalen Grenzen hinweg. Die Straße wurde zum paradoxen Symbol für Furcht, Mobilität und Freiheit.

Magnes Mabaso war bis 1998 Hausangestellte in Killarney, als, wie sie es ausdrückt, ihre "alte Dame starb". "Aber ich finde meinen neuen Job viel besser", und dann erzählt sie von dem Leben, das sie seither führt. Tagein, tagaus sitzt sie an der Ecke von Riviera- und Main Street und verkauft Erdnüsse, Zigaretten und Süßigkeiten. Dreißig bis vierzig Rand verdient sie am Tag und unterstützt damit noch ihre vier erwachsenen Kinder. Ein mit Plastik

months buying mealies from a farmer in Brits and getting up at 4am to journey to Noord Street, site of one of downtown's busiest taxi ranks. She arrives at 5am and makes the fire on which she will braai mealies all day, selling them for R3 each. On a good day, she can make R200.

Kubayi is one of many who, each year, between late October and May, participate in an intricate, colourful drama, as mealies, staple diet of South Africa's rural people, are brought to town and sold on the city's streets.

de la vie qu'elle s'est inventée pour remplacer son emploi de domestique. Elle est assise, tous les jours, au coin de Riviera et de Main, et vend des cacahuètes, des cigarettes et des bonbons aux banlieusards et aux piétons qui passent. Elle gagne 30 à 40 Rands par jour, somme avec laquelle elle aide ses quatre enfants désormais adultes. Une planche à repasser recouverte de plastique sert d'étalage, et les journaux posés par terre lui servent de tapis. Elle et ses amis s'assoient, au coucher du soleil, sur des

verkleidetes Eisengestell dient ihr als Verkaufsstand, Zeitungen auf dem Gehweg als Teppich. Bei Sonnenuntergang sitzen sie und ihre Freundinnen auf Orangenkisten, knabbern Erdnüsse und trinken Wasser aus Yoghurtbechern. "Jetzt kann ich mit meinen Freundinnen schwatzen, während ich arbeite", erklärt sie mir und verkauft schnell eine einzelne Zigarette für einen Rand an einen Kunden, der sein Taxi noch erwischen möchte. Gleich neben ihr spielt ein Mann, der Schuhe repariert, Karten mit seinen Freunden, und auf der

Aunt Eve Makoka, retired nursing sister, Kliptown

Tante Eve Makoka, infirmière à la retraite, à Kliptown

Aunt Eve Makoka war Krankenschwester in Kliptown - heute ist sie in Rente

Rural women in colourful Shangaan cloth, coal smoke rising from vacant lots, braziers carried by young men around the city's streets — these are only the visible signs of a complex configuration of informal urban-rural trade.

Unlike Kubayi, who is self-employed, Johanna Sibia, a young woman in her early 20s, sells for a man from Hammanskraal. During mealie season, he provides food and lodging for her in Bram Fischerville, a shack settlement near Dobsonville, Soweto, as does another mealie boss from Kwa-mhlanga. "We are well looked after," she said, telling me that she earns between R120 and R500 per day, depending on how much she sells. "Our parents told our boss to treat us like children. They even told him to punish us if we misbehave. But he treats us right. He gives us money for food and there is someone to cook for us when we get back in the evening."

Others are not so lucky. Lena Skosana comes from KwaNdebele and has been selling mealies since 1992. She, like others she works with, is paid just R20 per day, irrespective of her sales. "Our boss treats us very badly," she said. "We sleep in the open next to the truck. Sometimes people steal our clothes and blankets. We do not have a place to bath or change our clothes."

Many of these women are not here

cageots d'orange pour manger des cacahuètes crues et boire de l'eau dans des pots de yaourts. "Maintenant je peux m'asseoir et discuter avec mes amis tout en travaillant", explique-t-elle, en vendant une cigarette à 1 Rand à un homme qui s'apprête à attraper son taxi. A côté d'elle, un homme proposant un service de cordonnerie joue au cartes avec ses copains, pendant que, de l'autre côté de la rue, les vendeurs de légumes surveillent les enfants des uns et des autres.

A quelques pâtés de maison de cela, François Morgan se tient à l'intersection de Houghton Drive et de Harrow Road avec sa pancarte de mendiant, comme il le fait tous les jours depuis six ans. Issu d'une famille de 11 enfants, Morgan a grandi dans un orphelinat. Bien qu'il soit qualifié en tant que charpentier de construction et que plombier, il ne peut plus trouver de travail, une situation qu'il attribue à la discrimination positive. Au lieu de cela, il divertit les motoristes qui passent avec ses pancartes brillamment ironiques parodiant la vie de la classe moyenne, et qui lancent des appels tels que "Besoin d'argent pour réparer maison de vacances", "Besoin d'argent pour toilettage caniches" ou "www.pauvrefrère.com", ce qui lui permet de gagner entre 60 et 80 Rands par jour. Il m'a dit, une étincelle dans les yeux, qu'il "rêvait les messages qu'il faisait passer aux gens" chaque jour sur le chemin qu'il parcourt à pied entre son

anderen Straßenseite passen die Gemüsehändlerinnen gegenseitig auf ihre Kinder auf.

Ein paar Quadrate weiter steht François Morgan mit bemalten Pappkartonbildern in der Hand an der Kreuzung Houghton Drive/Harrow Road, so wie er dort jeden Tag seit sechs Jahren steht. Als eines von elf Kindern wuchs Morgan in einem Waisenhaus auf. Er ist Zimmermann und Klempner, aber obwohl er arbeitslos gemeldet ist, findet er keine Arbeit mehr, eine Tatsache, die er der "affirmative action" zuschreibt, den Maßnahmen zur beruflichen Förderung von Schwarzen. Und Morgan ist weiß. Nun unterhält er Autofahrer mit seinen herrlich ironischen Bildern auf Pappkarton, die das Leben der Mittelschicht auf die Schippe nehmen mit Sprüchen wie "Ferienhaus in Ordnung zu bringen", "Pfleger für Pudel gesucht" oder "www.armerbruder.com". Damit verdient er sechzig bis achtzig Rand am Tag. Mit einem verschmitzten Lächeln erzählt er mir, dass er morgens, wenn er von sich zu Hause — und das ist eine Bretterbude hinter dem Haus einer schwarzen Familie in Berea — zu seinem Arbeitsplatz geht, überlegt, "was die Leute anmacht".

Gladys Kubayi ist Ende vierzig und lebt in Chiawelo, Soweto. Seit 1994 kauft sie während der südafrikanischen Sommermonate von Ende Oktober bis Mai Maiskolben von einem Farmer in Brits. Morgens um vier macht sie sich auf den Weg nach Noord Street, zu einem

by choice. They have children to support and no way of doing so in their villages. By word of mouth they hear of farmers taking their stock to town and looking for sellers. Many end up on the city's streets for years, during which they build a solidarity and comaraderie. "Sometimes we gossip and fight," says Sibia, "but we do what we do because we don't want to be prostitutes or our children to become thieves."

Domestic workers, mealie sellers, hair cutters, the unemployed; their and

lieu de travail et son domicile, une cabane à l'arrière de la maison d'une famille noire à Berea.

Gladys Kubayi va sur ses cinquante ans et vit dans le quartier de Chiawelo, à Soweto. Tous les ans depuis 1994, elle consacre les mois d'été à l'achat des épis de maïs chez un fermier de Brits et se lève à 4 heures du matin pour aller jusqu'à Noord Street, où se trouve l'une des stations de taxi les plus bourdonnantes d'activité de la ville. Elle arrive à 5 heures et allume le feu sur lequel elle va cuire ses épis de maïs toute

der belebtesten Taxiplätze im Zentrum Johannesburgs. Um fünf Uhr kommt sie an, facht ein Feuer an und grillt den ganzen Tag über ihre Maiskolben. Sie verkauft sie für drei Rand das Stück. An einem guten Tag kann sie 200 Rand (100 ZAR = ca. 13 EUR) machen. Kubayi gehört zu der großen Schar fliegender Händler und Händlerinnen, die jedes Jahr Teil des komplizierten, aber farbenprächtigen Schauspiels sind, wenn die Maiskolben, die Hauptnahrung der Landbevölkerung in Südafrika, in die Stadt gebracht und auf den Straßen verkauft

Magnes Mabaso, street vendor in Killarney

Magnes Mabaso, vendeuse ambulante à Killarney

Magnes Mabaso, Straßenverkäuferin in Killarney

Gladys Kubayi braaing mealies at the Noord Street taxi rank

Gladys Kubayi grillant du maïs à Noord Street, gare routière

Gladys Kubayi beim Rösten von Maiskolben am Taxiplatz an der Noord Street

many others' presences on our streets have transformed Johannesburg. From being the ultimate zoned, controlled and compartmentalised city, it is now characterised by messy intersections and overlapping realities. Poverty has, for the first time, become visible. Ordinary, everyday lives, which were excluded from the city by western urban management practices, town planning codes or by the legal and administrative apparatus of apartheid, have brought distant geographical, social and cultural worlds into contact. In the spaces between corporatised communities and gentrified enclaves, an idea of the city as common ground for public life is beginning to emerge.

It may be anathema to middle-class notions of guarded space and fixed identities, but this is important territory. It allows livelihoods dependent on the solidarity of shared routines and the mobility of the road a way, however fragile, to survive. "This is my life," says Kubayi. "If I had any other means of survival other than sitting here and getting harassed by the police, I wouldn't be here at all. All I am trying to do is to make a living an honest way."

la journée, les vendant 3 Rands pièce. Les bons jours, elle peut gagner jusqu'à 200 Rands. Kubayi est l'une des nombreuses personnes qui, chaque année, entre la fin du mois d'octobre et le mois de mai, participent à la pièce de théâtre colorée qui se déroule dans les rues lorsque les épis de maïs, nourriture de base des habitants des régions rurales d'Afrique du Sud, sont apportés en ville y sont vendus — les femmes des milieux ruraux habillées de vêtements Shangaan colorés, la fumée de charbon qui s'élève des emplacements vacants, les brasiers transportés par de jeunes hommes dans les rues de la ville — ceux-ci ne sont que les signes visibles de la configuration complexe du commerce informel entre l'urbain et le rural.

Contrairement à Kubayi, qui travaille seule et est son propre patron, Johanna Sibia, une jeune femme d'une vingtaine d'années, vend pour un homme de Hammanskraal. Au cours de la saison du maïs, il lui fournit de la nourriture et un logement à Braamfisher, un camp d'habitation constitué de cabanes dans le quartier de Dobsonville, à Soweto, comme le fait un autre commerçant de maïs de Kwa-mhlanga. "On prend bien soin de nous", dit-elle, me disant qu'elle gagne entre 120 Rands et 500 Rands par jour, en fonction de la quantité qu'elle vend. "Nos parents ont dit à notre patron de nous traiter comme ses propres enfants. Ils lui ont dit de nous punir si nous nous comportions mal.

werden. Frauen vom Land in den bunten Kleidern der Shangaan, der Rauch von Kohlefeuern auf leer stehenden Grundstücken, junge Männer, die Kohlebecken durch die Straßen der Stadt tragen — dies sind die wenigen sichtbaren Zeichen eines sehr viel komplexeren, informellen Handels zwischen Stadt und Land.

Anders als Kubayi, die ihr eigener Boss ist, verkauft Johanna Sibia, eine junge Frau von Anfang zwanzig, für einen Mann von Hammanskraal. Während der Maiszeit erhält sie von ihm Essen und Unterkunft in Braamfisher, einer Bretterbudensiedlung in Dobsonville, Soweto; ein anderer Maiskolbenfarmer von Kwa-Mhlanga macht es ebenso. "Sie sorgen gut für uns", sagt Sibia und erzählt mir, dass sie zwischen 120 und 500 Rand am Tag verdiene, je nachdem, wie viel sie verkauft. "Unsere Eltern haben unserem Boss gesagt, er soll uns wie Kinder behandeln. Er soll uns sogar bestrafen, wenn wir uns daneben benehmen. Aber er behandelt uns gut. Er gibt uns Geld für Essen, und wenn wir am Abend zurückkommen, hat jemand schon für uns gekocht."

Nicht alle haben soviel Glück. Lena Skosana kommt aus Kwa-Ndable und verkauft Maiskolben seit 1992. Sie und andere, mit denen sie zusammen arbeitet, erhalten pro Person nur zwanzig Rand pro Tag, ganz gleich, wie viel sie verkaufen. "Unser Boss behandelt uns schlecht", sagt sie. "Wir schlafen im Freien neben

Mais il nous traite bien. Il nous donne de l'argent pour notre nourriture et il y a toujours quelqu'un pour cuisiner pour nous lorsque nous rentrons le soir."

D'autres n'ont pas autant de chance. Lena Skosana vient de Kwa-Ndable et vend des maïs depuis 1992. Elle est payée, comme d'autres avec qui elle travaille, seulement 20 Rands par jour, quel que soit le produit de sa vente. "Notre patron nous traite très mal", dit-elle. "Nous dormons dehors à côté du camion. Parfois, on se fait voler nos vêtements et nos couvertures. Nous ne disposons d'aucun endroit pour nous laver ou pour changer de vêtements."

Nombre de ces femmes ne sont pas ici par choix. Elles ont des enfants à nourrir et ne peuvent assumer cette charge dans leurs villages. Grâce au bouche à oreille, elles entendent parler de fermiers qui emmènent leur stock en ville et qui recherchent des vendeurs. Un grand nombre d'entre elles finissent dans les rues de la ville et y passe un certain nombre d'années, au cours desquelles elles développent une certaine solidarité et une certaine camaraderie. "Parfois nous nous racontons des ragots et nous nous battons", dit Sibia, "mais nous savons ce que nous faisons, parce que nous ne voulons pas devenir des prostituées ou que nos enfants deviennent des voleurs."

Les employés de maison, les vendeurs de maïs, les coiffeurs, les sans emploi; leur présence, ainsi que celle de dem LKW. Manchmal kommen Leute und stehlen uns unsere Kleider und Decken. Wir können nirgends baden oder uns umziehen."

Viele dieser Frauen sind nicht freiwillig hier. Sie haben Kinder, die sie ernähren müssen, aber in ihren Dörfern gibt es keine Arbeit. Untereinander hören sie von Farmern, die ihre Produkte zum Verkauf in die Stadt bringen und Verkäufer oder Verkäuferinnen suchen. Viele arbeiten jahrelang auf der Straße, und mit der Zeit entsteht zwischen ihnen ein Gefühl von Solidarität und Kameradschaft. "Es wird viel getratscht, und wir streiten auch", erzählt Sibia, "aber wir arbeiten hier, weil wir nicht als Prostituierte enden wollen, und unsere Kinder keine Diebe werden sollen."

Hausangestellte, Maiskolbenverkäufer und -verkäuferinnen, Leute, die Haare schneiden, die Arbeitslosen - sie und viele andere auf unseren Straßen haben Johannesburg verändert. Einst die ultimativ in Zonen und überwachte Abschnitte aufgeteilte, gerasterte Stadt, prägen sie nun schmutzige Kreuzungen und Welten, die aufeinander prallen. Zum ersten Mal wird Armut sichtbar. Haben bisher ein westlich orientiertes Stadtverwaltungssystem, Planungsverordnungen, Apartheidgesetze und -verwaltungsvorschriften das ganz gewöhnliche Alltagsleben aus der Stadt ausgeschlossen, kommen nun Welten miteinander in Kontakt, die sich bisher geographisch, gesellschaftlich und

nombreuses autres personnes dans nos rues ont transformé Johannesburg. D'une ville zonée, contrôlée et compartimentée à l'extrême dans le passé, elle se caractérise aujourd'hui par des intersections désordonnées et par des réalités qui se recoupent. La pauvreté est, pour la première fois, devenue visible. D'ordinaire, les vies de tous les jours, qui étaient exclues de la ville par des pratiques de gestion urbaine à l'occidentale, des codes de planification de la ville ou par l'appareil législatif et administratif de l'apartheid, ont fait se rencontrer divers mondes géographiques, sociaux et culturels. Dans les espaces qui se situent entre les communautés engendrées par le corporatisme et les enclaves élitistes, une idée de la ville comme terrain public pour la vie publique commence à émerger.

Il se peut qu'il s'agisse d'un anathème par rapport aux notions des classes moyennes de l'espace gardé et des identités fixées, mais il s'agit d'un territoire important. Cela permet aux gagne-pain dépendant de la solidarité des routines partagées et de la mobilité de la route d'avoir un moyen, quoi que fragile, de survivre. "C'est ma vie", déclare Kubayi. "Si je disposais d'autres moyens de survie que de rester assise ici et de me faire harceler par la police, je ne serais pas là du tout. Tout ce que j'essaie de faire, c'est de gagner de l'argent de manière honnête."

kulturell fremd waren. In den Räumen zwischen Firmenkomplexen und teuer sanierten Enklaven beginnt die Idee der Stadt als gemeinschaftlicher Grund für öffentliches Leben Gestalt anzunehmen.

Der Mittelschicht mit ihrer Vorstellung von überwachtem Raum und klar definierter Identität mag es nicht gefallen, aber dies ist wichtiges Terrain. Es können Auskommen und Lebensformen geschaffen werden, die auf Solidarität und Gemeinsamkeit basieren, und die Mobilität der Straße ist, wie problematisch auch immer, ein Weg zum Überleben. "Dies ist mein Leben", sagt Kubayi. "Wenn ich andere Verdienstmöglichkeiten hätte, als hier zu sitzen und von der Polizei belästigt zu werden, dann wäre ich gar nicht erst hier. Ich möchte nichts anderes als mein Leben auf ehrliche Weise verdienen."

THEME PARK CITY LA VILLE FETE FOR

NE THEMENPARKS – WELTEN FÜR SICH

today's aspiring world class cities are no longer primarily concerned with old-fashioned modernist aspirations like providing housing, efficient public transport, education, or work for the masses. Their priority is competing with each other for as much of the internationally circulating capital, goods and labour as they can. To do so, they not only have to offer a good climate for business.

They also have to display a lifestyle that appeals to the workers of international corporations — the highly mobile, highly paid, conspicuously consuming, post-industrial professional.

Johannesburg is no exception. "We need to be ambitious in the way we think, plan and act", said Kenny Fihla, head of finance, strategy and economic development on the city's mayoral committee. "This means thinking of ourselves as a player in the global economy." By 2030, the city's aim is to become "home to all major local headquarters and international companies operating throughout the subcontinent".

It is to just this market that Melrose Arch, a development adjacent to the M1 motorway to Pretoria, is designed to appeal. A R1 billion Sentinel Mining Industries retirement fund investment, it was conceptualised as a "post-industrial service centre", in other words, a high-tech live/work/play

les villes de classe mondiale qui suscitent l'inspiration dans le monde d'aujourd'hui ne se préoccupent quasiment plus des aspirations modernistes démodées que sont la fourniture de logement, l'efficacité des transports publics, l'éducation ou le travail des masses. Leur priorité est d'entrer en compétition les unes avec les autres pour amasser autant de capital, de biens et de main d'œuvre en circulation que possible. Pour cela, elles ne doivent pas se contenter d'offrir un climat propice aux entreprises. Elles doivent aussi exhiber un style de vie attractif pour les employés des sociétés internationales — pour le professionnel extrêmement mobile, particulièrement bien payé, qui consomme sans modération, de type post-industriel.

Johannesburg ne fait pas exception à cette règle. "Nous devons être ambitieux dans la manière dont nous pensons, planifions et agissons", a déclaré Kenny Fihla, directeur des finances, de la stratégie et du développement économique au comité de la mairie de la ville. "Cela signifie que nous devons nous penser comme un acteur de l'économie mondiale". D'ici à 2003, l'objectif de la ville est de devenir "un foyer d'accueil pour tous les sièges sociaux locaux majeurs ainsi que pour les sociétés internationales opérant sur le sous-continent.

C'est justement ce marché que Melrose Arch, un développement

den aufstrebenden Städten der Weltklasse, den "World Class Cities", geht es heute in erster Linie nicht mehr so sehr um altmodisch-modernistische Ziele wie Haus- und Wohnungsbau, leistungsfähigen öffentlichen Nahverkehr, Bildung oder Arbeit für die breite Masse. Vorrangig wetteifern sie untereinander um das in der globalen Welt vorhandene Potential an Kapital, Waren und Arbeitskraft. Dafür reicht nicht allein ein gutes Geschäftsklima. Sie müssen überdies einen Lebensstil bieten, der die Mitarbeiter internationaler Firmen anspricht — jene hochmobilen, gut verdienenden, teuer konsumierenden, post-industriellen Beschäftigten multinationaler Konzerne.

Johannesburg macht keine Ausnahme. "Wir müssen Ehrgeiz beweisen in der Art, wie wir denken, planen und handeln", sagt Kenny Fihla, zuständig für Finanz-, Strategie- und Wirtschaftsentwicklung in Johannesburgs Bürgermeisterkomitee. "Das bedeutet, dass wir uns selbst als "global player" in der internationalen Wirtschaft sehen müssen." Ziel der Stadt ist es, bis 2030 "Firmenstandort für alle größeren nationalen und internationalen Unternehmen zu werden, die auf dem afrikanischen Subkontinent tätig sind".

Genau diese Klientel hat Melrose Arch im Auge. Der neue Büropark an der Schnellstraße M1 nach Pretoria ist ein Pensionskasseninvestment der Sentinel Mining Industries in Höhe von 1 Milliarde

environment for today's corporate worker.

Melrose Arch has ripped up one of the city's oldest, most established residential suburbs, Melrose, to create, in the first of six phases, a 52 000-square-metre premixed design package. It includes offices, penthouses, shops, a hotel, health club, theatre, car showroom and a public square, offering a total lifestyle package to cosmopolitans including, rumour has it, head of the Reserve Bank, Tito Mboweni.

It has already attracted the attention of the international business community. One of its first tenants was Arthur Andersen and Associates, multinational accountants and auditors, who, at the end of 2001 moved 450 employees from their former premises in Dunkeld West into 6 500 square metres at Melrose Arch.

The move, said Daryll Jackson, the company's CEO, has been "sensationally successful". "Our staff love working here, productivity is up and this environment promotes the team work we require."

Andersen's open-plan offices are furnished with imported Herman Miller plug-in workstations and Museum of Modern Art Aaron chairs. The discreet meeting rooms are named after every citrus fruit in the family. An in-house Seattle Coffee Shop opens onto a bright, grassy courtyard. Employees

adjacent à la voie rapide M1 menant à Pretoria, a été conçu pour attirer. Avec un investissement de la caisse de retraite de Sentinel Mining Industries d'un montant de 1 milliard, ce lieu fut conceptualisé pour être un "centre de services post-industriel", en d'autres mots, un environnement high-tech répondant au concept logement/travail/divertissement pour l'employé en entreprise d'aujourd'hui.

La construction de Melrose Arch a entraîné la destruction de l'une des banlieues résidentielles les plus vieilles, banlieue également particulièrement bien établie: Melrose, pour créer, au cours de la première de six phases, un espace conceptuel en préfabriqué de 52 000 mètres carrés. Cet espace est constitué de bureaux, d'appartements terrasse, de magasins, d'un hôtel, d'un club de remise en forme, d'un théâtre, d'une salle d'exposition de voitures et d'une place publique, offrant aux habitants, dont l'un d'eux serait, selon la rumeur, Tito Mboweni, directeur de la Reserve Bank un espace de vie complet.

Cela a déjà attiré l'attention de la communauté internationale d'entreprises. L'un de ses premiers locataires fut Arthur Anderson and Associates, une multinationale de comptables et d'auditeurs qui, à la fin de 2001, délocalisa ses 450 employés de leurs anciens locaux de Dunkeld West dans 6500 mètres carrés à Melrose Arch. "Le déménagement", déclara Daryll Jackson,

Rand (100 ZAR = ca. 13 EUR) und ist ein als "post-industrielles Dienstleistungscenter" konzipiertes High-tech-Ambiente zum Leben, Arbeiten und zur Freizeitgestaltung für den modernen Firmenmitarbeiter.

Melrose Arch hat ein Loch in Johannesburgs ältestes und am besten etabliertes 'suburb', dem einst weißen Melrose, gerissen. In einer ersten von sechs Bauphasen wird auf 52.000 Quadratmeter ein komplettes Designpaket entstehen mit Büros, Penthäusern, Geschäften, einem Hotel, Fitnessclubs, Theatern, Ausstellungshallen von Autofirmen und einem öffentlichen Platz; das Terrain bietet den kosmopolitischen Bürgern, darunter auch, wie es heißt, dem Chef der Reserve Bank, Tito Mboweni, ein komplettes Lifestyle-Paket.

Melrose Arch hat bereits die Aufmerksamkeit der internationalen Business Community auf sich gelenkt. Einer der ersten, der einzog, war Arthur Andersen and Associates, ein multinationales Wirtschafts- und Rechnungsprüfungsunternehmen, das Ende 2001 mit 450 Mitarbeitern von seinem bisherigen Firmensitz in Dunkeld West in 6.500 Quadratmeter in Melrose Arch zog. Der Umzug, sagt Daryll Jackson, Generaldirektor des Unternehmens, "war sensationell erfolgreich. Unsere Mitarbeiter arbeiten sehr gern hier, die Produktivität ist gestiegen, und das Ambiente fördert die Teamarbeit, die für uns wichtig ist."

Melrose Arch, a live/work/play environment for the upwardly mobile

Melrose Arch, environnement /logement/travail/olivertissement pour la classe sociale montante

Melrose Arch, Wohn-, Arbeits- und Freizeitambiente für die Aufsteigergeneration

qualify for special rates from the hairdresser downstairs.

Equally important, and what initially attracted Andersen's global real estate group — the body that decides where their branches will be — is Melrose Arch's allusion to the traditional city. Its intimate streets, small-scale façades, a village square, lampposts, bollards, trees and benches are all familiar attributes of cities the world over. In fact, they are familiar to Johannesburgers, who will recognise the pattern in Parkview, Greenside or even Yeoville — the mixed-use suburban main street. Here people live above where they work, stop for coffee and a pastry on their way to the office, all know and greet each other and generally live like good neighbours. Even the local lumpen or homeless waif is spared a friendly wave.

There is one irony. Whereas elsewhere in the city Melrose Arch's model is falling apart — boarded-up windows, cracking pavements, parking problems, poor people lying about, low-paying tenants — here clients are moving in before the paint is dry, desperate to be at the forefront of trend. MGs, BMWs, a Mercedes 4x4 with the registration number "Noise 1 GP" are give-away signs of who hangs out in these coffee shops, these hairdressers, and who will frequent the pubs of the self-described "six star" Melrose Arch Hotel when it is complete.

le PDG de la société, a été "un succès sensationnel". "Notre personnel adore travailler ici, la productivité est en hausse et cet environnement nous garantit le travail d'équipe dont nous avons besoin.'

Les bureaux en plan ouvert d'Andersen sont meublées de stations de travail enfichables importées "Herman Miller" et de chaises "Aaron" du Musée d'Art Moderne. Les salles de réunion discrètes portent chacune le nom d'un agrume différent. Un Seattle Coffee Shop intra-muros y ouvre sur une court claire et verdoyante. Les employés bénéficient de prix spéciaux au salon de coiffure situé au rez-de-chaussée.

Un élément tout aussi important, et qui a d'ailleurs été ce qui dans un premier temps a attiré le groupe immobilier international d'Andersen - l'organe qui décide de l'endroit où les diverses branches vont être localisées - est l'allusion de Melrose Arch à la ville traditionnelle. Ses rues intimistes, ses petites façades, sa place de village, ses lampadaires, ses bornes, ses arbres et ses bancs sont tous des attributs familiers des villes du monde entier. En fait, on les retrouve très fréquemment à Johannesburg, où ce schéma — l'utilisation mixte de la rue principale de la banlieue — se reconnaît à Parkview, à Greenside, et même à Yeoville. Ici, les gens vivent au-dessus de leur lieu de travail, s'arrêtent pour prendre un café et une pâtisserie sur le chemin de leur bureau, tout le monde se connaît et se

Andersens Großraumbüros sind mit importierten Herman Miller plug-in-workstations und den passenden "Aeron"-Bürostühlen ausgestattet, wie sie auch im Museum of Modern Art in New York zu sehen sind. Die dezenten Konferenzräume sind nach den Früchten der verschiedenen Zitrusarten benannt. Ein Seattle Coffee Shop im Gebäude geht auf einen hellen, Gras bewachsenen Innenhof. Angestellte erhalten beim Friseur im Erdgeschoss Sonderpreise.

Ebenso wichtig aber — und dies war es auch, was Andersons Unternehmensorgan, das über die Firmensitze entscheidet, von Anfang zusagte — ist Melrose Archs Anspielung auf die traditionelle Stadt. Seine intimen Straßen, die stark gegliederten Fassaden, der Dorfplatz, Laternenpfähle, Poller, Bäume und Bänke sind vertraute Attribute von Städten überall in der Welt. Und sie sind auch Johannesburger Bürgern vertraut, die das Grundmuster in Parkview, Greenside und sogar in Yeoville wieder erkennen werden — die multifunktionale Hauptstraße des Viertels. Hier leben die Menschen in der Nähe ihrer Arbeit, trinken Kaffee oder essen ein Stück Kuchen auf dem Weg ins Büro, man kennt und grüßt sich und lebt im Allgemeinen in guter Nachbarschaft miteinander. Selbst die Obdachlosen des Viertels und die Straßenkinder werden mit einem freundlichen Wink bedacht.

Das Ganze ist nicht frei von Ironie. Während anderswo in der Stadt die

For this Main Street is a sanitised lifestyle package which conjures up an emotionally satisfying image of bygone times, while offering the most high-tech of services — raised-access flooring, a 178-camera closed-circuit television network and two levels of parking basement under the cobbles. It is the city as we wish it were (classy, secure and homogeneous), represented as an idealised fragment of what it was (snug, human-scaled and neighbourly) and accessible to those with enough disposable income to look like they belong. It all feels rather uncomfortably, up-marketly fake.

Graham Wilson, site architect, disagrees. "A public bus route runs through the development," he said. "Should the security situation change, we will pull down the perimeter fence and connect back into the surrounding fabric. This development aims to become part of the city."

Part of its success is the flamboyance of its 11 architects, each of whom designed one of its buildings, in an attempt to simulate the process by which cities develop over time. With a little more discipline, Melrose Arch might just have made it as Main Street. Thankfully we have been spared the boredom of that comforting image by the self-indulgence of our local architects, each seeming to want to outdo the other.

salue, et entretient généralement des relations de bon voisinage. Même le sous-prolétariat local et les enfants abandonnés sont gratifiés d'un salut amical. Il y a cependant une ironie à tout cela. Comme partout dans la ville, le modèle de Melrose Arch s'effrite — des vitrines bouchées, des trottoirs fissurés, des problèmes de parking, des vagabonds allongés ici et là, des locataires qui ne s'acquittent pas régulièrement de leur loyer; ici les clients s'installent avant même que la peinture n'ait fini de sécher, désespérés de se trouver à l'avant de la mode. Les MG, les BMW, un 4x4 Mercedes arborant une plaque d'immatriculation "Bruit 1GP", sont tous des indicateurs du type de personnes qui sortent dans ces cafés, qui font chez ces coiffeurs, et qui fréquentent le pub de l'Hôtel de Melrose Arch qui lors de son achèvement s'est auto-proclamé hôtel "six étoiles.

Car cette Main Street est un espace offrant un mode de vie aseptisé qui rappelle l'image émotionnellement satisfaisante des temps révolus, tout en offrant les services les plus high-tech — des sols à accès surélevés, un circuit de réseau télévisé fermé de 178 caméras et deux niveaux de parkings souterrains situés sous les pavés ronds des rues. C'est la ville telle que nous souhaitons qu'elle soit (classe, sécurisée et homogène), représentée par un fragment idéaliste de ce qu'elle était (confortable, à échelle humaine et de voisinage) et

Vorläufermodelle von Melrose Arch verfallen — verrammelte Fenster, aufgerissene Pflaster, Parkprobleme, herumlungernde Arme, Mieter, die sich kaum die Miete leisten können-, ziehen hier die Kunden ein, begierig Trendsetter zu sein, noch bevor die Farbe trocken ist. MGs, BMWs, ein Mercedes 4x4, für dessen provozierend "lautes" Nummernschild "Noise 1 GP" der Besitzer gern bezahlt hat, verraten, wer in den Coffee Shops und Friseurläden herumhängt, und wer später die Bars des nach eigenen Angaben "Sechs-Sterne"-Melrose Arch Hotels frequentieren wird, wenn es dann fertig ist.

Denn diese Hauptstraße ist ein keimfreies Lifestylepaket, das ein friedliches Bild längst vergangener Zeiten heraufbeschwört und gleichzeitig beste High-tech-Dienstleistungen offeriert — Installationshohlraumböden, ein Rundum-Überwachungssystem mit 178 Kameras und zwei unterirdischen Parkdecks. Es ist die Stadt, wie wir sie uns wünschen (edel, sicher und homogen), ein Fragment dessen, was sie in unseren Idealvorstellungen einmal war (gemütlich, menschlich und nachbarschaftlich) und zugänglich für jene, die über ein ausreichend hohes Einkommen verfügen, dass es aussieht, als ob sie dazugehörten. Das alles wirkt wie eine abgeschmackte Imitation auf hohem Niveau.

Graham Wilson, am Projekt beteiligter Architekt, hält dagegen. "Durch den

Melrose Arch's centrepiece is Andrew Makin's marvelous Hundertwasser muddle with a mortar-board-capped tower and colourful ceramic tiles that ooze out of every orifice. Nick Sack's building is exquisite, yet over-detailed, as if he tried to cram the whole of Buenos Aires into one building. Pedro Roos has adopted a more functional approach, exposing giant ducts and pipes over an escalator which descends to the underground parking, signposted as if to a subway station. Henning Rassmus has produced a slick brick and glass fragment of Berlin's reconstructed Potsdamer Platz. Little glimpses of everywhere have found their way onto this exotic Main Street. Walking around Melrose Arch feels like being a tourist in your own town.

Which is also what it feels like — though for very different reasons — to visit the Apartheid Museum. Located in Johannesburg's closest thing to a Coney Island pleasure park, the Apartheid Museum stands between a Nando's and a Chicken Licken "fly-through", and is flanked by screaming roller-coasters, a big wheel and the brass springboks of the Gold Reef City Casino. Given the inappropriateness of its site for a task as momentous as the institutionalising of apartheid's memory, the Apartheid Museum is wrapped in a fortress-like, 10-metre-

accessible à ceux disposant d'un revenu net suffisant pour avoir le sentiment d'appartenir à cet ensemble. Tout cela semble cependant plutôt inconfortable avec ses faux airs de luxe.

Graham Wilson, architecte de l'endroit, n'est pas d'accord. "Une voie de bus publics traverse le développement", dit il. "Dans le cas où la situation venait à changer concernant la sécurité, nous retirerions la clôture de sécurité et reconnecterions l'ensemble au tissu urbain environnant. Ce développement a pour but de s'intégrer à la ville."

Une partie de son succès tient à la flamboyance de ses 11 architectes, chacun d'entre eux ayant conçu l'un de ses bâtiments, dans une tentative pour stimuler le processus par lequel les villes se développement au cours du temps. Avec un peu plus de discipline, Melrose Arch aurait bien pu se contenter de Main Street. Heureusement, l'ennui de cette image réconfortante nous a été épargnée par l'auto-satisfaction de nos architectes locaux, chacun semblant vouloir surpasser l'autre. La pièce centrale de Melrose Arch est le merveilleux fouillis que constitue l'Hundertwasser d'Andrew Makins, un bâtiment constitué d'une tour couronnée d'un mortier et de carreaux de céramique multicolores qui dépassent de chaque orifice. Le bâtiment de Nick Sacks est exquis, mais comporte trop de détails, comme si l'architecte avait

Komplex führt eine öffentliche Buslinie", sagt er, "und wenn es eines Tages besser um die Sicherheit bestellt sein sollte, werden wir den Zaun niederreißen, der das Gelände umgibt, so dass es mit der Umgebung verschmilzt. Dieses Büroparkprojekt soll Teil der Stadt werden."

Ein Teil des Erfolges von Melrose Arch gebührt der Phantasie seiner elf Architekten. Jeder von ihnen hat ein Gebäude entworfen, womit der Versuch unternommen wurde, einen allmählichen Stadtentwicklungsprozess zu simulieren. Mit noch etwas mehr planerischer Disziplin hätte Melrose Arch wirklich eine Hauptstraße werden können. Glücklicherweise blieb uns die Langweiligkeit dieses beruhigenden Anblicks erspart - dank der hemmungslosen Bauwut unserer lokalen Architekten, die einer den anderen zu übertrumpfen versuchten.

Mittelpunkt von Melrose Arch ist Andrew Makins fantastisches Hundertwasserdurcheinander mit einem von einem überdimensionalen High-school-Käppchen bedeckten Turm und farbenprächtigen Keramikfliesen, die aus jeder Gebäudeöffnung herausquellen. Exquisit ist auch Nick Sacks Gebäude, leider mit allzu vielen Details, als ob er ganz Buenos Aires in ein Gebäude hineinpressen wollte. Pedro Roos hat einen funktionaleren Ansatz; über einem Aufzug, der zur Tiefgarage führt und beschildert ist, als ob es eine U-

Entrance to the Apartheid Museum, Gold Reef City

Musée de l'Apartheid, Gold Reef City

Das Apartheid Museum in Gold Reef City

high stone wall. Not surprisingly, its township nickname is Alcatraz.

Its exhibition spaces are buried under an artificially constructed mound of sloping earth planted with indigenous highveld grass. From the top of the mound, the city is visible as a muted silhouette on the horizon. Underneath, a sequence of cavernous spaces shapes the memory of apartheid's history — at once traumatic, shocking and bewilderingly absurd — and resists not only this city's tendency to trivialise everything, but also the ease with which it chooses to forget.

The Apartheid Museum is a very good building. Unused as we are in this country to very good buildings, its poetry evokes a strong sense of being somewhere else. Gabion walls, raw steel, packed stonework, rough concrete and face-brick, though at times unnecessarily derivative of recent buildings elsewhere, construct a neutral, abstract space in which the full brutality of apartheid is powerfully conveyed. In time, in my view, it will be counted among the other great museums of traumatic memory worldwide — the Holocaust Museum in Washington DC, Yad Vashem in Jerusalem and the extension to the Jewish Museum in Berlin.

Under construction at much the same time as the Apartheid Museum was another interior world, motivated,

essayé de concentrer l'intégralité de Buenos Aires dans un seul bâtiment. Pedro Roos a adopté une approche plus fonctionnelle, exposant des conduites et des tuyaux géants au dessus d'un escalator qui descend au parking souterrain, signalé comme le serait une station de métro. Henning Rassmus a reproduit un fragment superficiel de briques et de verre de la Potsdamer Platz reconstruite à Berlin. De petits bouts du monde entier ont trouvé leur place dans cette Main Street au caractère exotique. Se promener dans Melrose Arch donne le sentiment d'être un touriste dans sa propre ville.

Ce qui est également ce que l'on ressent — bien que ce soit pour différentes raisons — en visitant le Musée de l'Apartheid. Situé dans ce qui ressemble de très près à un parc de loisir tel que Coney Island à Johannesburg, le Musée de l'Apartheid se situe entre deux fast-food, un Nando's et un "drive-in" Chicken Licken, et est flanqué de montagnes russes hurlantes, d'une grande roue et des springboks cuivrés du Casino de Gold Reef City. Etant donné le caractère inapproprié du lieu pour une tâche aussi monumentale que l'institutionnalisation de la mémoire de l'apartheid, on a encerclé le Musée de l'Apartheid d'un mur de pierres de 10m de haut, l'ensemble faisant penser à une forteresse. Et c'est sans surprise que le surnom qui lui a été donné dans les township est celui d'"Alcatraz".

Bahnstation sei, verlegte er gigantische Rohrleitungen. Henning Rassmus hat aus Backstein und Glas ein smartes Fragment des wieder entstandenen Potsdamer Platzes in Berlin geschaffen. Abbilder, Eindrücke aus aller Welt haben ihren Weg in diese exotische Main Street gefunden. In Melrose Arch herumspazieren, ist, als ob man Tourist in der eigenen Stadt wäre.

Was man ebenso, wenn auch aus ganz anderen Gründen, bei einem Besuch des Apartheid Museums empfindet. Es liegt in einem Gelände, das man vielleicht am ehesten mit einem Coney-Island-Vergnügungspark vergleichen könnte, und wird von "Nando's"- und "Chicken-Licken"-Imibssketten, einer kreischenden Achterbahn, einem Riesenrad und den glänzenden Messing-Springböcken vor dem Golden Reef City Casino flankiert. Ein unangemessener Platz angesichts der großen Verpflichtung, die Erinnerung an die Apartheid zu repräsentieren. Das Museum ist von einer festungsähnlichen, zehn Meter hohen Steinmauer umgeben, und es überrascht nicht, dass es in den Townships "Alcatraz" genannt wird.

Die Ausstellungsräume befinden sich unter einem künstlich aufgehäuften Hügel, der mit einheimischem Gras bepflanzt ist, wie man es im 'hochveld' um Johannesburg herum findet. Von oben erblickt man die Silhouette der Stadt, hört das leise Grummeln des Verkehrs. Darunter erinnert eine Reihe von Kellergewölben an die Geschichte der

not by the social obligation to remember, but by the commercial imperative to forget (time, place or how much money you have already lost). Montecasino, the Tuscan gambling citadel in the northern suburbs, is an ungainly sprawl from the air. Inside, its authentically fake ornamental landscape wraps us in a fun-filled, never-ending twilight utopia, where the pigeons don't shit and the roofs cast shadows on the sky.

This gamblers' paradise was built in the late 1990s by Sogo Sun, Southern Sun's gaming division, backed by South African Breweries. At the time that Creative Kingdom — the concept architects — were working on it, Ken Rosevear, former CEO of Sun International, now development director of MGM Grand which operates the Montecasino (along with most others in the world), had just spent a holiday in Tuscany and loved it. He also knew that there was no other casino anywhere in the world in Tuscan theme and thought its "earthy feel" would appeal to South Africans. "So Tuscan it was," said Edmund Batley, of Bentel Abramson architects, who got the project built. "It was not a big intellectual decision, it just happened because Rosevear thought it would work." Batley told me that Montecasino is rated one of the top 10 casinos in the world, outstripping its South African counterparts by far. And

Ses salles d'exposition sont enterrées sous une colline de terre pentue artificiellement construite et plantée d'herbes indigènes du haut veld. Du haut de cette colline, la ville est visible telle une silhouette muette se dessinant à l'horizon. Au-dessous, une séquence d'espaces caverneux donne forme à la mémoire de l'apartheid — à un moment traumatisant, choquant et absurde à un point déconcertant — et résiste non seulement à la tendance de cette ville à tout vulgariser mais aussi à l'aisance avec laquelle elle choisit d'oublier.

Le Musée de l'Apartheid est un très beau bâtiment. Inhabitués comme nous le sommes dans ce pays aux très beaux bâtiments, sa poésie évoque très fortement le sentiment que l'on se trouve ailleurs. Des murs de gabion, de l'acier brut, des ouvrages de maçonnerie en pierre enfermés dans des cages, du béton brut et des briques de parement, bien que dérivatif parfois peu nécessaire des constructions récentes que l'on trouve partout ailleurs, façonnent un espace neutre, abstrait, dans lequel l'ensemble de la brutalité de l'apartheid est restitué. Avec le temps, de mon point de vue, ce musée fera partie des autres grands musées dédiés aux mémoires traumatisantes du monde — le Musée de l'Holocauste à Washington DC, Yad Vashem à Jérusalem et l'extension du Musée Juif à Berlin.

Consruit environ à la même période que le Musée de l'Apartheid, un autre

Apartheid, gleichzeitig traumatisch, erschreckend und auf verwirrende Weise absurd. Die Räume sperren sich gegen jeglichen Versuch, alles trivialisieren zu wollen, übrigens nicht nur in dieser Stadt, sondern auch anderswo, und widersetzen sich der Leichtigkeit, mit der man vergisst.

Das Apartheid Museum ist ein gelungener Bau. Seine Poesie gibt einem das Gefühl, irgendwo anders zu sein, umso mehr, als wir in diesem Land wenig gute Architektur kennen. Drahtschotterkästen, Rohstahl, kompaktes Mauerwerk, Rohbeton und Ziegelverblendungen, wenn auch manchmal unnötigerweise von anderen Neubauten abgeschaut, formen einen neutralen, abstrakten Raum, in dem die volle Brutalität der Apartheid ausdrucksstark vermittelt wird. Mit der Zeit wird meiner Meinung nach das Gebäude den anderen großen Museen der Welt zugerechnet werden, deren Aufgabe die Bewahrung traumatischer Erinnerungen ist, wie das Holocaust Museum in Washington DC, Yad Vashem in Jerusalem und der Libeskindbau des Jüdischen Museums in Berlin.

Fast zur gleichen Zeit wie das Apartheid Museum entstand eine andere Binnenwelt, nicht motiviert von der sozialen Verpflichtung der Erinnerung, sondern vom kommerziellen Imperativ des Vergessens (Zeit, Ort oder wie viel Geld man schon verloren hat). Montecasino, die toskanisch anmutende Spieler-Zitadelle in einem der nördlichen 'suburbs'

Rosevear still flies in regularly to advise on changes to the underwear hanging in its streets and to ensure that the flags draped in Piazza Duomo follow the fortunes of the teams in the Italian soccer league. With people like Rosevear attending to the details of the simulation, our Tuscany is arguably preferable to the real thing.

A stone's throw from Montecasino lies prestigious Fourways Gardens residential estate, where people pay a lot of money to come home to a suburban version of the African bush. South Africa's first security suburb, Fourways Gardens was laid out in 1986 by Anglo American Properties, when rumours of a "Norweto" (to mirror Soweto (South Western Township) on the north-western edge of the city) being planned by the then Transvaal Provincial Administration shocked Johannesburg's northern suburbs residents out of their peri-urban bliss. Norweto did not happen (though Diepsloot is a pretty good approximation), but Fourways Gardens did.

Its first phase is a walled, gated precinct of 420 houses. Each of its curving streets is planted with a different indigenous tree and named after it — Wild Pear Crescent, Paperbark Street, Soetdoring Way. It boasts clipped verges, cobbled crossings, an immaculate park along a watercourse, a clubhouse and a nature

monde intérieur, motivé non pas par l'obligation sociale du souvenir, mais pour l'impératif commercial de l'oubli (temps, lieu, et combien d'argent vous avez déjà perdu). Montecasino, la cité toscane du jeu située dans les banlieues nord, est une affreuse réplique du monde extérieur. A l'intérieur, ses paysages authentiques en toc vous enveloppent dans un brouillard utopique rempli de distractions, où les pigeons n'émettent pas la moindre déjection et les toits dessinent des ombres dans le ciel.

Ce paradis du jeu fut construit à la fin des années 1990 par Sogo Sun, la division jeu de Southern Sun, épaulée par les South African Breweries. Au moment où Creative Kingdom - les architectes de la conception du lieu - travaillaient sur ce projet, Ken Rosevear, ex-PDG de Sun International, et aujourd'hui directeur de MGM Grand qui gère le fonctionnement de Montecasino (ainsi que d'autres casinos dans le monde) venait juste de passer des vacances en Toscane et avait adoré l'endroit. Il savait également qu'il n'y avait aucun autre casino dans le monde construit sur le thème de la Toscane et pensa que l' "impression de naturel" attirerait les Sud-Africains. "On se mit alors d'accord sur le thème de la Toscane", déclara Edmund Batley, du cabinet d'architecture Bentel Abramson, qui prit en charge la construction du projet. "Ce n'était pas une décision intellectuelle importante, ça s'est juste

Johannesburgs, ist aus der Luft gesehen ein wuchtiger, wirrer Komplex. Drinnen umgibt uns eine authentisch nachgemachte Landschaft, die uns eine spaßerfüllte, nie endende, im künstlichen Zwielicht flimmernde Utopie vorgaukelt, wo die Tauben nicht scheißen und die Dächer Schatten auf den Himmel werfen.

Dieses Spielerparadies wurde Ende der 1990er von Sogo Sun, dem Unterhaltungssektor von Southern Sun, gebaut. Die südafrikanische Brauereigesellschaft, South African Breweries, unterstützten das Unternehmen. Zu der Zeit, als das Planungsarchitekturbüro Creative Kingdom an dem Projekt arbeitete, hatte Ken Rosevear, früherer Generaldirektor von Sun International und heute Direktor für die Abteilung Unternehmensentwicklung von MGM Grand, das sowohl Montecasino als auch die meisten anderen Spielbetriebe in der Welt unterhält, gerade Ferien in der Toskana gemacht; er liebte diese Region. Er wußte, dass es nirgends sonst wo auf der Welt ein Kasino mit toskanischem Flair gab, und er dachte sich, dass das "erdige Gefühl" die Südafrikaner ansprechen dürfte. "Und so wurde es die Toskana", sagt Edmund Batley vom Architekturbüro Bentel Abramson, das das Projekt realisierte. "Es war keine große intellektuelle Entscheidung, es passierte einfach, weil Rosevear dachte, dass es funktionieren würde." Batley erzählt, dass Montecasino zu den zehn besten Kasinos

reserve stocked with small buck, birds and a breeding zebra couple.

This tamed, suburban bushveld has broad appeal. Jonathan and Paddy Best, an Anglo American executive couple, have lived there for eight years. She loves it most of all "for its bird-life" and stocks feeders in her garden where a number of species breed. Jane Matthews, an energetic optometrist in her mid-30s with a large practice in Melville, likes its "aesthetic appeal" as well as the social life it offers her and her three young children

fait comme ça parce que Rosevear pensait que cela fonctionnerait". Batley me dit que Montecasino était classé parmi les 10 premiers casinos du monde, dépassant largement ses concurrents sud-africains. Et Rosevear y fait toujours régulièrement le déplacement en avion pour donner des conseils par rapport aux sous-vêtements qui sèchent dans ses rues et pour s'assurer que les drapeaux drapés dans le Piazza Duomo suivent les succès des équipes de la ligue de football italien. Avec des personnes telles que Rosevear

der Welt gehöre und alle anderen südafrikanischen Betriebe bei weitem überträfe. Und Rosevear fliegt noch immer regelmäßig ein und berät, wenn die in den Straßen flatternde Unterwäsche und die Fahnen der italienischen Fußballligavereine auf der Piazza Duomo entsprechend der Siege ihrer Mannschaften ausgewechselt werden müssen. Mit Leuten wie Rosevear, die bei der Kopie auf die kleinsten Kleinigkeiten achten, ist unsere Toskana womöglich der echten vorzuziehen.

Einen Steinwurf von Montecasino

Mrs Gulbun Quinlan, resident of Fourways Gardens residential estate, in her living room

Mrs Gulbun Quinlan, résidente du quartier résidentielle de Fourways Gardens, dans sa salle de séjour

Zu Hause bei Mrs. Gulbun Quinlan, Bewohnerin von Fourways Gardens

— from running clubs to holiday events programmes. Mrs Gulbun Quinlan, a Turkish-American whose husband heads the international operations of an American trucking company in Africa and Australasia, said she chose to live in Fourways Gardens seven years ago because she "likes to live in places where the trees are already grown. I move so often," she said, "I hate planting trees for someone else to enjoy."

As for many of their US compatriots, for the Quinlans Fourways Gardens has become home away from home. An estimated 45 percent of its properties are rented to American expatriates. July 4 is celebrated with Elvis look-a-likes, Cadillacs and hot dogs laid on by the home owners association; Halloween and Thanksgiving are bigger than Youth or Freedom Day, and estate flags were flown at half mast after September 11. As comforting as this is, Quinlan commented that Fourways Gardens is a bit of a "la-la land. It's a utopia," she said. "You forget what is out there and can easily let down your guard."

All of these scenic enclaves — Fourways Garden's America in the bush, Montecasino's Tuscan hill town, and Melrose Arch's Main Street — do the same thing. They hollow out parts of the city and, on the basis of idealised images, construct urban

pour s'occuper des détails des lieux, notre Toscane est discutablement préférable à la région d'origine.

A une courte distance de Montecasino se trouve le complexe résidentiel de Fourways Gardens, où les gens payent des sommes d'argent considérables pour rentrer à la maison dans une version suburbaine de la savane africaine. Première banlieue en terme de sécurité, Fourways Gardens a été développée en 1986 par Anglo American Properties, lorsque la rumeur d'un "Norweto" (pour imiter le nom de Soweto (South Western Township) à la bordure nord-ouest de la ville) planifié alors par l'Administration Provinciale du Transvaal tira les résidents des banlieues nord de Johannesburg de leur béatitude péri-urbaine. Norweto ne vit jamais le jour (quand bien même Diepsloot en soit une approximation plutôt bonne), mais Fourways Gardens naquit.

Au premier abord, il s'agit d'une enceinte murée et gardée de 420 maisons. Chacune de ses rues sinueuses est plantée d'une espèce d'arbre indigène différente et nommée en fonction de cette espèce - Rue de la Poire Sauvage, Rue du Paperbark, Allée de Soetdoring. Ce lieu se compose d'accotements parfaitement tondus, de carrefours pavés, d'un parc immaculé qui s'étend le long d'un cours d'eau, d'un pavillon réservé à la communauté et d'une réserve naturelle où l'on trouve de petites antilopes, des oiseaux et un

entfernt liegt der noble Wohnpark Fourways Gardens, wo Leute eine Menge Geld bezahlen, um in einer suburbanen Version des afrikanischen Buschs zu leben. Es war Südafrikas erstes gesichertes 'suburb', das 1986 von "Anglo American Properties" gebaut wurde. Zu dieser Zeit waren Gerüchte aufgekommen, wonach die damalige Transvaal Provinzverwaltung beabsichtigte, im Nordwesten Johannesburgs ein "Norweto" (als Gegenstück zu Soweto, South Western Township) zu errichten. Diese Pläne rissen die Bewohner von Johannesburgs nördlichen 'suburbs' aus ihrer geschützten peripheren Glückseligkeit. Norweto kam nicht (obwohl Diepsloot schon sehr nahe an das heran kommt), aber Fourways Gardens kam.

In einem ersten Bauabschnitt wurde ein mit einer Mauer umgebenes und von Toren abgeriegeltes Gelände mit 420 Häusern erschlossen. Jede seiner in Bögen verlaufenden Straßen sind mit einer anderen einheimischen Baumart bepflanzt und danach benannt - der Wild Pear Crescent nach der Wildbirne, die Paperbark Street nach einem dem Teebaum verwandtem Baum oder der Soetdoring Way nach einer einheimischen Akazienart. Das Gras an den Straßenrändern wird sauber geschnitten, Kreuzungen und Übergänge sind gepflastert, es gibt einen gepflegten Park mit Wasserlauf, ein Clubhaus und ein Tiergehege mit verschiedenen

places appealing to the desire, nostalgia or paranoia of people who can pay to be there. None of them have much, if any, connection to the rest of the city or its history. The city is being remade as a collection of juxtaposed fragments. The gritty, complex city, as opposed to its glitzy, idealised counterpart, has highways, crime, suburban sprawl, vacant office space, neglected buildings, congested traffic, poor people, McDonald's. But it has been obscured and upstaged. Simulated glimpses of what cities once

couple de zèbre reproducteurs.

Cette savane arbustive parfaitement maîtrisée, suburbaine, attire beaucoup de monde. Jonathan et Paddy Best, un couple de cadres supérieurs anglo-américains, vivent ici depuis huit ans. Si Paddy aime l'endroit, c'est en particulier pour "sa vie avicole" et les mangeoires de son jardin où un grand nombre d'espèces se reproduisent. Jane Matthews, une ophtalmologiste au caractère dynamique d'environ 35 ans qui possède un cabinet important à Melville, aime son "attrait esthétique"

Antilopenarten, Vögeln und einem Zebrapaar.

Dieses gezähmte, suburbane 'bushveld' übt einen großen Reiz aus. Jonathan und Paddy Best, ein anglo-amerikanisches Ehepaar mit gutem Einkommen, leben schon seit acht Jahren hier. Sie liebt es vor allem "wegen der Vögel" und hat Futtertrichter im Garten aufgestellt, wo verschiedene Vogelarten brüten. Jane Matthews, eine agile Augenärztin Mitte dreißig mit einer großen Praxis in Melville, liebt den "ästhetischen Appeal" und das soziale Leben, das das

Walking the dogs, Fourways Gardens Residential Estate

Promenade des chiens, à Fourways Gardens, quartier résidential

Wohnanlage Fourways Gardens - Spaziergang mit Hunden

Fake façades fronting one of Montecasino's internal streets

Fausses façades en face de l'une des rues intérieures de Montecasino

Kunst der Imitation: Fassaden in Montecasino

were are celebrated as signs of development, while the city they represent, or even copy, decays and disintegrates.

This is the Johannesburg of tomorrow. A city of disappearing suburbs, a forgotten central business district, trendy enclaves, simulated history and unwelcome poor.

The boosterist policies recently adopted by the local authority in its 2030 plan will ensure that it remains that way. Public space, public amenities and urban citizenship will become things of the past. Privately owned spaces — Sandton Square, the Rosebank Zone, Montecasino, Melrose Arch, and others not yet conceived will increasingly function as its civic squares, but never assume its civic responsibilities. For like commercial ventures everywhere, their only concern will be to ensure that their consumers are not interfered with and have fun.

Maybe at the end of the day, we are just a mining town after all. Where most of the people live out-of-sight lives in appalling conditions so that some of the people can get rich quick; where people don't plant things in the earth and watch them grow, but stake their claim, exploit its wealth, and move on.

Perhaps, despite all attempts to reconfigure our economy, our politics and our society, it is this unconscious

ainsi que la vie sociale que le complexe lui offre ainsi qu'à ses trois jeune enfants — depuis les clubs de course à pied aux programmes d'activités spécial vacances. Mme Gulbun Quilan, une femme de nationalité turque américaine dont l'époux est à la tête des opérations internationales d'une société de transport américaine en Afrique et en Océanie, déclara qu'elle avait choisi de venir vivre à Fourways Gardens sept ans plus tôt parce qu'elle aimait "vivre dans des endroits où les arbres avaient déjà atteint l'âge adulte. Je déménage si souvent", dit-elle, "je déteste planter des arbres pour que quelqu'un d'autre en profite."

Tout comme bon nombre de leurs compatriotes américains, pour les Quinlans, Fourways Gardens est devenu leur maison loin de chez eux. On estime que 45 pourcents des propriétés du quartier sont louées à des expatriés américains. Le 4 juillet y est célébré avec des sosies d'Elvis, des Cadillacs et des hot-dogs préparés par l'association des propriétaires de maisons; Halloween et Thanksgiving y sont plus importants que la Journée de la Jeunesse ou de la Liberté sud-africaines, et les drapeaux du complexe furent mis en berne après le 11 septembre. Pour aussi réconfortant que ce soit, Quinlin m'a affirmé que Fourways Garden était une "sorte de lieu fictif. C'est une utopie", déclara-t-elle. "Vous oubliez la réalité de l'extérieur et vous pouvez facilement oublier de rester sur vos gardes."

Anwesen ihr und ihren drei kleinen Kindern bietet — von Sportclubs bis zu Ferienprogrammen. Mrs. Gulbun Quinlan, eine Amerikanerin türkischer Herkunft, deren Mann die internationalen Geschäfte eines amerikanischen Speditionsunternehmens in Afrika und in der austral-asiatischen Region leitet, erzählt, dass sie vor sieben Jahren entschieden habe, hierher nach Fourways Gardens zu kommen, weil sie "in Gegenden leben möchte, wo die Bäume schon groß sind. Ich ziehe so oft um", erklärt sie, "und ich habe keine Lust, Bäume zu pflanzen, an denen sich dann später andere erfreuen."

Wie für so viele ihrer US-amerikanischen Landsleute ist auch für die Quinlans Fourways Gardens ein Zuhause weg von Zuhause geworden. Rund 45 Prozent der Objekte sind an amerikanische Bürger vermietet. Der 4. Juli wird von der Bewohnergemeinschaft mit Elvis-Imitatoren, Cadillacs und gegrillten Würstchen gefeiert. Halloween und Thanksgiving sind größere Ereignisse als der Tag der Freiheit oder der Jugend, und Fourways Gardens' Fahnen wehten nach dem 11. September auf Halbmast. So wundervoll beruhigend das alles ist, Fourways Gardens sei doch irgendwie eine heile Welt, meint Quinlin. "Es ist eine Utopie. Man vergisst, was draußen los ist, und lässt schnell alle Aufmerksamkeiten fallen."

Alle diese Themenpark-Enklaven — Fourways Gardens' Amerika im Busch,

history of self-interested indifference that will continue to shape Johannesburg's future.

Toutes ces enclaves paysagères — le Fourways Garden américain dans la savane, la ville collinaire toscane de Montecasino, la Rue Principale de Melrose Arch — ont le même effet. Elles évident des parties de la ville et, sur la base d'images idéalisées, construisent des espaces urbains faisant appel au désir, à la nostalgie et à la paranoïa de ceux qui peuvent payer pour y vivre. Aucune d'entre elles ne possède beaucoup de connexions avec le reste de la ville ou avec son histoire, si ce n'est aucune. La ville est reconstituée comme une collection de fragments juxtaposés. La ville caillouteuse, complexe, par opposition à ses contreparties fastueuses et idéalisées, est composée d'autoroutes, de crime, d'étendues suburbaines, d'espaces de bureaux vacants, de bâtiments négligés, d'embouteillages, de pauvres, de McDonald's. Mais elle a été obscurcie et s'est vue rejetée en arrière-plan. Des aperçus simulés de ce que les villes furent un temps sont célébrés comme des signes du développement, pendant que la ville qu'ils représentent, ou même copient, se délabre et se désintègre.

C'est le Johannesburg de demain. Une ville aux banlieues qui disparaissent, un centre d'affaires oublié, des enclaves à la mode, une histoire simulée et des pauvres que l'on préfèrerait ne pas voir.

Les politiques amplificatrices récemment adoptées par les autorités locales dans leur programme de 2003

die toskanische Hügelstadt von Montecasino und Melrose Archs' Hauptstraße — bewirken dasselbe. Sie höhlen Teile der Stadt aus und bauen auf der Grundlage von idealisiert übersteigerten Bildern städtische Plätze, die die Wünsche, Sehnsüchte oder die Paranoia derjenigen anspricht, die dafür bezahlen können. Keiner dieser Komplexe hat, wenn überhaupt, einen großen Bezug zur Stadt oder ihrer Geschichte. In einer Ansammlung von aneinander gereihten Fragmenten wird die Stadt nachgeahmt. Die wirkliche, ungeschminkte, komplexe Stadt hat — im Unterschied zu ihrem glitzernden, idealisierten Pendant — Autobahnen, Verbrechen, quirlige, wuchernde Viertel, leer stehende Büroräume, heruntergekommene Gebäude, Abgase, Armut, McDonalds. Aber all das wird verschleiert und verdrängt. Simulierte Abbilder dessen, was Städte einmal waren, werden als Zeichen von Entwicklung gefeiert, während gleichzeitig die Stadt, die sie darstellen, ja sogar kopieren, verkommt und zerfällt.

Dies ist das Johannesburg von morgen. Eine Stadt verschwindender 'suburbs', ein vergessenes Geschäftszentrum, einem Trend folgende Enklaven, simulierte Geschichte und Arme, die unwillkommen sind.

Die vor kurzem von der Stadtverwaltung in ihre "Joburg 2030 Vision" aufgenommenen Strategien werden gewährleisten, dass es so bleibt.

vont s'assurer que cela ne change pas. L'espace publique, les aménagements publiques et la citoyenneté urbaine vont devenir des éléments du passé. Les espaces publiques privatifs — Sandton Square, les complexes de Rosebank Zone, de Montecasino, de Melrose Arch et encore bien d'autres qui n'ont pas encore été conçus, vont de plus en plus fonctionner comme des places publiques, mais n'assumeront jamais leurs responsabilités civiles. Pour les entreprises commerciales qui fleurissent de partout, leur seule inquiétude sera de s'assurer que leurs consommateurs ne sont pas dérangés et qu'ils puissent passer de bons moments.

Peut-être qu'au bout du compte, nous ne sommes après tout qu'une ville minière. Où la plupart des personnes vivent des vies à l'écart dans des conditions dramatiques pour que certaines personnes puissent s'enrichir rapidement; où les gens ne plantent rien dans la terre et regardent leurs productions pousser, mais revendiquent leurs droits, exploitent les richesses, et passent à autre chose. Peut-être que malgré toutes les tentatives pour reconfigurer notre économie, notre politique et notre société, c'est cette histoire inconsciente d'indifférence engendrée par l'intérêt personnel qui va continuer à donner forme au futur de Johannesburg.

Öffentlicher Raum, öffentliche Einrichtungen und eine innerstädtische Bewohnerschaft werden der Vergangenheit angehören. Private Räume, wie Sandton Square, die Rosebank Zone, Montecasino, Melrose Arch und andere, die noch nicht einmal auf dem Papier stehen, werden zunehmend als städtische Plätze fungieren, doch nie ihre Verantwortung für die Stadt übernehmen. Denn wie allen kommerziellen Unternehmen geht es ihnen nur darum, sicherzustellen, dass ihre Kunden ungestört Spaß haben.

Vielleicht sind wir am Ende doch nur eine Minenstadt. Wo die meisten Leute unter erschreckenden Bedingungen, aber außer Sichtweite leben, so dass wenige sehr schnell reich werden können; wo Leute nicht mehr pflanzen und das Heranwachsende beobachten, sondern ihren Grund und Boden abstecken, den Reichtum ernten und dann weiterziehen. Trotz aller Versuche, unsere Wirtschaft, unsere Politik und unsere Gesellschaft neu zu gestalten, ist es vielleicht diese nicht bewusst wahrgenommene Geschichte von egoistischer Gleichgültigkeit, die auch weiterhin Johannesburgs Zukunft prägen wird.

KASI KUL'CA KASI K

6

'CA TOWNSHIPLEBEN

Soweto today is many places and has many faces. Unlike the singularity of its former image as the sprawling precise of the high apartheid township, of uniformity and oppression, violence and squalor, today it is a site of multiple re-imaginings and re-inventions, of evolving urban lifestyles, invented identities and reconfigured spaces. A site where, more than any other, the dimensions of the new South Africa are being figured out.

Pat Lephunya, a former civic activist and fiery orator in the days of Johannesburg's Metropolitan Chamber, the forum that negotiated the city's transition to democratic local government, is now the Director of Region 6, the administrative area of the city embracing a large chunk of Soweto. I met him in his offices, ironically housed in the premises of the former Soweto Town Council, the hated black local authority against which he waged war in the 1980s.

Lephunya, now comfortably rounder than he was in his activist days, rattles off the achievements of his first three years in office: garden refuse sites created in Protea and Mapetla; public swimming pools heated in Dobsonville and Lenasia; the Zondi depot converted into a waste recycling centre; unused schools and council office space handed over to communities for economic activity;

aujourd'hui, Soweto, ce sont de nombreux lieux et de nombreux visages. Contrairement à la singularité de son image du passé qui en faisait un résumé étendu du township du haut apartheid, d'uniformité et d'oppression, de violence et de misère odieuse, c'est aujourd'hui un lieu où l'on ré-imagine constamment et où l'on réinvente, un lieu où les styles de vie urbains évoluent, où s'inventent des identités et où les espaces sont reconfigurés. Un lieu où, plus que partout ailleurs, les dimensions de la nouvelle Afrique du Sud se découvrent.

Pat Lephunya, ancien activiste de la société civile et orateur fougueux à l'époque de la Chambre Métropolitaine de Johannesburg, est désormais le Directeur de la Région 6, la région administrative de la ville qui embrasse une large portion de Soweto. Je l'ai rencontré dans ses bureaux, abrités, ironie du sort, dans les enceintes de l'ancien conseil municipal de Soweto, l'autorité locale noire haït contre laquelle il était en guerre dans les années 1980.

Lephunya, désormais considérablement plus enveloppé qu'il ne l'était lorsqu'il était activiste, débite à toute allure les résultats obtenus lors de ses trois premières années à ce poste — création de décharges consacrées aux déchets biodégradables à Protea et à Mapetla, piscine publiques chauffées à Dobonsville et à Lenasia, la reconversion du dépôt de Zondi en un centre de

Soweto heute sind viele Orte und viele Gesichter. War es früher einzig und allein Symbol für das wuchernde, von schlimmster Apartheid geprägte Township, für Gleichförmigkeit, Unterdrückung, Gewalt und Elend, so ist es heute ein Ort, wo sich eine Vielfalt neuer Ideen und Vorstellungen entwickelt, städtischer Lebensstil wächst, neue Persönlichkeiten zur Entfaltung kommen und neu gestaltete Räume entstehen. Soweto — das ist ein Ort, wo sich deutlicher als anderswo die Dimensionen des neuen Südafrika erkennen lassen.

Pat Lephunya, ehemaliger Aktivist der Soweto Bürgerbewegung ("Soweto Civic Association") und glühender Redner in den Tagen von Johannesburgs Metropolitan Chamber, wo der Übergang zur Demokratie diskutiert wurde, ist inzwischen Verwaltungsdirektor von Region 6, Johannesburgs 6. Verwaltungsbezirk, zu dem ein Großteil Sowetos gehört. Ich treffe ihn in seinem Büro, das — Ironie des Schicksals — im Gebäude des früheren Soweto Town Council's untergebracht ist, jener verhassten schwarzen Bezirksbehörde, die von der Apartheid-Regierung eingesetzt wurde, und gegen die er in den 1980ern kämpfte.

Lephunya, heute ein gutes Stückchen rundlicher als in seinen Tagen als Aktivist, rasselt die Erfolge seiner ersten drei Jahre im Amt herunter — die Schaffung von Gartenabfalldeponien in Protea und Mapetla, öffentliche Schwimmbäder mit

Mofolo Park transformed into a recreation area that rivals Johannesburg's Zoo Lake "where you are lucky to find a spot on weekends". It is only when he starts speaking of the remaining health hazards of asbestos roofing and the fossil fuels still burnt by many people who cannot afford electricity, that I feel on vaguely familiar turf — something still remains of my embedded, but obviously fast receding, image of Soweto.

Sofasonke Street runs through the heart of Orlando East. It is not a very remarkable street, but it is long and old; a line of discontinuous vectors intersecting the numerous circles and squares that formed the pattern of the prize-winning township plan laid out in 1933. It was a street uniformly lined for nearly 60 years by dusty verges and numbered matchbox houses, except at its centre, where the Orlando East Administration offices, a symbol of apartheid oppression, aggressively occupied the centre of a diamond-shaped, palisade-fenced island. Today the street is signed and tarred; its verges are decorated, clipped and mown; garbage bins are wheeled out for collection; walls of precast concrete, yellow brick, ornate steelwork, or wagon-wheel motifs define the edges of private properties; extensions of corrugated iron, concrete slabs or plastered brickwork with tiled roofs have transformed the original

recyclage des déchets, le transfert des écoles non utilisées et des espaces de bureaux du conseil aux communautés pour leur activité économique ; la transformation de Mofolo Park en un Zoo Lake propre à Soweto, "où vous avez de la chance si vous y trouvez un espace libre le week-end", me dit-il. C'est seulement lorsqu'il se met à parler des dangers sanitaires qui subsistent à cause des toitures en amiante et aux sources d'énergie fossile toujours brûlées par les nombreuses personnes qui ne peuvent pas se permettre de payer l'électricité, que je retrouve un domaine vaguement familier - quelque chose subsiste toujours de l'image profondément incrustée en moi, mais qui s'efface forcément rapidement, de Soweto.

Sofasonke Street passe par le cœur d'Orlando Est. Il ne s'agit pas d'une rue particulièrement impressionnante, mais c'est une rue ancienne et longue; une ligne de vecteurs discontinus qui se croisent avec les nombreux cercles et places qui forment la trame de ce township qu'un prix décora et établit en 1933. Il s'agissait d'une rue uniformément bordée durant quasiment 60 ans par des bas-côtés poussiéreux et par de petites maisons numérotées, sauf en son centre où les bureaux de l'Administration d'Orlando Est, symboles de l'oppression de l'apartheid, occupaient de manière agressive le centre d'un îlot en forme de diamant et entouré d'une palissade.

Warmwasserbecken in Dobsonville und Lenasia, die Umwandlung der alten Mülldeponie in Zondi in ein Abfallrecyclingcenter, die Übergabe von leer stehenden Schulen und Bezirksämtern an die Gemeinden für wirtschaftliche Aktivitäten; die Sanierung von Sowetos Mofolo Park, "wo Sie froh sein können, wenn Sie am Wochenende noch ein freies Plätzchen ergattern", lacht er. Aber dann kommt er auf die noch immer vorhandenen Gesundheitsrisiken zu sprechen, die von den Dächern aus Asbestmaterial ausgehen, und dass immer noch viele mit Holz und Kohle kochen, weil sie sich Elektrizität nicht leisten können, und ich fühle ich mich auf halbwegs vertrautem Gelände: Etwas von meinem tief verwurzelten, aber offensichtlich immer mehr verblassenden Bild von Soweto ist doch noch vorhanden.

Sofasonke Street führt mitten durch das Herz von Orlando Ost. Es ist keine besonders bemerkenswerte Straße, aber lang und alt. In Windungen und Kurven durchschneidet und kreuzt sie zahlreiche Kreisel und Plätze, die das Muster des 1933 preisgekrönten Townshipplans bildeten. Eine Straße, die sich sechzig Jahre lang einförmig dahin zog, mit staubigen Rändern und nummerierten Einheitshäuschen, Matchbox- oder Streichholzschachtelhäuser genannt. Nur in der Mitte thronte wuchtig und aggressiv die Verwaltung von Orlando Ost, Symbol der Apartheidunterdrückung, eine von

houses into bloated, makeshift loxion (township) villas. Public telephone outlets, doctors' surgeries and tuckshops ply trade from passers-by. The Kopani Funeral Parlour at the intersection of Sofasonke and Mofakeng streets has become a two-storeyed monolith (evidence of its thriving business) and the former administrative offices have become the City of Johannesburg's Region 6 People's Centre. It is here that I arranged to meet Ruby Mathang, the African National Congress councillor for the area.

The People's Centre is pastel-green and air-conditioned. Benches, potted plants, a water dispenser and gold-framed photographs of Johannesburg's mayor, Amos Masondo, and former president Nelson Mandela make it indistinguishable from any other People's Centre elsewhere in the city. What is unusual are the competing radio stations — YFM and Kaya — blaring simultaneously from different ends of the waiting-room, ensuring that all tastes are catered for. Mathang arrives 45 minutes late, greets the members of his constituency in the hall, and introduces me to his colleague, a former youth activist who is now chairperson of the local Community Policing Forum. "Previously walking in here would have branded you as a collaborator," he says. "But people are slowly getting

Aujourd'hui, la rue dispose de signalisation et est goudronnée ; ses bas-côtés sont décorés, taillés et tondus. Les poubelles sont roulées à l'extérieur pour le ramassage des ordures; des murs de béton préfabriqué, des briques jaunes, des extensions de tôle ondulée, de la maçonnerie en briques crépies, des toits en tuiles ou des dalles de béton ont transformé les maisons d'origine en villas (de township) conçues avec des matériaux de fortune ; des petits magasins de téléphonie publique, des cabinets médicaux, des boutiques de provisions exercent leurs fonctions grâce aux passants ; le Salon Funéraire Kopani, au croisement de Sofasonke et de Mofakeng, est devenu un monolithe à deux étages (l'évidence de la bonne marche de ses affaires) et les bureaux de l'administration sont devenus le Centre Communautaire de la Région 6 de Johannesburg. C'est là que je me suis arrangée pour rencontrer Ruby Mathang, Conseiller ANC du quartier.

Le Centre Communautaire est peint en vert pastel et est équipé de la climatisation. Des bancs, des plantes en pots, un distributour d'eau et des photographies du Maire, Masondo, encadrées en doré, et de l'ancien Président Mandela font qu'il est impossible de distinguer cet endroit des autres Centres Communautaires partout ailleurs dans la ville. Tout ce qui fait la différence, ce sont les stations radio en

Palisaden geschützte Insel mit dem Umriss eines geschliffenen Diamanten.

Heute ist die Straße geteert, und es gibt Straßenschilder; Blumen schmücken die Ränder, der Grassaum ist sauber geschnitten und gemäht; Mülltonnen werden an den Abfuhrtagen herausgerollt; Mauern aus Betonfertigteilen, aus gelben Ziegeln, verzierten Metallgittern oder mit Wagenradmotiven versehen, bilden die Grenzen zwischen privatem Besitz und Boden; Anbauten aus Wellblech und Backsteinmauern mit Ziegeldächern und Fliesen haben die alten Häuschen in aufgeblasene Möchtegern-Townshipvillen verwandelt. Öffentliche Telefonstellen, Arztpraxen, Läden mit Süßigkeiten und anderen Knabbereien haben eröffnet; Kopani Funeral Parlour, das Beerdigungsinstitut an der Kreuzung von Sofasonke- und Mofakeng Street, ist heute ein mächtiger zweistöckiger Kasten (Beweis für ein boomendes Geschäft), und aus dem alten Verwaltungsgebäude wurde das Bürgerzentrum von Region 6. Hier habe ich mich mit Ruby Mathang, dem Bezirksabgeordneten des ANC verabredet.

Das Bürgerzentrum ist pastellgrün gestrichen und klimatisiert. Mit seinen Bänken, Topfpflanzen, einem Wasserspender und goldgerahmten Fotografien von Johannesburgs Regierendem Bürgermeister Amos Masondo und dem früheren Präsidenten Nelson Mandela unterscheidet es sich in nichts von anderen Bürgerzentren sonst wo in der Stadt. Lediglich die miteinander

over this and learning to embrace their new institutions."

Mathang is a full-time town-planning student at Wits University, a councillor, and he is in charge of the ANC's 2004 Gauteng election campaign. He is upbeat about the changes that democracy has brought to Soweto residents. "Every Saturday and Sunday here in Orlando East," he says, "we used to run out of water. People would have to drive to other areas to fetch it. We have replaced water and sewer pipes, tarred roads,

concurrence — YFM et Kaya, qui beuglent simultanément aux deux extrémités de la salle d'attente, pour s'assurer que tous les goûts sont prix en compte. Mathang arrive avec 45 minutes de retard, salue les membres de sa circonscription électorale dans le hall, et me présente à son collègue, un ancien jeune activiste et président du Forum Politique Communautaire local. "Avant, si l'on vous avait vu marcher ici, on vous aurait catégorisé comme un collaborateur", dit-il. "Mais les gens s'habituent progressivement au

konkurrierenden Radiosender YFM und Kaya, die gleichzeitig von beiden Seiten der Wartehalle um die Wette plärren, geben ihm seine eigene Note und sorgen dafür, dass für jeden Geschmack etwas dabei ist. Nach 45 Minuten kommt Mathang, er grüßt seine Wahlanhänger in der Halle und stellt mich seinem Kollegen vor, einem ehemaligen Jugendaktivisten und Vorsitzenden des örtlichen Gemeindeforums für öffentliche Ordnung. "Wer früher hier hineinging, wäre als Kollaborateur gebrandmarkt worden", sagt er. "Aber die Leute kommen langsam

Pat Lephunya, Director of Region 6, outside his administrative offices

Pat Lephunya, Directeur de la Région 6, à l'extérieur de ses bureaux administratifs

Pat Lephunya, Verwaltungsdirektor von Johannesburgs Region 6, vor seinem Bürokomplex

**Thokoza Park at Regina Mundi —
Johannesburg Region 10**
\

Thokoza Park – Région 10, Johannesburg

Thokoza Park in Johannesburg, Region 10,
Soweto

installed electric lights. The impact on people's daily lives has been immeasurable. But, the biggest change has been a mindset one," he says. "Ten years ago, we heard gunshots every hour. We resolved everything through violence — politics, family squabbles, everyday conflicts. It was part of our way of life. Now all that has changed. Tolerance, discussion and democracy are beginning to be entrenched."

Solomon Moripe, the chairperson of the Channel Youth Club in neighbouring Meadowlands, agrees. "The most important change in Soweto over the last 10 years," he says, " is the way we see life. We have a sense of dignity, belonging and a respect for other people's rights. Before, even I thought nothing of slapping my girlfriend around. It was part of being a man. Every night we heard women screaming on the street. Now I know that that is wrong. I do not do it any more, and if I see one of my friends doing it, I tell him to stop."

The Channel Youth Club is an organisation started in 1998 by a group of youths with dreams of improving their lives. At the time, Moripe was a Wits Technikon graduate in human resource development, but most of the other founder-members had just matriculated, with no prospects of employment in the formal market. "We wanted to change this mindset," says Moripe, "to give people a sense that it

changement et apprennent à soutenir leurs nouvelles institutions."

Mathang est étudiant à plein temps en Aménagement du Territoire à l'Université de Wits et est Conseiller et responsable de la campagne d'élection de l'ANC pour 2004 pour la province du Gauteng. Il est impressionné par les changements que la démocratie a apportés aux résidents de Soweto. "Chaque samedi et chaque dimanche, ici, à Orlando Est", dit-il, "nous manquions souvent d'eau. Les gens devaient se rendre dans d'autres quartiers pour aller en chercher. Nous avons remplacé les canalisations d'eau et d'égout, nous avons bitumé les routes, installé l'éclairage électrique. L'impact sur les vies quotidiennes des habitants a été sans commune mesure. "mais", dit-il, "le défi le plus important concernait les mentalités. Il y a dix ans, on entendait des coups de feu toutes les heures. Nous résolvions tout par la violence — la politique, les querelles familiales, les conflits de tous les jours. Cela faisait partie de notre vie de tous les jours. Maintenant, tout cela a changé. La tolérance, la discussion et la démocratie sont des idées qui commencent à s'ancrer dans les esprits."

Solomon Moripe, Président du Channel Youth Club dans le quartier avoisinant de Meadowlands, est d'accord. "Le changement le plus important à Soweto au cours des 10 dernières années", déclare-t-il, "est la

darüber hinweg und lernen, ihre neuen Institutionen anzunehmen".

Mathang ist Vollzeitstudent für Stadtplanung an der Witwatersrand Universität, Bezirksabgeordneter und zuständig für die Wahlkampagne des ANC 2004 in der Provinz Gauteng. Er ist begeistert von den Veränderungen, die die Demokratie den Bewohnern von Soweto gebracht hat. "Jeden Samstag und Sonntag", sagt er, "ging uns normalerweise hier in Orlando Ost das Wasser aus. Die Leute mussten zum Wasserholen regelmäßig in andere Stadtteile fahren. Wir haben Wasser- und Abwasserrohre erneuert, die Straßen geteert und elektrisches Licht verlegt." Der Alltag der Menschen hat sich unwahrscheinlich verändert. "Die größte Veränderung aber", fährt er fort, "geschah in den Köpfen der Menschen. Vor zehn Jahren hörten wir jede Stunde Gewehrschüsse. Wir lösten alle Probleme mit Gewalt — politische Probleme, Familienstreitereien, jeden alltäglichen Konflikt. Das war Teil unserer Lebensweise. Heute hat sich das alles verändert. Toleranz, eine Gesprächskultur und Demokratie beginnen sich durchzusetzen."

Solomon Moripe, Vorsitzender des Channel Youth Club, eines Jugendclubs im benachbarten Meadowlands, pflichtet ihm bei. "Die entscheidendste Veränderung, die wir in Soweto in den letzten zehn Jahren erlebt haben, ist die Art und Weise, wie wir jetzt das Leben

is possible to take the initiative, to make a living, that even if you do not have a job to go to, that you can make it on your own." The club did this by formalising relationships with schools in the area and hosting talk-shows, debates, public-speaking competitions and peer-group studies for children after school, all aimed at confidence-building and life-skills development. Today all its original members are employed or self-employed; the Channel Youth Club is a registered non-governmental organisation and PropCom, Johannesurg's property management agency, is finalising the transfer of land to the club for the building of a learning centre. Moripe has left his former employment at Standard Bank and runs his own training consultancy from home. Business is so good that it has outgrown his mother's Meadowlands house and he will soon be moving to the suburbs.

Is this inevitable? Is Soweto just a place to leave? Mathang, the ANC councillor, thinks it is. "The older generation referred to the rural areas as home," he says. "Now, since 1994, people have seen this [Soweto] as their place, their home. Since they now own their houses, they have settled, put money into improving them. But it is quite natural to move as soon as your economic status has improved. It is a question of social match."

manière dont nous considérons la vie. Nous avons un sens de la dignité, de l'appartenance à un lieu, et un respect pour les droits d'autrui. Avant", dit-il, "même moi, cela ne me dérangeait pas de gifler ma petite amie de temps à autre. Cela faisait partie du rôle d'un homme. Chaque nuit, nous entendions des femmes hurler dans la rue. Maintenant, je sais que ce n'est pas bien de faire ça. Je ne le fais plus et si je vois l'un de mes amis agir de la sorte, je lui dis d'arrêter."

Le Channel Youth Club, que dirige Moripe, est une organisation consacrée à la jeunesse qui a été établie en 1998 par un groupe de jeunes qui rêvaient d'une vie meilleure. Alors que Moripe disposait d'un diplôme développement en ressources humaines du Technikon de Wits, la plupart d'entre eux avaient tout juste obtenu leur baccalauréat, et ne disposaient d'aucune possibilité d'emploi sur le marché du travail officiel. "Nous voulions changer les mentalités", déclare-t-il, "pour faire comprendre aux gens qu'il était possible de prendre des initiatives, de vivre de quelque chose, et que même si vous ne vous rendiez pas au travail parce que vous n'aviez pas d'emploi, vous pouviez vous créer votre propre emploi." Ce qu'ils firent en développant une relation avec les écoles du quartier et en organisant des "talk shows", des débats, des concours d'art oratoire, et des groupes d'études constitués par affinité après l'école,

sehen. Wir haben ein Gefühl für Würde und Zusammengehörigkeit bekommen und respektieren die Rechte des anderen. Davor", so Moripe weiter, "habe ich mir überhaupt nichts dabei gedacht, wenn ich meine Freundin geschlagen habe. Das gehörte zum Mannsein dazu. Jede Nacht hörten wir Frauen auf der Straße schreien. Heute weiß ich, dass das falsch ist. Ich tue es nicht mehr, und wenn ich sehe, dass einer meiner Freunde es tut, sag' ich ihm, er soll damit aufhören."

Der von Moripe geleitete Channel Youth Club ist eine Jugendorganisation, die 1998 von einer Gruppe von Jugendlichen gegründet wurde. Sie träumten davon, etwas aus ihrem Leben zu machen. Während Moripe sein Studium in Human Resources am Witwatersrand Technikum damals schon beendet hatte, fingen die meisten gerade erst zu studieren an, ohne Aussichten auf dem Arbeitsmarkt. "Wir wollten das Bewusstsein verändern", sagt Moripe, "Leuten das Gefühl geben, dass es möglich ist, selbst die Initiative zu ergreifen und sich ein Leben aufzubauen. Dass du es schaffen kannst, selbst wenn du keinen Job hast". Sie nahmen Kontakt zu Schulen im Viertel auf und organisierten Talkshows, Diskussionen, öffentliche Redewettbewerbe und Hausaufgabengruppen für Schulkinder mit dem Ziel, das Selbstbewusstsein der Jugendlichen zu stärken und Fähigkeiten zu entwickeln, die sie fürs Leben brauchen. Heute haben alle ersten

Others disagree. "I will never leave Kasi," says Sarah Nkwane, an Orlando West resident. In her mid-twenties, Nkwane, wearing long braids under an MTN cap, is articulate, ambitious, beautiful and streetwise. She went to a private school in Johannesburg and speaks like a "bourgeois", a term for those who come from the middle-class Diepkloof, on the northern boundary of Soweto. Divorced, with a three-year-old child, an almost-completed accounting degree from the University of South Africa and her own manicure business, she has just bought a house in a newly developed area near Gold Reef City. "Even though I might live in the suburbs, this will always be my home," she says, articulating a common sentiment among the city's upwardly mobile youth. "Look at Zola," says Nkwane, referring to the host of the Zola 7 actuality show on SABC 1."He sleeps in the suburbs with his white girlfriend, but he gets up in the morning and comes back here, to sit in cheap car-washes with his friends and eat sadza and nyama on the street. This is his home. Life in the suburbs is boring."

It is the likes of Zola, a former gangster turned media celebrity, who are the new role models for Soweto's youth. As they negotiate the uncharted borderlands between township and suburb, street and mall, life and death, the values and models provided by

toutes ces activités visant à développer la confiance et les aptitudes à se prendre en charge. Aujourd'hui, tous les membres d'origine de ce club sont employés ou ont monté leur propre entreprise; le Channel Youth Club est désormais une ONG officielle et PropCom, l'agence de gestion des propriétés de la ville est en train de finaliser le transfert d'un terrain pour le club pour la construction d'un centre d'apprentissage. Moripe lui-même a quitté son ancien poste à Standard Bank et dirige son propre service de consultation depuis son domicile. Les affaires vont si bien qu'il ne dispose pas de suffisamment d'espace dans la maison de sa mère à Meadowlands et va bientôt déménager en banlieue.

Est-ce que cela est inévitable ? Est-ce que Soweto n'est qu'un endroit destiné à être quitté ? C'est ce que pense Mathang, le Conseiller ANC. "La plus vieille génération fait référence au milieu rural lorsqu'elle mentionne la maison", déclare-t-il. Maintenant, depuis 1994, les gens perçoivent l'endroit comme leur quartier, leur maison. Depuis qu'ils peuvent désormais posséder leur maison, ils se sont installés, ils ont dépensé de l'argent pour les améliorer. Mais c'est quelque chose de relativement naturel", dit-il, "que de déménager dès que votre statut économique s'améliore. C'est une question de correspondance sociale."

D'autres ne sont pas d'accord. "Je

Mitglieder des Clubs eine Anstellung gefunden oder konnten sich selbständig machen; Channel Youth Club ist eine eingetragene Nichtregierungsorganisation (NGO), und PropCom, die städtische Liegenschaftsbehörde, ist dabei, der Organisation ein Stück Land zu übertragen, auf dem ein Lernzentrum entstehen soll. Moripe selbst hat seinen Job bei der Standard Bank aufgegeben und führt sein eigenes Consultancy-Büro von zu Hause aus. Die Geschäfte laufen so gut, dass das Unternehmen in dem Haus seiner Mutter in Meadowlands aus allen Nähten platzt, und er bald in eines der 'suburbs' umziehen wird.

Ist das unvermeidlich? Ist Soweto nur noch ein Ort, von dem man weg möchte? Mathang, der ANC-Abgeordnete glaubt es. "Die ältere Generation nannte die ländlichen Gegenden ihr 'home', ihr Zuhause", sagt er. "Seit 1994 sehen die Leute dies jetzt hier als ihr Zuhause, ihr 'home'. Sie haben jetzt ihre eigenen Häuser, haben Geld hineingesteckt, um sie auszubauen und schöner zu machen. Aber, und das ist ganz natürlich", fährt er fort, "sobald es dir wirtschaftlich besser geht, wirst du wegziehen. Es ist eine Frage des sozialen Umfelds."

Andere sind nicht seiner Meinung. "Nein, ich werde das Township nie verlassen", sagt Sarah Nkwane, die in Orlando West wohnt. Sie ist Mitte zwanzig, trägt lange Zöpfe unter ihrer Baseballkappe, auf der das Logo des südafrikanischen

The Hector Peterson Museum
in Orlando West at night

Le Musée Hector Peterson vu
de nuit à Orlando West

Das Hector Peterson Museum
in Orlando West bei Nacht

politics or church have been long displaced. The language they speak, the cell phones they use, the clothes they wear, the cars they drive, the music they listen to, the alcohol they drink and where and how they party are the signifiers of newly constructed identities. Politics is just another fraudulent path to self-advancement. It is the media celebrities, the musicians, the soccer players and the criminals who model the good life (and how to get there) to which they aspire.

Part of this life is HIV Aids. "If one is not infected, one is affected," says Kgomotso Tlhoacle, one of the Channel Youth Club's star public speakers. "We still go to funerals almost every weekend; people still talk about the disease as a bewitchment; it is an epidemic we have still not found ways to deal with." But, she adds, "slowly people are feeling safer to disclose their status, support groups are being set up and information is changing people's perspective."

"Our parents think we are crazy," Moletsane Koena and his brother Lebohang tell me. "They call our lifestyle lost, open-minded. It makes no sense to them. It intimidates them. They see their cultural values disappearing, people losing respect for each other. Individualism is replacing commonly-held human values. They are worried." Pause. "I must admit though", concedes Lebohang, father of

ne quitterai jamais Kasi", déclare Sarah Nkwane, résidente d'Orlando Ouest. Agée d'une vingtaine d'années, Nkane, qui porte de longues tresses sous sa casquette MTN, parle bien, est ambitieuse, belle, et connaît bien le monde de la rue. Elle a fait sa scolarité dans une école privée de Johannesburg et parle comme une "bourgeoise", un terme employé pour désigner ceux qui sont issu du quartier des classes moyennes de Diepkloof, à la frontière Nord de Soweto. Divorcée et à charge d'un enfant de trois ans, avec un diplôme de comptabilité de l'UNISA presque en poche, et un commerce de manucure à Melville, elle vient d'acheter une maison pour elle-même et pour sa fille dans l'un des nouveaux quartiers en développement près de Gold Reef City. "Même s'il se peut que je parte vivre en banlieue", dit-elle, "Soweto sera toujours chez moi", décrivant un sentiment commun parmi les jeunes de plus en plus mobiles de la ville. "Regardez Zola", dit Nkwane, faisant référence au présentateur du Talk Show Zola 7 sur SABC 1. Il dort en banlieue avec sa petite amie blanche, mais il se lève le matin et revient ici, pour s'asseoir dans les stations de lavage de mauvaise qualité avec ses amis et manger du sadza et du nyama dans la rue. C'est là, sa maison. La vie dans les banlieues n'est pas intéressante."

Ce sont les personnes comme à Zola, ancien gangster reconverti en

Mobiltelefonunternehmens MTN prangt. Sie kann sich gut ausdrücken, ist ehrgeizig, schön und kennt sich aus auf den Straßen ihrer Stadt. Sie ging auf eine Privatschule in Johannesburg und spricht wie eine "Bürgerliche", eine "bourgeoise" — ein Name, der denen gegeben wird, die aus dem Mittelschichtviertel Diepkloof in den nördlichen Außenbezirken von Soweto kommen. Sie ist geschieden, hat ein drei Jahre altes Kind, fast ihr Studium der Buchhaltung an der Fernuniversität von Südafrika (UNISA) abgeschlossen und ist Besitzerin eines eigenen Manikürestudios in Melville. Gerade hat sie für sich und ihre Tochter ein Haus auf einem neu erschlossenen Baugrund nahe Gold Reef City gekauft. "Selbst wenn ich mal in einem 'suburb' leben sollte", betont sie, "wird dies hier immer mein Zuhause sein", und spricht damit aus, was die allgemeine Gefühlsstimmung der nach oben strebenden Stadtjugend ist. "Schau dir Zola an", sagt Nkwane und meint damit den Moderator der Zola 7 Talk Show beim südafrikanischen Fernsehsender SABC 1. "Er schläft im 'suburb' bei seiner weißen Freundin, aber morgens kommt er hierher zurückgefahren, sitzt mit seinen Freunden in billigen Autowaschanlagen herum und isst auf der Straße 'Sadza' und 'Nyama', Maisbrei mit Fleisch. Hier ist sein Zuhause, das Leben in den 'suburbs' ist langweilig."

Es sind Typen wie Zola, die sich vom Gangster zum Medienstar verwandelt

a seven-month-old child, "when I hear children abusing their parents, I think maybe they have a point. Certain traditional things should not be forgotten. I agree with our deputy president when he says that moral regeneration is needed."

We are sitting in the Koenas' home in Naledi Extension 1, on the far western edge of Soweto. In front of it, what was once open veld is now crammed with newly built houses. Their mother, a nurse at present working on contract in the UK, moved there when, as part of the former government's mid-1980s drive to create a black middle class, she was able to buy it through the First Time Home Owners subsidy scheme. They have lived there ever since.

"While previously the township was just a place to sleep and we did everything else outside, this has changed," the Koenas tell me. "Right here, in Protea North, we have a good school called Rashome High; we have a Spar and a Shoprite in Dube, and Soweto now has a night-life — restaurants, clubs, shebeens that have been upgraded into pubs where you can listen to live entertainment and buy food. It is becoming a nice environment to live in." Moletsane, a fifth-year architecture student, feels so positive about Soweto and the lifestyle it offers him that he intends opening up an architectural practice here once he

célébrité des médias, qui sont les nouveaux modèles à imiter pour les jeunes de Soweto. Pendant qu'ils négocient les limites non fixées entre le township et la banlieue, la rue et le centre commercial, la vie et la mort, les valeurs et les modèles que transportent les hommes politiques ou les hommes d'église ont depuis longtemps été mis de côté; le langage qu'ils adoptent, les téléphones portables qu'ils utilisent, les vêtements qu'ils portent, les voitures qu'ils conduisent, la musique qu'ils écoutent, l'alcool qu'ils boivent et la manière dont ils s'amusent — tout cela constitue les signes des identités qui viennent de se développer. La politique n'est qu'un autre chemin frauduleux pour la promotion personnelle. Ce sont les célébrités des médias, les musiciens, les footballeurs et les criminels qui jouent le rôle de modèle de la bonne vie (et de comment y arriver) à laquelle ils aspirent.

Une partie de cette vie est le VIH/Sida. "Si l'on n'est pas infecté, on est affecté", déclare Kgomotso Tlhoacle, l'une des oratrices stars du Channel Youth Club. "Nous assistons toujours à des enterrements quasiment chaque week-end; les gens parlent toujours de la maladie comme d'une malédiction; c'est une épidémie pour laquelle nous n'avons toujours pas trouvé de solution. Mais petit à petit", ajoute-t-elle, "les gens sont moins réticents à divulguer leur statut, des groupes de soutien se forment et

haben, die nun die neuen Vorbilder für Sowetos Jugend sind. Wenn sie über die schmale Grenzlinie zwischen Township und Suburb, zwischen Straße und Mall, Leben und Tod sprechen, gelten die Werte und Vorbilder, die Politik und Kirche anbieten, schon lange nicht mehr. Die Sprache, die sie sprechen, die Handys, die sie benutzen, die Kleidung, die sie tragen, die Autos, die sie fahren, die Musik, die sie hören, der Alkohol, den sie trinken, und wie und wo sie ihre Partys feiern — das sind die Symbole einer neu aufgebauten Identität. Politik sei nur ein anderer, ein betrügerischer Weg, um weiter zu kommen. Es sind die Medienstars, die Musiker, Fußballspieler und die Kriminellen, die das gute Leben vorführen (und zeigen, wie man dorthin gelangt), das die Jugendlichen auch für sich erstreben.

Zu diesem Leben gehört Aids. "Selbst wenn man nicht mit dem Virus infiziert ist, ist man betroffen", sagt Kgomotso Tlhoacle, eine der beliebtesten Rednerinnen bei den öffentlichen Debatten des Channel Youth Club. "Wir gehen fast jedes Wochenende zu Beerdigungen; die Leute glauben noch immer, dass die Krankheit den Leuten angehext würde; wir haben noch keinen Weg gefunden, wie wir mit dieser Krankheit umgehen sollen", sagt sie. "Aber ganz allmählich bekommen die Leute mehr Mut und verschweigen nicht mehr, wenn sie Aids haben. Unterstützergruppen entstehen, und

Thokoza Park on a Sunday Journée du dimanche à Thokoza Park Sonntag im Thokoza Park

has graduated. "So many professionals are making a living here now, he says — doctors, dentists, lawyers — but no architects yet. I think I will be the first to do it."

Not everyone is as positive. Thabo Motoung, a curio trader outside the Hector Peterson Museum in Orlando West, is bitter. He is a qualified electrician and plumber and was employed as a labourer during the construction of the building. Since then he has been out of work. He sits outside the museum trying to entice tourists to buy the third-hand Zimbabwean curios he buys at Bruma Lake, without much success. "The bus drivers tell the tourists not to buy our goods," he tells me, "so the tourists go in and out of this building, and the only ones who benefit are the ones inside."

The Hector Peterson Museum is one of the few architecturally significant buildings to have been built in Soweto since 1994. It commemorates the 1976 student riots against Afrikaans as a medium of education in township schools. It was designed by Mashabane Rose Architects, who, with the Apartheid Museum at Johannesburg's Gold Reef City, the Slave Museum in Cape Town and the Rock Art Museum at the University of the Witwatersrand under their belts, are fast becoming the most sought-after museum architects in the country. The Hector Peterson Museum

l'information modifie la "perspective" des individus."

"Nos parents pensent que nous sommes fous", me déclarent Moletsane Koena et son frère Lebohang. "Ils pensent que notre style de vie est dépravé, trop ouvert. C'est une chose qu'ils ne peuvent comprendre. Ça les intimide. Ils voient leurs valeurs culturelles disparaître, les gens perdre le respect de l'autre. L'individualisme remplace les valeurs que les hommes ont habituellement. Ils sont inquiets." Pause. "Je dois tout de même admettre", avoue Lebohang, père d'un bébé de sept mois, que "lorsque j'entends des enfants abuser leurs parents, je pense qu'ils ont peut-être raison. Certains éléments traditionnels ne devraient pas être oubliés. Je suis d'accord avec notre vice-président lorsqu'il dit qu'il est nécessaire que se fasse une régénération morale."

Nous sommes assis dans la maison de Koena à Naledi Extension 1, à la limite Ouest de Soweto. En face de la maison, ce qui un temps n'était qu'une espèce de savane ouverte, est désormais envahit par des maisons nouvellement construites. Leur mère, une infirmière qui travaille actuellement par contrat au Royaume-Uni, a déménagé dans ce quartier lorsque, sous l'impulsion de l'ancien gouvernement à créer une classe moyenne noire dans les années 1980, elle parvint à se l'acheter grâce au plan

Informationen helfen, die Lebensperspektive der Leute zu verändern."

"Unsere Eltern denken, wir seien verrückt", erzählen mir Moletsane Koena und sein Bruder Lebohang. "Sie halten die Art, wie wir leben, für ein verlorenes Leben, wir sind ihnen viel zu aufgeschlossen. Sie begreifen es nicht. Es macht ihnen Angst. Sie sehen, wie ihre eigenen kulturellen Werte verschwinden, wie Leute den Respekt vor einander verlieren. Anstelle von Werten, die bisher für allgemein gültig gehalten wurden, macht sich Individualismus breit, und sie sind besorgt." Pause. "Ich muss zugeben", räumt Lebohang, Vater eines sieben Monate alten Kindes, ein, "wenn ich höre, was für Worte Kinder heute gegenüber ihren Eltern benutzen, glaube ich, dass die Alten vielleicht Recht haben. Bestimmte Traditionen sollten nicht in Vergessenheit geraten. Ich stimme unserem Vize-Präsidenten zu, wenn er sagt, dass wir eine moralische Wiederbelebung brauchen."

Wir sitzen in Koenas Haus in Naledi Extension 1, am äußersten westlichen Ende von Soweto. Vor dem Haus lag früher offenes Feld, heute ist es völlig zugebaut mit neuen Häusern. Die Mutter der beiden Brüder, die Krankenschwester ist und zur Zeit in Großbritannien arbeitet, zog hierher, als die damalige Regierung Mitte der 1980er die Schaffung einer schwarzen Mittelschicht propagierte, und sie so das Haus mit Hilfe eines

is an enigmatically mute, monumentally scaled red brick box. From inside its windows define precise views into the distant space of the township, framing significant spots for the history it commemorates — the Orlando Police Station, the Morris Isaacson School, activist Jeff Moropeng's house. A sprouting brown grass line, the so-called "line of fire", connects its entrance to the site of the slaying of Hector Peterson (the first student to be killed in the riots), up Moema Street. But more immediately, it severs itself from its context, turning its back on Uncle Tom's (the adjacent cultural centre), on trader Motoung's house and on its potential to develop a local economy. "These tourists cannot even speak English," says the 70-year-old mother of Mboyisa Makhuba, the young man carrying Hector Peterson in the now iconic portrait of the riots. She sits next to Motoung selling t-shirts printed with her son's image and other '76 paraphernalia. "They come from Germany, Holland and France, but because we cannot communicate with them, we do not sell much."

Such is the nature of the emerging social and spatial economy of Soweto. For some, democracy has opened up a space of opportunity; the township has expanded, has become just one element in a complex network of interconnected lived space — the township, the town, the mall, the

de subvention nommé "Propriétaire de Maison pour la Première Fois." Depuis lors, c'est là qu'ils ont toujours vécu.

"Alors qu'avant", me dit-elle, "le township n'était qu'un lieu ou dormir, et que toutes les autres activités se passaient à l'extérieur, les choses ont changé. Ici, à Protea North, il y a une bonne école qui s'appelle Rashome High; nous avons un Spar et un Shopright dans Dube et Soweto possède maintenant sa vie nocturne — des restaurants, des boîtes de nuits, des débits d'alcool qui ont été transformés en pubs où l'on peut écouter de la musique live et acheter à manger. C'est devenu un environnement agréable à vivre." Moletsane, étudiant en cinquième année d'architecture, est si positif par rapport à Soweto et au style de vie qui lui est proposé qu'il envisage d'y ouvrir un cabinet d'architecture une fois diplômé. "Tellement de professionnels ont désormais un emploi ici, dit-il — des médecins, des dentistes, des avocats — mais il n'y a pas encore d'architectes. Je pense que je serai le premier à installer mon cabinet ici."

Tout le monde n'est pas aussi positif. Thabo Motoung, un vendeur de souvenirs qui travaille à l'extérieur du Musée Hector Peterson à Orlando Ouest, est amer. Il est qualifié en tant qu'électricien et que plombier et avait été employé comme ouvrier durant la construction du musée. Depuis lors, il n'a pas retrouvé de travail. Il se tient

Finanzierungssystems der "First Time Home Owners" kaufen konnte. Seit dieser Zeit lebt die Familie hier.

"Während das Township früher nur eine Schlafstadt war", erzählen sie mir, "und wir alles andere außerhalb machten, hat sich das nun geändert. Hier in Protea Nord gibt es jetzt eine gute Schule, die Rashome High; wir haben einen 'Spar' und eine Shopright-Kaufhalle in Dube, und Soweto hat jetzt sogar sein Nachtleben. Es gibt Restaurants und Clubs, 'shebeens' — die traditionellen Bierhallen — haben sich zu Pubs gemausert, wo man Lifemusik hören und essen kann. Es ist schön hier zum Leben geworden." Moletsane, Architekturstudent im fünften Studienjahr, ist so zuversichtlich, was Soweto und den Lebensstil betrifft, den es ihm bietet, dass er hier ein Architekturbüro aufmachen möchte, sobald er mit dem Studium fertig ist. "So viele Hochschulabsolventen leben und arbeiten hier schon", sagt er, "Ärzte, Zahnärzte, Rechtsanwälte — aber noch keine Architekten. Ich denke, ich werde der erste sein, der das macht."

Nicht jeder ist so zuversichtlich. Thabo Motoung, Souvenirverkäufer vor dem Hector Peterson Museum in Orlando West, ist verbittert. Er ist gelernter Elektriker und Klempner und hatte am Bau des Museums mitgearbeitet. Aber danach fand er keine Arbeit mehr. Jetzt sitzt er vor dem Museum und versucht — ohne großen Erfolg -, Touristen Souvenirs zu verkaufen, die eigentlich aus Simbabwe

suburb. The city is fluid, dynamic, malleable, interpretable. For others, it has closed down; disappointed expectations have brought new expulsions and exclusions, a new sense of being on the outside, of stasis and isolation. New urban imaginaries and practices have failed to take hold. The geographies of apartheid have remained, intractable.

These are the dimensions of the emerging post-apartheid township landscape. Receding and yet returning, held within a network of disconnected spaces and experiences, the former homogeneity of its landscape ruptured by diverging practices and identities, it is being reconfigured according to the multiple logics of difference. Soweto, once one, once set apart and closed off, is today a site of multiple identities, moving in many directions all at once.

assis à l'extérieur du musée et essaie, d'attirer les touristes à acheter les souvenirs de troisième main qui viennent du Zimbabwe et qu'il achète à Bruma Lake, sans grand succès, "Le chauffeur de bus dit aux touristes de ne pas acheter nos souvenirs", me dit-il, "alors les touristes rentrent et sortent de ce bâtiment, et les seuls qui bénéficient de leur présence sont ceux qui se trouvent à l'intérieur."

Le Musée Hector Peterson est l'un des bâtiments important d'un point de vue architectural à avoir été bâti à Soweto depuis 1994, en commémoration des luttes étudiantes de 1976 contre l'instauration de l'Afrikaans comme langue d'enseignement dans les écoles des townships. Conçu par Mashabane Rose Architects qui, avec le Musée de l'Apartheid à Gold Reef City, le Musée de l'Esclavage au Cap et le Musée d'Art Rupestre à l'Université du Witwatersrand (entre autres) à leur tableau d'honneur, deviennent rapidement les seules architectes spécialisés dans l'édification de musées dans le pays, ce musée est une boîte de briques rouges énigmatiquement muet et aux proportions monumentales. De l'intérieur, ses fenêtres définissent des vues précises de l'espace distant du township, encadrant des points significatifs pour l'histoire que ce musée cherche à commémorer — le Commissariat d'Orlando, l'école Morris

kommen, und die er wiederum vom Touri-Markt in Bruma Lake, Johannesburg Ost, erwirbt. "Die Busfahrer sagen den Touristen, sie sollen unsere Ware nicht kaufen", erzählt er mir, "also gehen die Touristen rein ins Museum und kommen wieder raus, und die einzigen, die davon profitieren, sind die da drinnen."

Das Hector Peterson Museum gehört zu den wenigen architektonisch interessanten Gebäuden, die seit 1994 in Soweto entstanden. Es erinnert an die Schüleraufstände von 1976, die sich gegen das Afrikaans richteten, der Unterrichtssprache in den Schulen der Townships. Entworfen wurde das Museum vom Architekturbüro Mashabane Rose Associates, die sich bereits u.a. mit dem Apartheid Museum in Gold Reef City, dem Sklavenmuseum in Kapstadt und dem Rock Art Museum an der Witwatersrand Universität einen Namen gemacht haben und inzwischen zu den meist gefragten Museumsarchitekten in Südafrika gehören. Mit diesem Vorhaben gelang ihnen ein mystischer, stiller Bau aus rotem Backstein von monumentaler Größe. Von innen heraus geben die Fenster den Blick frei auf das Township und bilden den Rahmen für die wichtigsten Plätze der Geschichte, an die es erinnert — die Orlando Polizeistation, die Morris Isaacson Schule, das Haus des Studentenführers Jeff Moropeng. Eine Linie aus braunem Gras, die so genannte "Feuerlinie", verbindet den Museumseingang mit der Stelle in Moema

Issacson, la maison de l'activiste Jeff Moropeng. Une ligne naissante d'herbe brune, appelée "ligne de feu" joint l'entrée à l'endroit où Hector Peterson (le premier étudiant à être tué) fut abattu, en haut de Moema Street. Mais plus immédiatement, cela le dissocie de son contexte, tournant le dos de Uncle's Tom (le centre culturel adjacent), et de la maison de Motoung, le commerçant, et de son potentiel à développer une économie locale. "Ces touristes ne peuvent même pas parler Anglais", affirme la mère, âgée de 70 ans, de Mboyisa Makhuba, le jeune homme qui porte Hector Peterson sur le portrait iconique des combats, et qui se tient assise prêt de Motoung et vent des t-shirts imprimés à l'effigie de son fils ainsi que d'autres attirails sur les années 76. "Ils viennent d'Allemagne, de Hollande et de France, mais parce que nous ne pouvons pas communiquer avec eux, nous ne vendons pas beaucoup."

Telle est la nature de l'économie sociale et spatiale émergente de Soweto. Pour certains, la démocratie a ouvert un espace d'opportunités ; le township s'est étendu, est devenu un simple élément du réseau complexe des espaces vécus interconnectés — le township, la ville, le centre commercial, la banlieue. La ville est fluide, dynamique, interprétable. Pour d'autres, cet espace s'est fermé; des attentes déçues ont entraîné de nouvelles expulsions et de nouvelles exclusions,

Street, wo Hector Peterson (der erste Schüler, der umkam) erschossen wurde. Aber seiner nächsten Umgebung verweigert es sich, dreht dem angrenzenden Uncle Tom-Kulturzentrum den Rücken zu, wendet sich ab von Motoung, dem Souvenirhändler, und verschließt sich seinen Möglichkeiten, diesem Viertel zu wirtschaftlicher Entwicklung zu verhelfen. "Die Touristen können ja kein Englisch", bemerkt die 70-Jahre alte Mutter von Mboyisa Makhuba, des jungen Mannes, der auf dem inzwischen zur Ikone gewordenen Bild von den Schüleraufständen Hector Peterson trägt. Sie sitzt neben Motoung und verkauft T-Shirts mit dem Foto ihres Sohnes und andere Erinnerungsstücke der '76er. "Sie kommen aus Deutschland, Holland und Frankreich, aber weil wir nicht mit ihnen kommunizieren können, verkaufen wir nicht viel."

So ist es bestellt um die neu entstehende soziale und räumliche Ökonomie von Soweto. Einigen hat die Demokratie Raum für Möglichkeiten und Chancen geöffnet; das Township ist expandiert, ist ein Element innerhalb eines komplexen Netzwerkes von untereinander verbundenen Lebensräumen geworden - das Township, die Stadt, die Mall, die 'suburbs'. Die Stadt ist fließend, dynamisch, anpassungsfähig, vieldeutig. Anderen hat sich die Stadt verschlossen; enttäuschte Erwartungen brachten neue Vertreibungen, neues Ausgeschlossensein; ein neues Gefühl

un nouveau sentiment d'appartenir à l'extérieur, un sentiment d'immobilité et d'isolation. Les nouvelles imageries urbaines et les nouvelles pratiques urbaines n'ont pas réussi à prendre. Les géographies de l'apartheid ont subsisté, irrétractables.

Voici donc les dimensions émergeantes du paysage du township post-apartheid. S'estompant mais,, revenant, tenues dans un réseau d'espaces et d'expériences déconnectées, l'ancienne homogénéité de son paysage rompue par des pratiques et des identités divergentes, elles se reconfigurent selon les logiques multiples de la différence. Soweto, à un moment une seule et même entité, à un moment mis à l'écart et fermé, est aujourd'hui un lieu aux identités multiples, prenant plusieurs directions à la fois.

von Außen-vor-sein, von Stillstand und Isolierung. Neue Vorstellungen von einem städtischen Leben und seinen Lebensformen haben nicht gegriffen. Die Geographie der Apartheid hat sich gehalten. Hartnäckig.

Dies sind die Dimensionen der neuen Post-Apartheid-Townshiplandschaft. Verblassend und doch wiederkommend, gefangen in einem Netz von voneinander getrennten Räumen und Erfahrungen, ihre frühere Geschlossenheit zerbrochen an sich nun unterscheidenden Praktiken und Identitäten, gestaltet sich diese Landschaft neu nach der mannigfaltigen Logik der Unterschiede. Soweto, einst eins, einst isoliert und ausschlossen, ist heute ein Ort vieler Identitäten, die alle gleichzeitig in unterschiedliche Richtungen streben.

ACKNOWLEDGEMENTS

Photographers

Lori Waselchuk Cover, 4, 12, 16, 22, 28, 32, 38, 44, 52, 60, 74, 79, 82, 96, 106, 111, 118, 134, 138, 143, 144, 148, 152

Sydney Seshibedi (© Sunday Times) 35, 41, 47, 56, 59, 65, 66, 71, 87, 101, 102, 113, 114, 131, 133
Lindsay Bremner 2, 90, 93, 122, 126

Translators
German – Petra Reategui
French – Murielle Mars, Sylvie Kaninda and Bernard Cointault

Map
GIS / Global Image

Proofreader
Michael Collins

Copy Editor
Laura Grant

Design and layout
Adam Rumball and Thabo Matlejoane
Mad Cow Studio, a division of STE Publishers.

ANGLOGOLD ASHANTI

Thanks to AngloGold Ashanti for their generous sponsorship of this book.

Lindsay Bremner holds the position of Chair of Architecture at the University of the Witwatersrand, Johannesburg. Prior to this, she was Chair of Planning, Urbanisation and Environmental Management on the Greater Johannesburg Transitional Metropolitan Council. She is Currently completing her Senior Doctorate entitled "Thinking Citiness from Johannesburg: Writings 1990-2004." Professor Bremner is married with two children.

Lindsay Bremner occupe les fonctions de Professeur en Architecture à l'Université de Witwatersrand à Johannesburg. Mais avant cela, elle était Responsable de la Planification, de l'Urbanisme et de la Gestion de l'Environnement dans le Conseil Métropolitain de Transition de Johannesburg et son Agglomération. Elle est, pour le moment, en train de terminer une Thèse de Doctorat intitulée: "Réflexions sur les Caractéristiques de Johannesburg: Les Ecrits de 1990 à 2004." Le Professeur Bremner est mariée et mère de deux enfants.

Lindsay Bremner bekleidet den Lehrstuhl fuer Architektur an der Universitaet Witwatersrand in Johannesburg. Davor hatte sie den Lehrstuhl fuer Planung, Verstaedterung und Umwelt-Verwaltung des Groesseren Johannesburger Uebergangs-Stadtrates inne. Gegenwaertig bringt sie ihre Doktorarbeit mit dem Titel "Thinking Citiness from Johannesburg: Werke von 1990-2004" zum Abschluss. Professor Bremner ist verheiratet und hat zwei Kinder.